T0330440

Applied Evolutionary Economics and the Knowledge-based Economy

Applied Evolutionary Economics and the Knowledge-based Economy

Edited by

Andreas Pyka

Associate Professor

and

Horst Hanusch

Professor and Chair in Economics, University of Augsburg, Germany

Edward Elgar
Cheltenham, UK • Northampton, MA, USA

Published by
Edward Elgar Publishing Limited
Glensanda House
Montpellier Parade
Cheltenham
Glos GL50 1UA
UK

Edward Elgar Publishing, Inc.
136 West Street
Suite 202
Northampton
Massachusetts 01060
USA

A catalogue record for this book
is available from the British Library

Library of Congress Cataloguing in Publication Data
European Meeting on Applied Evolutionary Economics (3rd : 2003 : University
of Augsburg)
   Applied evolutionary economics and the knowledge-based economy / edited
by Andreas Pyka and Horst Hanusch.
      p. cm.
   Selected papers from the 3rd European Meeting of Applied Evolutionary
Economics, April 2003 at the University of Augsburg.
      1. Technological innovations–Economic aspects–Congresses. 2. Information
technology–Economic aspects–Congresses. 3. Knowledge management–
Congresses. 4. Industries–Technological innovations–Economic aspects–
Congresses. 5. Technology transfer–Economic aspects–Congresses.
6. Evolutionary economics–Congresses. I. Pyka, Andreas. II. Hanusch, Horst.
III. Title.

   HC79.T4E97   2003
   330,9′051–dc22   2005049465

ISBN-13: 978 1 84376 903 3
ISBN-10: 1 84376 903 4

Printed and bound in Great Britain by MPG Books Ltd, Bodmin, Cornwall

Contents

Contributors

Giulio Bottazzi   S. Anna School of Advanced Studies, Pisa, Italy.

Norhene Chabchoub   Université du Québec à Montréal, Canada.

Robin Cowan   MERIT, Universiteit Maastricht, The Netherlands.

Bernd Ebersberger   Fraunhofer-Institut ISI, Karlsruhe, Germany.

Emmanuelle Fauchart   Laboratoire d'économétrie, CNAM Paris, France.

Dominique Foray   Ecole Polytechnique, Lausanne, Switzerland.

Philip Gunby   University of Canterbury, New Zealand.

Horst Hanusch   Institute of Economics, University of Augsburg, Germany.

Bart Los   Groningen Growth and Development Center and SOM Research School, Groningen University, The Netherlands.

Michael Menhart   Münchner Rückversicherung, Germany.

Piergiuseppe Morone   University of Napoli 'l'Orientale', Italy.

Lionel Nesta   Observatoire François des Conjonctures Economiques, Département de Recherche sur l'Innovation et la Concurrence, Sophia-Antipolis, France.

Jorge Niosi   Department of Management and Technology, Canada Research Chair on the Management of Technology, Université du Québec à Montréal, Canada.

Alessandro Nuvolari   Faculty of Technology Management, Eindhoven Centre for Innovation Studies (ECIS), Eindhoven University of Technology, The Netherlands.

Andreas Pyka   Institute of Economics, University of Augsburg, Germany.

Angelo Secchi   S. Anna School of Advanced Studies, Pisa, Italy.

Erik Stam   Erasmus Research Institute of Management (ERIM), Erasmus University Rotterdam, and Urban and Regional research centre Utrecht (URU), Utrecht University, The Netherlands, and Max Planck Institute of Economics, Growth and Public Policy Group, Jena, Germany.

Richard Taylor   Centre for Policy Modelling, Business School of Manchester Metropolitan University, UK.

Bart Verspagen   Eindhoven Centre for Innovation Studies (ECIS), Faculty of Technology Management, Eindhoven University of Technology, The Netherlands.

Nick von Tunzelmann   Science and Technology Policy Research (SPRU), University of Sussex, UK.

Arnold Wentzel   Economics Department, University of Johannesburg, South Africa.

Preface

The present book is the outcome from the third European Meeting of Applied Evolutionary Economics (EMAEE) which took place in April 2003 at the University of Augsburg. The conference was entitled as this volume 'Applied Evolutionary Economics and the Knowledge-based Economies'. The different contributions of this book are a selection of conference papers and deal with various aspects of knowledge-based economies. They also demonstrate how far developed the applied fields of evolutionary economics already are. The various chapters show that evolutionary economics has left the nursery of new academic approaches and offers important insights for the understanding of socio-economic processes of change and development strongly affecting especially the industrialized world.

As organizers of the conference we would also like to use the opportunity of this volume to express our thanks to those who played a considerable role in the success of the conference. We would like to express our warm thanks to Thomas Grebel and Markus Balzat who creatively managed the local organization. Furthermore, important thanks go to Bernd Ebersberger, Koen Frenken, Werner Hölzl, Vanessa Oltra and Paul Windrum and their outstanding work in the scientific committee. Of course, thanks also to our keynote speakers Uwe Cantner, Phil Cooke, Gunnar Eliasson, Ernst Helmstädter, Franco Malerba, Stan Metcalfe, Fritz Rahmeyer and Paolo Saviotti who importantly contributed to the high intellectual level of the conference.

The conference would not have been possible without the support of various public institutions and private firms. First of all, we would like to express our deepest thanks to the DFG (German Research Foundation) and the State of Bavaria for financial support. In addition, Zeuna Stärker (automotive industry), PCI (chemical products), Deutsche Bank and Stadtsparkasse Augsburg supported the conference. We must also gratefully acknowledge a donation by the Friends of the University of Augsburg. Finally, the Augsburger bakery Wolff, the dairy producer Zott, the juice company Burkhart, the fruit company Fruchthof Nagel, the brewery Hasenbräu, the Stadtwerke Augsburg and Saeco coffee deserve our deepest thanks.

1. Introduction

The increasing importance of knowledge for almost all economic affairs is a global phenomenon which severely challenges economics at least since around the last 25 years. The World Bank states in its 1998/1999 development report:

> For countries in the vanguard of the world economy, the balance between knowledge and resources has shifted so far towards the former that knowledge has become perhaps the most important factor determining the standard of living.. . . Today's most technologically advanced economies are truly knowledge based. (World Bank, 1999)

How is this challenge accepted within economics in its most recent history?

DEVELOPMENT AND QUALITATIVE CHANGE

Within academia it is now also almost 25 years since the famous book of Richard Nelson and Sidney Winter *An Evolutionary Theory of Economic Change* was published. This book summarizing the research of the two authors has to be considered the hallmark of a shift in the economic reasoning on growth and development leaving behind the traditional equilibrium-oriented analysis and opening up a new research programme. This research programme is suited for the analysis of dynamic development processes including prominently not only quantitative but also *qualitative change* which is a condition-sine-qua-non for understanding the important transformation processes going on in present day economies.

COMPLEXITY

In its early years this new research programme quickly establishes a connection to new approaches coming from *complexity theory* (for example Kauffman, 1993), in order to develop the analytical tools which allow dealing with the rich dynamics of real economic systems. Uncertainty irresolvably connected to innovation, heterogeneous actors combining their various competences and capabilities, and close interactions between these actors leading to non-linearities put the traditional toolkit of economics into question and demand for new approaches able to cope with pattern formation and disruptive change observable in real world economic systems.

KNOWLEDGE-BASED ECONOMIES

A further severe difficulty comes from the empirical side. Without doubt economic evolution is most strongly affected by innovation diffusing through the economic system and by this permanently changes its composition. Innovation is made up by knowledge accumulation and learning processes which empirically confronts economics with severe measurement problems and makes life for empirically oriented economists difficult. Knowledge is often no longer only an intangible input into a production function but often also the output of the production processes, for example, in knowledge intensive service industries and therefore demands for an adequate measurement in particular also in its qualitative dimension. Gunnar Eliasson was among the first authors addressing these important questions already in the 1980s and he also first coined the notion of the *knowledge-based* information *economy* in a book published in 1990.

EUROPEAN MEETING OF APPLIED EVOLUTIONARY ECONOMICS

In a way the sequence of the European Meetings of Applied Evolutionary Economics (EMAEE) reflects these developments and demonstrates how highly developed evolutionary economic reasoning and especially its empirically and applied fields, which today can best be labelled as Neo-Schumpeterian Economics (Hanusch and Pyka, 2005), already are. The first meeting which took place in 1999 in France was focused on the methodological developments, in particular new empirical methods and simulation techniques allowing to analyse also the *qualitative dimension* of economic change (Saviotti, 2003). The second meeting took place in 2001 in Austria and was organized around the central topic of complex systems shedding light on the multifaceted sources of *complexity* in economic life (Foster and Hölzl, 2004). And the third meeting organized in 2003 in Germany, which this volume is about, was thematically focused on *knowledge-based economies* and prolific approaches allowing the economic analysis of knowledge-driven dynamics.

KNOWLEDGE-BASED ECONOMIES AND THE KNOWLEDGE-ORIENTATION IN ECONOMICS

Permanent change in the impact, speed and direction of innovation processes leads to continuous development and qualitative change strongly visible especially in industrialized economies. On the one hand, new companies and often even new industries emerge, whereas established firms are confronted with severe transformation processes. On the other hand, these changes exert a crucial impact on the development potential of regions and whole economies. In this perspective competition is no longer only price competition, but increasingly gains an extremely important innovation dimension. Competition for innovation determines the international market position of firms, as well as the competitiveness of regions and national states within the framework of a growing international division of labour.

So-called key technologies, such as information and communication technologies (ICT) and modern biotechnology play a decisive role in these development processes. Industries applying and improving these technologies are in the centre of interest for financiers, politicians, industrial actors, and in particular for creative entrepreneurs. The development in these industries will not only lead to important innovations for science and technology, but they are also the foundation for economic, social and organizational changes in the twenty-first century.

Beyond these processes stands the transformation of economies to so-called knowledge-based economies. The decisive difference with respect to traditional manufacturing-based economies has to be seen in the dominant role for economic welfare which is played today by knowledge creation and diffusion processes. However, only to push forward the scientific and technological frontiers (*exploration*) is not sufficient to cope with these pervasive developments. What additionally counts is to be prepared for permanent transformation processes of the whole economic system which is strongly connected with the effective *exploitation* and use of the various kinds of new knowledge in a preferably broad set of economic activities.

Of course, the knowledge effects are most obvious in knowledge-intensive industries such as ICT and biopharmaceuticals. Also in knowledge-intensive service industries, like business consultancy and financial industries, they become more and more visible. Without doubt, however, at least indirectly all sectors of an economy are affected by the increasing importance of knowledge (for example new labour organization, the increasing use of information, communication and network technologies, life-long learning and so on). To highlight these developments some authors even use the term *weightless economy* (see Quah, 1995) emphasizing the fact that today knowledge and information account for the major share of economic transactions.

Traditional neoclassical analysis cannot deal with the rich complexity and dynamics characterizing the knowledge-based economy. It is beyond the scope of this introduction to discuss in detail the criticism of the restrictive assumptions underlying the mainstream economic reasoning. A major discussion on the basis of evolutionary economics can be found among others, in Dopfer (2001), Clark and Juma (1987), Silverberg (1988) and Saviotti (2003). Here it is sufficient to mention three major points, which are of outstanding importance in the discussion of economic development processes. These points are also constitutive for that strand of literature which is concerned with industry evolution and technological progress and can be coined Neo-Schumpeterian economics (see Hanusch and Pyka, 2006). Here, instead of the incentive-orientation of neoclassical industrial economics, a knowledge-orientation is underlying the investigation of industries and innovation processes in particular. First of all, Neo-Schumpeterian economics wants to explain how innovations emerge and diffuse over time. A specific feature of these processes is uncertainty, which cannot be treated adequately by drawing on stochastical distributions referring to the concept of risk. Therefore, one has to get rid of the assumption of perfect rationality, underlying traditional models, instead the concepts of bounded and procedural rationality are invoked. Consequently, actors are characterized by incomplete knowledge bases and capabilities. Closely connected, the second point concerns the important role heterogeneity and variety plays. Due to the assumption of perfect rationality, in traditional models homogeneous actors and technologies are analysed. Heterogeneity as a source of learning and novelty is by and large neglected, or treated as an only temporary deviation from the representative agent and the optimal technology. Finally, the third point deals with the time dimension in which learning and the emergence of novelties take place. By their very nature, these processes are truly dynamic, meaning that they occur in historical time. The possibility of irreversibility, however, does not exist in the mainstream approaches, relying on linearity and optimal equilibrium states.

Thus, traditional economic theories, summarized here as incentive-based approaches, with their focus on rational decisions only and based on marginalistic reasoning, are excluding crucial aspects of actors' various competences and multifaceted interactions, which are influenced by a couple of factors lying by their very nature beyond the scope of these approaches, for instance factors such as learning, individual and collective motivation, trust, and so on. It is the role of such factors the knowledge-orientation of Neo-Schumpeterian economics explicitly takes into account.

By switching from the incentive-based perspective to knowledge-orientation Neo-Schumpeterian economics realizes a decisive change in the analysis of transformations of economic systems. In this light the introduction of novelties mutate from rational calculus to collective experimental and problem solving processes (Eliasson, 1991). The capabilities of the actors are no longer perfect, instead a gap between the competences and difficulties which are to be mastered opens up (Heiner, 1983). There are two reasons responsible for this competence-difficulty gap when it comes to innovation. On the one hand, technological uncertainty introduces errors and surprises. On the other hand, the very nature of knowledge avoids an unrestricted access to it. Knowledge in general, and new technological know-how in particular, are no longer considered as freely available, but as local (technology specific), tacit (firm specific), and complex (based on a variety of technologies and scientific fields). To understand and use the respective know-how specific competences are necessary, which have to be built up cumulatively in the course of time. Following this, knowledge and the underlying learning processes are important sources for the observed heterogeneity among agents. Heterogeneity again is a necessary prerequisite for innovation, growth and prolific development. It opens up new opportunities for creativity and learning. Accordingly, it is the self-propagating dynamics of the above process, linking knowledge creation to heterogeneity and vice versa, which is driving the transformation of economic systems and development in terms of economic growth.

This process of endogenous re-structuring of economic systems based on knowledge and accompanied by creativity, learning and innovation leading to increasing differentiation and specialization (Saviotti and Pyka, 2004) is placed centrally in Neo-Schumpeterian economics. It has to be understood adequately and constitutes a persistent challenge for theoretical and applied economics. The contributors to this book try to face these challenges. They concentrate on the specificities of knowledge-based economies in reality, they innovatively introduce new methodologies and empirical tools in order to capture the underlying dynamics and thus help to improve our understanding of the Neo-Schumpeterian dimensions of modern knowledge-based economies.

OVERVIEW

Part I of the book is entitled 'Knowledge and cognition' and includes two chapters dealing very generally with the implications of considering knowledge creation and diffusion processes. The first chapter 'Conjectures, constructs and conflicts: a framework for understanding successful innovation' is written by Arnold Wentzel and introduces a conceptual framework of how invention, innovation and entrepreneurship, which collectively is referred to as imagineering, takes place at the individual level with the aim to improve our understanding of the underlying dynamics driving knowledge-based economies. Wentzel highlights the importance of the cognitive approach for economics and shows possibilities of its application.

Robin Cowan and co-authors in their chapter 'Learning from disaster' address questions of knowledge generation focusing on the important role of failure. In the literature on innovation this is usually neglected and leads to the well known success bias. According to their reasoning, a disaster is an opportunity to produce knowledge, to reduce the probability of future disasters and to improve the performance of technological systems. In their view disasters are considered as uncontrolled experiments which lead to knowledge in areas which were not considered before. Obviously, a whole set of organizational conditions and incentive mechanisms come into play determining the direction of learning from disaster, the kinds of things to be learned, and the extent to which this learning is diffused to other actors. In their chapter the authors develop a framework to identify the problems raised by processes of learning from disaster which can be considered as an important source of disruptive change on the micro- meso- and macro-level of an economy.

Studies of particular knowledge-based industries are the general topic of Part II of the book. Lionel Nesta starts with his chapter on 'The value of knowledge integration in biotechnology'. The author examines the relationship between the characteristics of the firms' knowledge base and the stock market value of 99 firms active in biotechnology during the 1990s. By using panel data regression models the author shows that the measure of knowledge integration better explains the variance of a firm's market value than the more conventional variable of knowledge capital. Following this kind of analysis, profitable and research-intensive firms reach higher levels of market value, a rationale symptomatic for knowledge-based economies.

The next chapter by Norhene Chabchoub and Jorge Niosi entitled 'The anchor tenant hypothesis revisited: computer software clusters in North America' is dealing with another knowledge intensive industry, namely ICT. Chabchoub and Niosi are interested in the geographically clustering behaviour of high technology companies. Several explanations can be found in the literature: a common labour pool, a shared infrastructure, and knowledge externalities. A more recent hypothesis suggests that anchor tenant firms are at the basis of these externalities. The chapter examines the patterns of geographical concentration of invention in North American computer software firms. The research is based on 220 publicly quoted computer hardware and software firms operating in the USA and Canada, and the patents they obtained from the US Patent and Trademark Office between 1986 and 2002. Chabchoub and Niosi confirm the importance of anchor corporations in the software industry. They add new theoretical elements to the anchor hypothesis from a detailed observation of the evolution of the main software clusters in North America. The results of their work are showing important strategic issues for companies as well as for technology policy, where to foster the emergence of technology clusters is highly in vogue.

The last chapter of Part II deals with knowledge intensive service industries. In particular Michael Menhart and co-authors focus on 'Industry dynamics in the German insurance market'. Empirical research in organizational ecology has mainly focused on analysing founding and mortality rates using life history data of the organizations. Menhart *et al.* extend this approach in several ways. Most interestingly they chose a population of service organizations, in particular the German insurance companies. The development dynamics in this industry is obviously caused by the innovative activities of existing organizations and not by entry decisions. They further discuss potential connections between organizational ecology and the theory of industry life cycles and extend the analysis to the relationship between innovative activities and population dynamics. The study examines the effects of population density, former events and organizational size and age structure in the population of insurance companies on the number of product innovations generated. Furthermore, a concept for an insurance specific industry life cycle with a non-typical maturation and degeneration phase is developed.

Part III of the book is devoted to the important geographical dimension of knowledge-based economies. The first chapter 'A process model of locational change in entrepreneurial firms: an evolutionary perspective' by Erik Stam addresses the geographical dimension of entrepreneurial behaviour. He tackles the question 'How do changes in the spatial organization of entrepreneurial firms come about?' Stam's main purpose is to provide a concept of the process of locational change. The process model of locational change he is introducing for this purpose is constructed on the basis of an empirical study of 109 locational events during the life course of 25 young firms in knowledge intensive sectors. The model maps both internal and external variation and selection processes. With the help of his model, Stam delivers an important contribution to the development of a theory of the geographical dimension of entrepreneurship.

Alessandro Nuvolari, Bart Verspagen and Nick von Tunzelmann highlight in their chapter 'The diffusion of the steam engine in eighteenth-century Britain' the geographical dimension in diffusion processes. The authors have a twofold purpose in mind. The first is to provide a thorough reconstruction of the early diffusion of steam power technology by providing new estimates for the timing, the pace and the geographical extent of steam engine usage during the eighteenth century. The second goal is to assess the factors influencing the adoption of steam engine technology in this period. In particular, the chapter pays attention to the process of spatial spread of steam technology during the eighteenth century. The focus on the geographical aspects of the diffusion process is motivated by the fact that in the diffusion literature it is increasingly argued that a proper understanding of the processes of economic change taking place during the British industrial revolution needs to be based on a regional perspective.

Piergiuseppe Morone and Richard Taylor in their chapter 'Knowledge diffusion with complex cognition' analyse the mechanisms which dominate the phenomenon of knowledge diffusion in a process labelled *interactive learning*. The authors examine how knowledge spreads in a network in which agents interact by word of mouth. The target of their simulation is to test whether knowledge diffuses homogeneously or whether it follows some biased path, and its relation with the network architecture. They also numerically investigate the impact of an ICT platform on the knowledge diffusion process.

The final Part IV of the book deals with measurement and modelling issues for knowledge-based economies. Bart Los introduces 'A non-parametric method to identify nonlinearities in global productivity catch-up performance'. The last decade has witnessed a host of articles on empirical assessments of the strength of global convergence in productivity growth rates. Linear specifications of the convergence equation implicitly assume that the more backward a country is, the more opportunities there are for rapid catch-up. This assumption neglects the widespread feeling that very backward countries often lack the capabilities to assimilate the technologies at the global frontier. Such a lack of 'absorptive capacity' would call for a nonlinear estimation framework to explain the actual patterns of convergence and divergence. In the literature a bell-shaped relationship and a rather complex method to estimate a piecewise-linear regression equation are alternatively discussed. Bart Los extends the latter approach, in the sense that he proposes and analyses a very simple and appealing test for the significance of the nonlinearities. The chapter concludes with a limited number of applications to a productivity dataset. The Total Economy Database of the Groningen Growth and Development Center is used for an analysis of aggregate productivity convergence. In particular, Bart Los is considering two measures of absorptive capacity as threshold variables, the initial labour productivity gap to the world leader and the average number of years of schooling of the adult population.

The last chapter by Giulio Bottazzi and Angelo Secchi introduces 'Self-reinforcing dynamics and the evolution of business firms'. Recent empirical analyses on different datasets have revealed a common exponential behaviour in the shape of the probability density of corporate growth rates.

In their chapter Bottazzi and Secchi propose a simulation model that, under rather general assumptions, provides a robust explanation of the observed regularities. The model is based on a stochastic process describing the random partition of a number of 'business opportunities' among a population of identical firms. With the help of their model, Bottazzi and Secchi exactly reproduce the empirical finding in the limit of a large number of firms. Furthermore, the authors show that even in moderately small industries the asymptotic results can also be found.

REFERENCES

Clark, N. and C. Juma (1987) *Long Run Economics – An Evolutionary Approach to Economic Growth*, London: Pinter Publishers.

Dopfer, K. (2001) 'Evolutionary economics: framework for analysis', in K. Dopfer (ed.), *Evolutionary Economics: Program and Scope*, Boston and Dordrecht: London: Kluwer Academic Publishers, pp. 1–44.

Eliasson, G. (1991) 'Modelling the experimentally organized economy', *Journal of Economic Behaviour and Organization*, **16** (1–2), 153–82.

Eliasson, G., S. Fölster, T. Lindberg, T. Pousette, and E. Taymaz (eds.) (1990) *The Knowledge-Based Information Economy*, The Industrial Institute for Economic and Social Research, Stockholm.

Foster, J. and W. Hölzl (2004) *Applied Evolutionary Economics and Complex Systems*, Cheltenham, UK and Northampton, MA, USA: Edward Elgar.

Hanusch, H. and A. Pyka (eds.) (2006) *The Elgar Companion to Neo-Schumpeterian Economics*, Cheltenham, UK and Northampton, MA, USA: Edward Elgar, (forthcoming).

Heiner, R. A. (1983) 'The origin of predictable behaviour', *American Economic Review*, **73**, 560–95.

Kauffman, S. A. (1993) *The Origins of Order: Self-Organization and Selection in Evolution*, New York: Oxford University Press.

Nelson, R. and S. Winter (1982) *An Evolutionary Theory of Economic Change*, Cambridge, MA: Belknap Press.

Quah, D. (1995) 'Regional convergence clusters across Europe', Centre for Economic Performance Discussion Paper, No. 274.

Saviotti, P. P. (2003) *Applied Evolutionary Economics, New Empirical Methods and Simulation Techniques*, Cheltenham, UK and Northampton, MA, USA: Edward Elgar.

Saviotti, P. and A. P. Pyka (2004) 'Economic development by the creation of new sectors', *Journal of Evolutionary Economics*, **14** (1), 1–36.

Silverberg, G. (1988) 'Modelling economic dynamics and technical change: mathematical approaches to self-organization and evolution', in G. Dosi, C. Freeman, R.R. Nelson, G. Silverberg and L. Soete (eds), *Technical Change and Economic Theory*, London and New York: Pinter Publishers.

World Bank (1999) *World Development Report*, Oxford University Press, Washington.

PART I

Knowledge and Cognition

2. Conjectures, constructs and conflicts: a framework for understanding imagineering

Arnold Wentzel

Invention, innovation and entrepreneurship (collectively referred to as imagineering), while not totally disregarded, have attracted relatively little attention in mainstream economic research. A possible reason for this is that economists tend to pay more attention to phenomena that they can place within a mathematical or econometric model. Entrepreneurship and invention do not fit well into such models (Barreto, 1989; Magee, 2000), and it is therefore difficult to generate consistent results from their incorporation into economic models.

Another reason for the superficial treatment of imagineering is that imagineering, especially invention, is not seen as so important and that it is therefore sufficient to treat it as exogenous to the analytical systems of economists (Magee, 2000). Schmookler's (1966) counter-argument would be that imagineering is not only a form economic activity (which is sufficient to merit extensive attention from economists) but it also affects economic development. Mokyr (1990) argued that technologically progressive economies have always shown considerable flair in invention and innovation, and by implication, those are the economies where imagineering is given most attention. As the economy becomes ever more knowledge-based, these arguments gain in strength, and may lead economists to change their views and look deeper into the dynamics of imagineering.

One of the premises of this chapter is that part of the reason why few attempts have been made to model imagineering is that its dynamics are not fully understood. Following on from this premise, the aim of this chapter is to present a conceptual framework of how successful imagineering takes place at the level of the individual, in order to create an improved understanding of the underlying dynamics of imagineering. Even though this chapter is but one step towards a more complete framework, the current framework will suggest that introducing the dynamics of imagineering into economic models is within reach of economists.

INVENTION, INNOVATION AND ENTREPRENEURSHIP

This section provides the context for the rest of the chapter. Here I shall justify why I propose to investigate imagineering at the level of the individual, why I group invention, innovation and entrepreneurship under the collective noun of 'imagineering' and review previous theories of imagineering.

Basic Concepts

Let's first clarify the basic concepts. Ames (1961) makes the following distinction: invention is a flow of prototypes of articles never made before or processes never used before, and innovation takes place once the invention becomes part of a commercial transaction and a price is attached to it. It is the entrepreneur who converts the invention into economic value, or the one that translates the possibilities into action. While the entrepreneur does not need to be an inventor, innovation or entrepreneurship can only occur if there is invention. Invention, innovation and entrepreneurship are therefore closely related and complementary. The sequence of invention, innovation and entrepreneurship suggested by Schumpeter, Schmookler (1966), Maclaurin (1953) and Markman *et al.* (2002) shows that this complementarity is generally accepted.

Of the elements of imagineering, invention is the one that is least understood and studied (Gorman and Carlson, 1990). Invention itself is an aggregated concept, and can be further divided into different levels of invention. This disaggregation is necessary, because as will be argued later, many misconceptions have been created by failing to distinguish between different kinds of invention. One useful classification has been provided by Altshuller, who after a review of over 200 000 Russian patents distinguished five levels of invention (Terninko *et al.*, 1998: 13):

1. *Level one*: Apparent or conventional solution, that is the solution is by means of methods well known within the specialty (32 per cent of patents);
2. *Level two*: Small invention inside the paradigm. This involves the improvement of an existing system, usually with some compromise (45 per cent of patents);
3. *Level three*: Substantial improvement within the technology. The solution leads to a substantial improvement of the existing system (18 per cent of patents);
4. *Level four*: Invention that occurs outside the technology. This means a new generation of design using science, not technology (4 per cent of patents);

5. *Level five*: A major discovery or originating a new science (1 per cent of patents).

The review of patents has since been expanded worldwide to over two million patents, and it was found that the percentages have remained stable over the last 50 years (Domb and Dettmer, 1999).

Treating Invention, Innovation and Entrepreneurship as One Concept

If invention, innovation and entrepreneurship are closely related and complementary, it should not be surprising to find a number of similarities between them at the level of the individual. In general, authors have pointed out that invention, innovation and entrepreneurship have the same sources and deliver outputs that are in essence very similar. Some of the similarities between them are:

1. The output of inventive, innovative and entrepreneurial activities all deliver something that is new, either psychologically or historically (Johannessen *et al.*, 2001).
2. Creativity pervades all three elements of imagineering (Beattie, 1999). While this may be obvious in the case of invention and possibly innovation, it is not often regarded as important to entrepreneurship. Schumpeter, however, argued that the desire to be creative motivates the entrepreneur (Scott, 1989); while according to a study by Hills and Shrader (1998) most entrepreneurs regard themselves as creative. Mitchell *et al.* (2002) regards creativity as the essence of opportunity recognition (which Kirzner saw as central to entrepreneurship). Hench and Sandberg (2000) further demonstrate that entrepreneurs not only recognize opportunities, but create new ones in the process.
3. When engaging in any one of the elements of imagineering, connections are created where none existed before. The function of the entrepreneur as the creator of new connections is obvious from Timmons' definition of entrepreneurship as the pursuit and creation of opportunities without regard to the available resources (Mitchell *et al.*, 2002).
4. All three elements of imagineering are in response to imperfect knowledge and uncertainty. The existence of uncertainty is what distinguishes invention from routine activities (Redelinghuys, 2000). In fact, uncertainty is a prerequisite for any creative activity (Rizzello, 1999); without it no imagineering needs to occur.

So, all elements of imagineering exist because of uncertainty, are enabled by creativity and create new connections in the economic system. This alone, however, is not sufficient to justify grouping invention, innovation and entrepreneurship under a single collective noun. Since this chapter is to investigate imagineering at the level of the individual, one also needs to show that all elements of imagineering are similar, specifically at the level of individual cognition.

Simon (1983) argued that even though all activities on the continuum from discovery to development address different substantive problems, and that the psychological processes (including cognition) that underlie them are similar. Though Simon was not clear what these similarities are, the literature mainly suggests the following cognitive similarities:

1. None of the elements of imagineering involve pure deductive thinking. According to Redelinghuys (2000), for something to be an invention, it must not be deducible from the current state of art. Similarly, Rizzello (1999) states that innovation cannot be derived from a succession of previous decision-making events.
2. All the elements involve non-rational thinking and imagination. A person, such as an entrepreneur, who pursues opportunities while disregarding resources, will not be described by an economist as being a rational actor. Langlois (1987) explains that an entrepreneur would not be able to fulfil his function if he did not engage in 'extra-logical' thinking. The role of imagination in inventing and innovating is also emphasized by Loasby (2001a) and Maclaurin (1953). One specific instance of non-rational thinking that is essential to all three elements is the leap of conjecture (Beattie, 1999).
3. To successfully engage in any of the three elements, one has to be able to resolve contradictions. Redelinghuys (2000) regards the discovery and removal of contradictions as crucial to invention while Beattie (1999) and Hills and Shrader (1998) point out the importance of contradictions to guiding the actions of entrepreneurs.
4. All the elements of imagineering involve imperfect perception. Successful entrepreneurs' cognition is known to entail counterfactual thinking, a belief in small numbers, affect infusion, a self-serving bias, over-confidence and the planning fallacy (Mitchell *et al.*, 2002). All of these create and are the result of imperfect perception. The 'attacker's advantage' of innovating firms are as a result of imperfect perception of the risks and returns of an innovation (Foster, 1986). Rizzello (1999) goes as far as stating that the true microfoundation of any theory of change should be based on imperfections in perception.
5. The processes underlying all three elements are enabled by previous knowledge. Entrepreneurs are better able to recognize opportunities if they have some degree of knowledge of the relevant field (Ardichvili

and Cardozo, 2000). This is also true for innovation in organizations (Nonaka *et al.*, 2000) and obviously for any inventor.

6. A certain level of preparedness or alertness is necessary to engage in any one of the three elements. This is an idea that is central to Kirzner's work, and is confirmed by Ardichvili and Cardozo (2000).

The points made above support Simon's argument that all activities on the continuum from discovery to development involve the same psychological processes. Given that the paper will investigate invention, innovation and entrepreneurship by looking at individual cognition, there is sufficient justification for joining them into one cognitive concept ('imagineering'), if only to make it easier to refer to them collectively in this chapter. Imagineering is named after one of the results that invention, innovation and entrepreneurship have in common, namely the engineering of imagination.

Previous Theorizing on Imagineering

A quick review of past economic literature, starting with the so-called neoclassical views, may be in order here to place the contribution of this study in a theoretical context. Neoclassical theories, based on the notion of general equilibrium, have no place for any kind of change. There is no allowance for the progression of time, uncertainty, surprise or choice, and hence no room for any imagineering (Loasby, 2001b). It treats all forms of imagineering as exogenous to the economic system (Schmookler, 1966). Even if it admits the possibility of imagineering taking place, it regards it as a black box. Any imagineering is simply seen as moving the market towards completeness – imagineering takes place until every single possible need is satisfied and every possible state is hedged (Lewis and Mizen, 2000). Loasby (2001b) further criticizes the neoclassical approach as disregarding the role of cognition in human action.

It is therefore clear that an economic theory of imagineering has to be developed outside the limiting assumptions of the general equilibrium approach. According to Ruttan (1997), three major schools developed as a result:

1. Inducement theories: This school originated with Hicks and was elaborated on by economists such as Ahmad (1966), who believed that innovation was induced by changes in factor prices. Another inducement theory was what Ruttan calls the 'demand-pull' tradition as espoused by Griliches (1957) and Schmookler (1966). Schmookler's main finding was that demand was more important than the supply of knowledge and technological advances in determining the direction

and extent of inventive activity. There is certainly some support for the demand-inducement theory – inventors such as Edison and Bell are known to have been driven by market forces in their inventive efforts (Gorman and Carlson, 1990). However, over the years Schmookler's theory has attracted a lot of criticism, notably from Rosenberg (1974). Many authors have also pointed out the failure of demand-inducement to explain the development and adoption of important innovations such as eyeglasses (Maldonado, 2001), antibiotics (Townes, 1983) and lasers (Townes, 1983). Koen and Kohli (1998) showed that demand can only drive incremental invention (Altshuller's levels 1 to 3), but not any kind of radical invention (levels 4 to 5). The reason for this is that the market can only demand what it is aware of – demand often lies latent only to be awakened by an advance in knowledge or technology. This seems to have been true in the case of the fluorescent light (Hamberg, 1963), computers (Neubauer and Lank, 1998), copiers (Lewis and Mizen, 2000) and watches (Proctor, 1998). Despite the criticism, inducement theories represented an advance since they allowed economists to treat imagineering as an endogenous variable. It did, however, disregard supply factors and still treated the dynamics of imagineering as a black box. The understanding of the inducement school is shown in Figure 2.1.

2. Evolutionary theories: These theories follow on from the work of Nelson and Winter (1982). Imagineering is seen to start with a search for better techniques with successful techniques being selected by the market. Once a technique is established, it is imitated and becomes a routine that encapsulates the knowledge created by the imagineering (Ruttan, 1997). Of all the economic theories of imagineering, this theory comes closest to giving us insight into what happens inside the black box.

3. Path dependence theories: Path dependence theories give more attention to the role of technology and knowledge in determining the rate and direction of imagineering. It points out that imagineering efforts are constructed on past knowledge (Ardichvili and Cardozo, 2000) and technological paradigms, and hence tend to follow irreversible technological trajectories (Dosi, 1982). The trajectories constrain search

Figure 2.1   The black box approach to innovation

efforts within certain zones and limit the power of market inducement to influence imagineering efforts. Path dependence theory represents a theoretical advance since it gives a greater role to the supply side, that is the state of technology and knowledge. It still does not explain how imagineering takes place at the level of the individual and it carries a flavour of Ogburn's view that inventions are inevitable. Fleming (2001) suggests that the idea of trajectories may be too narrow a description, since innovation is the result of interdependent webs of combinations of technologies. At the base of Fleming's criticism is Schumpeter's (1912) idea that imagineering is due to the formation of new combinations. Redelinghuys (2000) points out that the combinative theory is closely related to path dependence theories since networks of prior combinations determine the new combinations, recombinations and uncombinations that are made. One can only recombine or uncombine what already exists and he refers to this phenomenon as the phylogeny law of inventions. The combinative theory of imagineering is developed in more detail later. Fleming (2001) draws attention to the relationship of combinative theory to the evolutionary theory of imagineering, in that imagineers do a local search for new combinations that are selected by the market.

Despite the contributions that these theories have made to economists' understanding of imagineering, there is still one main concern: the actual process of imagineering remains a black box (Kline, 1995; Magee, 2000). For example, how are better techniques created, how do heuristics develop, how do technological paradigms form, how does a price change create an invention, or how are the best combinations found and integrated? To the extent that these questions remain unanswered, our understanding of imagineering will be limited and 'new ideas' will still very much be treated as exogenous to economists' analytical systems (Weitzman, 1996).

All of the imagineering theories have one thing in common – they are based on microfoundations. If despite their micro-approach they are still unable to open the black box, it requires researchers to go even deeper to the micro-micro level as Leibenstein (1979) suggested. In order to replace the black box rationality (which is mainly derived from neoclassical theory) one needs to investigate the cognition of economic agents (Denzau and North, 1994). We need to investigate that which underlies imagineering micro-behaviour of individuals, that is, cognitive states, thinking processes and thinking tools.

COGNITION IN ECONOMICS

Herbert Simon believed that 'Economics will progress as we deepen our understanding of human thought processes' (Rizzello, 1999: 79). Assuming that cognition is a fruitful departure point, this section starts with reviewing the role that cognition plays in neoclassical theory and to what extent it has been explored by economists. Since some people may not regard cognition as a suitable subject for economic research, the section also considers why there is a need to understand cognition in economics.

The Theories

There is no role for any kind of thinking in neoclassical economics. Neoclassical theory assumes an integral field, where everything is connected to everything else in the most optimal way (Potts, 2000). No resources are assumed to be available for cognition since cognition is only needed in an environment where imperfect knowledge and uncertainty exist.

Any reference to cognition is inconsistent with neoclassical theories, but in cases where such theories do refer to cognition and the mind, a distorted picture arises. Their idea of the mind is that of a container (Arthur, 2000), all minds are assumed to be the same and in the highly unlikely case of cognition having to take place, it is assumed that cognitive abilities are perfect and unbounded (Rizzello, 1999). If any cognition takes place it is of a purely deductive nature; economic agents only engage in logical and probabilistic reasoning. In mathematical general equilibrium models, there is of course no room for any kind of thinking that is inconsistent with mathematical reasoning.

The lack of attention to cognition is somewhat surprising considering that economists such as Adam Smith and Alfred Marshall considered it to be particularly important (see Loasby, 2001a; Rizzello, 1999). More recently, Hayek and Simon stand out as the economists who paid the most attention to cognition. Simon's concepts of bounded rationality, procedural rationality and satisficing need no introduction. Though many people are familiar with Hayek's writings on knowledge (see Hayek, 1945), his work on mind and cognition is less known, especially his book *The Sensory Order* (Hayek, 1976 [1952]).

Cognition in economics therefore clearly has a long and proud lineage. This raises the question of why economists have paid so little attention to it. It may be that economists do not believe that it is important to consider the role of cognition in economic theories and policy-making.

But do Economists Need to Understand Cognition?

To claim that economic theory guides economic agents in making choices, economists have to be concerned with the underlying process of choice-making. Without an understanding of cognition, there can be no under-standing of choice. Cognition not only determines how agents make choices, it also determines how they generate alternatives and how they interpret the reality to which they respond. One can go as far as saying that no agent experiences reality directly, and that it is cognition that brings forth the world that we perceive and respond to (Von Krogh, *et al.*, 2000).

Without a cognitive theory of imagineering, one has to rely on the study of behaviour without knowing what forces drive that behaviour. Simon (1983: 4569) expressed his dissatisfaction with the behaviourist approach to imagineering when he said: 'In building a theory of scientific discovery or invention, a scientist's behaviors are the data – the phenomena we seek to explain – not the direct source of theory . . . We use terms such as 'judge-ment', 'intuition' and 'creative insight' to name and label . . . But labels are not explanations.'

Some authors have pointed out that without an understanding of cogni-tion, and specifically of cognition of individuals, economists will be unable to understand developments in the knowledge-based economy and are likely to suggest inappropriate policies:

1. Cognition results in the creation and application of knowledge. Without an understanding of cognition, it is virtually impossible to understand the role that knowledge plays in organizations (Nonaka *et al.*, 2000) and the economy as a whole;
2. As the role of cognition in entrepreneurial success is increasingly being acknowledged, it is attracting more attention in recent research on entrepreneurship (Mitchell *et al.*, 2002). Not only is an understanding of cognition important to enhance our micro-understanding of imagineering, it is also important if we want to be able to determine and understand the broader social and economic forces involved in technological progress (Gorman and Carlson, 1990);
3. Kline (1995) suggests that economic theory that ignores the cognitive perspective will constrain the areas that economists explore and may thus lead to misconceived policy. Arthur (2000) speculates that this was indeed the case with the collapse of the Soviet Union in the early 1990s. A cognitive perspective on economic change would have led econo-mists to make more appropriate policy recommendations, which rec-ognized that Russians were not simply a collection of empty minds

with given endowments and preferences. As it were, it seems a general equilibrium perspective led to imbalanced recommendations that made the economic and social situation worse.

When it comes to the study of imagineering, some economists may argue that a focus on individual cognition is misplaced since invention and innovation are no longer done by independent individuals, but by large corporations in their research laboratories.

The view that large corporations and their teams of scientists and problem-solvers are the real drivers of invention and innovation has been generally accepted (by Schumpeter, among others). Few researchers have actually investigated to what extent this is true. Most simply point out that the majority of patents are registered by corporations, without considering the inventive level of the patents or the actual conversion of patents into innovations.

The only study that I am aware of is a study by Hamberg (1963), conducted at a time when the belief that the corporation is the main source of invention was already well established. He points out that consensus-driven, risk-averse corporations with groups of relatively average scientists focused on producing defensive patents are unlikely to generate inventions that go beyond Altshuller's levels one or two. Radical invention is most likely to happen outside the confines of a corporation, and corporations are more likely to purchase (not generate) radical inventions once they show potential. Incremental inventions (being more obvious and easier to generate) contribute more to the patent pool than radical inventions. Furthermore, a far greater proportion of inventions by independent inventors tend to be converted into innovations than corporate inventions (Hamberg, 1963), while corporations can take up to 20 years to turn their inventions into innovations (Sarett, 1983; Townes, 1983), if at all. So while corporations may well deliver a greater quantity of inventions, it is independent inventors whose work is most likely to lead to entrepreneurial ventures. In the end, all imagineering originates in the individual, and this is sufficient to justify a focus on the cognition of individuals.

CONCEPTUAL FRAMEWORK FOR UNDERSTANDING IMAGINEERING

In this section, the phenomena that make up a cognitive theory of imagineering is first discussed separately and then integrated into a cognitive conceptual framework. Since this conceptual framework does not include many of the important variables highlighted by economic theories of imagineering, these variables are then added in order to produce a more general economic conceptual framework.

Cognitive Phenomena Important to Imagineering

From the discussion of the cognitive similarities between the elements of imagineering it is clear that the phenomena which need to be investigated and related in a cognitive theory of imagineering are: mental constructs, heuristics, routines, contradictions, conjectures, deduction, imagination and other kinds of connective thinking. They are all addressed in this section.

Making Connections: Deduction and Imagination

Most successful innovations appear obvious and logical in hindsight, which creates the belief that one only needs deductive thinking to be a successful innovator. Deduction, however, plays only a small role in the imagineering process. For instance, Hume said: 'no kind of reasoning can give rise to a new idea', Einstein said: 'There is no logical path leading to laws' and Rabinow (the inventor of machine character recognition) said: 'Inventing is not done logically' (Weber and Llorente, 1993: 67). Entrepreneurs are also known to engage in non-logical thinking (Mitchell *et al.*, 2002). Foster (1986) described the limited use of deduction as the source of the 'attacker's advantage' often attributed to entrepreneurs.

Deduction is usually only of use in the generation of level one inventions; it is impossible for deduction to deliver anything that lies outside the predetermined path of logic. It is only by escaping from deductive rationality that one can engage in radical innovation. Deduction does become much more useful in later stages of imagineering when the implications of discoveries and inventions are explored and when innovations are tested, de-bugged and adjusted.

While deductive thinking connects the unconnected along a fairly predetermined and predictable path, imagination creates connections that did not previously exist in the realm of experience. All deductive reasoning is based on assumptions (everything that lies between 'if' and 'then'). The assumptions themselves exist prior to any reasoning – their source is imagination. Deductive rationality cannot exist without imagination (Sinnott, 1959).

Inducement theories of imagineering are open to criticism because they don't acknowledge the role of latent demand. People can only demand what exists or is obvious to them. Existing demand is unlikely to induce imagineering that goes beyond the obvious. Here is where imagination comes in.

By creating that which cannot be seen, it releases the latent demand that makes room for invention and innovation to succeed (Loasby, 2001a).

Before new combinations can be formed, they have to be imagined. New markets, products, services, production methods, sources of supply or ways of organizing must first be imagined before any entrepreneur can generate commercial transactions from them. Without imagination, imagineering is not possible.

Imagination expresses itself in a way of thinking that can be described as making a leap of conjecture. The leap takes the imagineer outside what is known or observed and enables him to make new connections. These ideas are not new to economics, and can be traced back to Adam Smith who believed that speculation is the source of innovation (Loasby, 2001a).

As deductive reasoning cannot exist without imagination, so the reverse is also true. Poincaré (1924) saw the result of imagination as the departure point for rationality – it takes over where imagination stops. Once a new combination is imagined, it has to be brought back into the world of the known; it has to be converted into something that people can associate with. Once an innovation turns out to be successful, it also has to be translated into a routine. Deduction makes this possible, and so ensures that the gains that arise from exercising imagination are preserved (Bartlett, 1958).

Mental Constructs and Contradictions

Knowing that imagination enables imagineers to leap outside the known, the question is, what is this 'known' that they leap from? Hayek believed that we cannot experience reality directly – we create an image of the 'known' which we adjust as time goes by. This image through which we filter our experience is called a mental model or construct. Denzau and North (1994) define mental constructs as internal representations that individual cognitive systems create to interpret the environment. Such constructs comprise things such as goals, rules or assumptions, categories, exceptions, and methods for discovery and translating experience into constructs (Holland *et al.*, 1986).

Mental constructs are the filter through which we observe and consider the information generated by our experience. They limit our ability to perceive certain objects, relationships or events. Scientific theories can create mental constructs and distort scientists' perception – as Einstein said: 'It is the theory that determines what we can observe'. Mental constructs originate in our personal and collective experience, and since every person's experience is different, every person's mental constructs may be different. It can therefore easily happen that different people will interpret the same data differently.

So if imagination is employed to make a leap of conjecture, the leap is not made from actual experience, but from and out of a mental construct. Mental constructs limit the perception of individuals and whole communities, and so by leaping outside a mental construct, one is able to perceive what has not been perceived before. Leaping outside a personal construct may lead to psychological creativity only, while leaping outside a collective construct may give rise to historical creativity.

New combinations lead to innovations, but even though all economic agents are aware of the elements that could be combined, their mental constructs prevent them from creating the connections that may lead to an innovation. Boden (1994) argues that this is exactly what happened with Kekulé's discovery of the benzene molecule. Kekulé knew everything that he needed to know to make his discovery, that is snakes and loops, but personal and collective mental constructs initially prevented him from making the connection that led to the discovery. Along the same lines, Savransky (2000) lists three conditions for invention to take place – each condition involves observing something that has been there all along but nobody was able to see.

No leap of conjecture can completely escape the mental construct it leaps from. Mental constructs form the base of the leap and still influence the direction and quality of the leap. Leaps can lead to several new ideas, of which the vast majority can never be converted into inventions, innovations and new ventures. The mental construct's influence returns here by controlling the selection of the ideas that will be allowed to develop into inventions (Holton, 1979). Mental constructs and imagination are complementary, and mental constructs guide, focus and limit the range of imagination (Von Krogh *et al.*, 2000).

The purpose of mental constructs is not simply to maintain cognitive stability, but rather to create the conditions required to generate the new knowledge that facilitates imagineering. Since mental constructs are simplifications and translations of reality, it will be common for mental constructs to be inconsistent with reality, and even for the mental constructs of the same person to be contradictory.

If mental constructs were perfectly congruent with reality, there would be no need to create knowledge and no reason for imagineering. However, a world of change means that agents constantly need to create knowledge in order to adjust to the mismatch between the data they perceive and their preceding experiences (Rizzello, 1999). Incongruence between mental constructs and experience, alerts agents to the need to create new knowledge and directs them to the areas where new knowledge and imagineering are most urgently required. Denzau and North (1994: 26) make the point in relation to entrepreneurship: 'An ideological entrepreneur who learns of an incoherence . . . could utilize this in order to help reinterpret that ideology in ways more suitable to the entrepreneur's goals'. The apparent weakness of mental constructs therefore turns out to be their most useful attribute.

The idea that incongruence triggers the process of imagineering is not new to economists, management scientists (cf. Hampden-Turner, 1990) or scientists. For instance, Loasby (2001a) mentions that Adam Smith believed that anomalies were an important stimulus for the creation of new knowledge. Drucker (1985) developed a classification of the sources of innovation and entrepreneurship, and six of the eight sources he mentions cause or create incongruence and lead to imagineering.

To deal with incongruence, agents are forced to examine their mental constructs and make their assumptions explicit. Argyris (1980) refers to these assumptions as the 'undiscussables' and they constrain learning and imagineering for as long as they are hidden. If the agent wants to learn and 'imagineer', he must find the assumptions that reinforce the incongruence and use these assumptions as a launching pad from which to make leaps of conjecture. One way to find hidden assumptions is to rephrase the incongruence as a contradiction (Goldratt and Cox, 1992), which brings us back to the idea mentioned earlier, that successful imagineering usually involves the resolution of a contradiction. This goes some way to explain Nonaka and Toyama's (2002) argument that innovative firms are normally those that are good at resolving contradictions.

Economists prefer to use the concept of trade-off instead of contradiction, and normally map it as a curve with a negative slope. Trade-offs are important to Dosi's notion of a technological trajectory, which he defines as 'the activity of technological process along the economic and technological trade-offs defined by a paradigm' (Dosi, 1988: 1128). Like Dosi, Ahmad (1966) explains that innovation can be shown as a resolution of trade-offs such as the one illustrated in Figure 2.2. An innovation can be

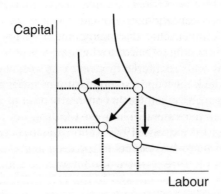

Figure 2.2   Innovation as a resolution of trade-offs

something that allows a firm to produce the same output with less capital and labour, or increasing output without needing to sacrifice more capital and labour, as indicated by the inward shift of the isoquant.

The existence of mental constructs inevitably leads to contradictions, and the market (itself a mental construct) cannot be relied on to resolve such contradictions. Economic agents therefore need to employ methods to assist them in making assumptions explicit, making leaps of conjecture from these assumptions and resolving contradictions. The heuristics employed are influenced by the mental construct, and in turn the heuristics, as part of a mental construct, leads to adjustments to the mental construct. Once a heuristic proves itself to be useful, it will become part of the imagineer's repertoire of routines. A prolific inventor such as Edison was believed to have generated his inventions with only a handful of heuristics (Gorman and Carlson, 1990).

Given the purpose of mental constructs, they cannot be right or wrong. Prince (1975) demonstrates how 'wrong' mental constructs can lead to new combinations that become successful innovations. In fact, if a mental construct becomes more accurate, variety will suffer and the ability of the agent to engage in imagineering will decline.

In the next section, all the basic elements of cognition involved in imagineering will be integrated into a single cognitive framework.

A COGNITIVE CONCEPTUAL FRAMEWORK OF IMAGINEERING

The early view of imagineering on the individual level was that it was unfathomable – a process of courting serendipity through the hard work of trial-and-error. Representative of this view was Thomas Edison's comment that success is 99 per cent perspiration and 1 per cent inspiration, or Louis Pasteur with his comment that 'discovery comes to the prepared mind'. As long as our understanding is limited to this view, it is only possible to introduce imagineering into economic models as an exogenous variable at a fairly aggregated level. Our understanding of how individual imagineering has, however, advanced much further since the days of Edison. The first milestone in the development of our post-Edison understanding of the practice of successful individual innovation was the understanding that innovation does not involve deductive reasoning, but a leap of conjecture.

In a letter written in 1952, Einstein outlined a model for thinking that led him to his discoveries and is reproduced from Holton (1979) as Figure 2.3. This model captures the cognitive dynamics, not only of scientific discovery, but also of imagineering.

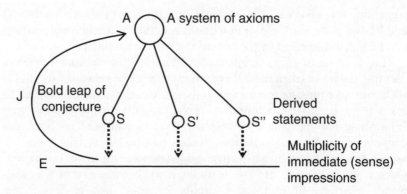

Figure 2.3   Einstein's model of scientific discovery

The aspiring 'imagineer' who wants to create an invention, innovation or new venture, needs to imagine it first. If the imagineer is to create something that is truly novel, he needs to break out of his experience (E) by making a bold leap of conjecture (J). If the leap is successful it will lead to an axiom (A), or a new idea that has not been thought of before. At this stage, the new idea is still vulnerable to criticism, as it has not been properly connected to the collective experience yet. The axiom's implications need to be translated into statements (S), in other words the new idea needs to be connected to other elements to form a useful new combination. The collection of statements forms a discovery (or an invention or innovation) that has to be tested against experience (E). Einstein deliberately left a gap between the arrows and the line representing experience, to indicate that leaping and testing does not occur in relation to direct experience, but in relation to the mental construct based on experience. Einstein's process makes it clear exactly how individuals can consistently practise successful imagineering: by applying techniques that facilitate breaking out of existing mental constructs.

Einstein could not explain how someone should make leaps of conjecture to potentially useful axioms, except for stating that it depended on intuition (Holton, 1979). De Bono (1969, 1992) provided the solution here with his development of tools (which he called lateral thinking) designed for breaking out of mental constructs. Instead of mental constructs, De Bono referred to the mind as a self-organizing system, preceding the work on self-organization by Ilya Prirogine by several years.

After de Bono's contribution, the next question was where innovators should focus their attention once they had mastered the techniques for breaking out of mental constructs. There are an infinite number of possible leaps that can be made. Goldratt and Cox's (1992) dialectical mapping

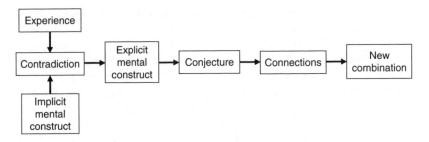

Figure 2.4   Cognitive framework of imagineering

technique (called the 'evaporating cloud') filled in this piece of the puzzle. The evaporating cloud allows one to define all problems as trade-offs or contradictions. It shows how one can draw out the assumptions behind a trade-off and use these assumptions as focus points for innovative efforts (see Scheinkopf, 1999).

Once the assumptions underlying a contradiction have been made explicit and used as the basis to leap to a potentially novel idea, this idea needs to be connected to other elements in the form of a new combination. This new combination must then be refined and tested through the use of mainly deductive reasoning and be turned into a market transaction. It also needs to be connected to the collective mental constructs of the relevant community through communication based on deductive reasoning.

The cognitive framework of the practice of successful imagineering on an individual level integrates all these milestones (see Figure 2.4). The framework makes it clear that innovation is the result of leaping outside existing mental constructs by resolving trade-offs or contradictions.

An agent starts out with a set of experience and a mental construct of which he is not aware. The mental construct at some point will deliver predictions that are not borne out in experience. The comparison of experience and the implicit mental construct leads to incongruence, which can be phrased as a contradiction. The contradiction could be a problem, an unexpected failure or a constraint, which is then the start of the process that leads to innovation. Becoming aware of the contradiction allows the agent to identify the underlying assumptions, and in turn this process makes the mental construct explicit. The assumptions included in the mental construct that seem to be at the root of the incongruence can then be challenged by using them as reference points for conjectural thinking. Once a conjecture leads to potentially useful ideas, those ideas are tested and verified through a process of deductive reasoning and finally connected to other ideas or objects to form a useful new combination.

The TRIZ approach, probably the most comprehensive review of inventions confirms this framework. A process for systematic innovation developed by Altshuller, is based on a worldwide review of over two million patents. According to the TRIZ approach, there is one thing all inventions from levels two to five have in common – they resolve a contradiction. TRIZ offers tools that enable the aspiring inventor to break free of mental constructs by tapping the mental constructs of other fields outside his expertise. This is done with the aid of 40 inventive principles and a contradiction table (see Savransky, 2000).

The framework as given is not static, but an iterative process. The first iteration starts with a dramatic leap of conjecture, and leads to a major invention or discovery (level five). At that point the new the invention or discovery creates a new field or science, but its usefulness is not immediately obvious. When the implications of the invention or discovery are drawn into the collective mental construct, it challenges conventional wisdom and generally accepted assumptions in the area. It exposes new contradictions and makes the dimensions of past contradictions invalid. The new contradictions create a base for the development of innovations and new ventures. Since the initial invention has created various incongruities, these incongruities create problems that can only be solved by going through the process again. Innovators and entrepreneurs make their leaps of conjecture and find new combinations with other technologies, which leads to useful ('killer') applications (level four) for the initial invention or discovery. Once this round is completed, the next round (level three) begins, probably triggered by other new combinations that now become possible or by problems experienced with the current generation of innovations. Moving to levels two and one, innovations involve making the more obvious combinations and improvements.

Innovations at each level create a 'splash' of incongruence in the current mental constructs, which creates further opportunities for inventors and entrepreneurs. The consequence is that the basic contradiction exposed at level five is continuously resolved. At level one, the limit of the resolution of the initial contradiction is reached, so that no improvement can be made without sacrificing something. This process is reminiscent of Dosi's (1982) notion of technological paradigms and trajectories – with the paradigm defined at level five and the trajectory being the progression from level five to level one. The iterative process is not one-directional, imagineering activity can take place at all levels simultaneously, and it is not necessarily the case that a trajectory has to reach level one before a new level five invention appears.

Once most imagineering takes place on level one, the field is ripe for a new level five invention or discovery, which makes past dimensions of the trade-off or contradiction invalid and exposes a new basic contradiction.

With the emergence of a level five discovery, one of the dimensions of the previous paradigm's trade-off becomes irrelevant and new dimensions enter. Dosi (1988) illustrates how this happened in thermionic valves, but as a simpler illustration, one could imagine how this re-dimensionalization of trade-offs could have happened with something like the book. In the days of the medieval scribes, the trade-off was between quantity and quality. Gutenberg's printing press resolved this trade-off by making it possible to produce higher quantity and higher quality simultaneously. Modern printing presses made the quantity aspect increasingly irrelevant as the speed of book production increased. Instead a new dimension was introduced, so that the trade-off that now concerned the market probably became one between cost and quality.

A trajectory can indeed be exhausted as Kirzner suggested. Schmookler (1966) believed that this could not happen for as long as demand existed, and cited as evidence the fact that a seemingly exhausted area such as horseshoes, had an increase in the number of patents until 1910 when motor vehicle technology arrived. This is not, as Schmookler suggests, proof that exhaustion can never occur as long as there is demand, since most of the horseshoe inventions were almost certainly incremental inventions – there were no radical inventions (Altshuller's levels four to five) in horseshoe technology in the latter part of the period. Inventions and new ventures can be created for as long as other elements are available with which to form new combinations. However, without radical inventions and discoveries, new trajectories are unlikely to be created, and old trajectories will deliver little more than improvements and refinements. Thomson's (1987) study of sewing machines confirms that demand drives new inventions, but that such inventions are usually of an incremental nature. Since the market cannot resolve contradictions (Nonaka and Toyama, 2002), it is unable to create radical inventions.

The cognitive framework makes it clear how the cognition of agents can be modelled, but it is incomplete if the insights of economists are ignored. The role of the market, uncertainty, path dependence, personality and knowledge are among the factors that need to be added to the framework.

A More Comprehensive Conceptual Framework of Imagineering

Market forces do influence the rate and direction of imagineering. Inventors such as Edison and Bell were known to have been motivated by the possibility of appropriable personal financial gain (Schmookler, 1966; Gorman and Carlson, 1990), but financial gain seems to be less of a driving force to the scientist who wants to create new knowledge. This is not to say that knowledge and market forces are in opposition, instead they are complementary. The market cannot enable imagineering to the extent that knowledge creation and complementary technologies can (Rosenberg, 1974), but the market is a much stronger motivator of imagineering. However, even if the motivation that market induces is at its strongest, it cannot lead to imagineering in the case of latent demand, that is where users have not yet been able to imagine new possibilities.

Even if the market cannot resolve contradictions, it certainly determines which trade-offs or contradictions are most important (Da Silveira and Slack, 2001). But one could go further than that – the market actually creates the incongruence that can be phrased as contradictions. The incongruence is created for example when the relative price of a production factor changes (Ahmad, 1966) or when income changes (Schmookler, 1966). However, without enabling knowledge, no change in relative prices can lead to the needed invention (for example, cure for cancer); it can only increase the intensity of the incongruence. Dosi (1988) also states that relative price changes can influence the rate of progress, selection criteria and direction within a technological trajectory, but cannot on its own give rise to a new trajectory.

Other factors that may influence imagineering efforts are the traits of the imagineer and uncertainty. Uncertainty triggers imagineering by creating opportunities for incongruence to emerge and to be exposed. Shackle (1972: 416–417) said that 'uncertainty involves . . . the entertainment of rival, mutually exclusive hypotheses'. In other words, uncertainty is itself a kind of contradiction, which in turn may trigger imagineering.

Previous research (see Grebel, 2002) has shown that there are certain traits that distinguish the entrepreneur from the non-entrepreneur. As Schumpeter pointed out, there is also a difference between the inventor and the entrepreneur and Markman *et al.* (2002) investigated this further. They found that the distinction between the entrepreneurial and the non-entrepreneurial inventor can be explained by the traits of inventors, specifically by their mental constructs concerning events (regretful thinking) and their own abilities (self-efficacy).

A more comprehensive framework can now be offered, combining the cognitive framework with the effect of market-inducement, knowledge, uncertainty and traits. This is shown in Figure 2.5.

Four boxes are added from Figure 2.4. All new combinations create new knowledge, which feeds into agents' mental constructs. This takes care of the path-dependence one is likely to observe in imagineering. New combinations do not lead to a commercial transaction unless the originator of the new combination possesses certain entrepreneurial traits. Once transactions take place, they have an influence on the relative prices of inputs and related products, and the price changes in turn become part of the agent's experience. Uncertainty is not shown separately, since uncertainty is, as per Shackle's definition, already included as a kind of contradiction.

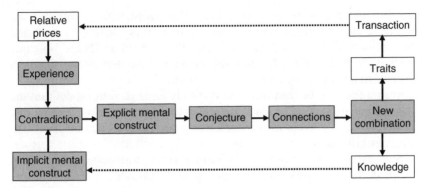

Figure 2.5   Synthesis of various approaches to innovation

The given framework offers a synthesis of the inducement, path-dependence and combinatorial theories of innovation. It also indicates where further empirical research needs to focus and what elements and relationships have to be included when imagineering is modelled. Given a framework such as the one in Figure 2.5, the remaining questions are first if imagineering can be modelled at all, and second if such modelling is desirable. These issues are addressed in the next section.

CAN IMAGINEERING BE MODELLED AND WITH WHAT RESULTS?

No attempt will be made to present a simulation or mathematical model of imagineering in this chapter. For now, I will simply explore to what extent the elements and relationships mapped in Figure 2.5 have been modelled before. The argument is that if they have been modelled before, it should be possible to construct a comprehensive agent-based simulation model of imagineering.

Modeling of imagineering is too complex to be done without the aid of computer simulation. Most people would argue that computational modelling of imagineering is impossible since computers cannot create something that has not been given beforehand. Neural networks work on this basis – it appears as if neural networks learn, but all possible connections are given to them in advance. When such a program 'learns' all it really does is change the strengths of existing connections or activating connections that have been latent. No new connections are created, and hence no real learning or imagineering takes place.

Some simulation models of creativity worked along similar lines, but instead of pre-existing relationships they contained a number of pre-programmed heuristics. The model used these heuristics to make 're-discoveries' from a given set of data. Simon (1983) explains how one such model (called BACON) was able to induct a number of mathematical laws from an unorganized set of data. While this model did not produce anything that can be regarded as historically creative, it did show that the use of heuristics could be modelled. In addition, it demonstrated that discoveries could be made with a small set of heuristics, as was the case with Thomas Edison.

Successful work has also been done on mental constructs. Arthur (2000) mentions his own work and that of Sargent as examples of computational models that simulated how agents adjust their mental constructs based on their experience. Their models do not lead to imagineering, but the work of Holland *et al.* (1986) moves closer. Holland and his colleagues developed a program where agents created their own mental constructs on the basis of their experience. Their program, called PI, was able to recategorize within mental constructs if there were a mismatch with experience. PI was not only able to engage in deductive reasoning as one would expect, but also in retroductive, abductive and analogical thinking. Abductions, retroductions and analogies are all ways of thinking that enable people to make leaps of conjecture.

Holland *et al.*'s (1986) program could also form new concepts by combining existing concepts. It found combinations that may lead to new concepts by looking for conflicting expectations between the existing concepts and reconciling the conflicts through the use of certain heuristics. In the search for potentially useful combinations, those that contained no conflicts were ignored. This showed how the resolution of contradictions, that lead to new combinations, could be modelled.

The originator of a new combination becomes an entrepreneur once the new combination is converted into value through a market transaction. The distinction between the entrepreneurial and non-entrepreneurial inventor lies in their traits. Grebel (2002) showed that is possible to introduce the role of entrepreneurial traits in an economic model.

In short then, computational models are able to simulate all the cognitive aspects contained in this chapter's conceptual framework, that is the use of heuristics, conjectural thinking, the creation of mental constructs, the identification of incongruence, the adaptation of a mental construct as a result of incongruence, the resolution of contradictions that result from incongruence, the formation of new combinations triggered by a contradiction and the role of traits in the entrepreneurial venture that follows. Given the potential for computational modelling of creativity, it should therefore not be surprising if a computer program were to produce a patentable invention. This did indeed happen with a program called EURISKO (Boden, 1994). Designing a program that produces a patent is, however, not the same as modelling imagineering, but it does suggest that agent-based modelling of imagineering is not out of the reach of computational economists.

With proper training, methodologies such as TRIZ and Synectics (see Prince, 1970) seem to be able to produce invention on demand, which may suggest that imagineering is controllable to some extent. If it is controllable, does that not mean that imagineering would stop because everyone will produce the same ideas? Not necessarily, because creativity depends on mental constructs which vary from person to person. Different mental constructs mean different contradictions will be perceived and hence different new combinations will emerge. So far from destroying imagineering, even if everyone mastered the perfect recipe for imagineering, it would more likely lead to a proliferation of new ideas, and not the multiple discovery of the same idea (Magee, 2000).

Different mental constructs is also the reason why it would be difficult to predict the direction of especially radical imagineering. A small difference in mental constructs between the agents in a model and the agents in real life will be sufficient to lead to divergent results.

However, the purpose of models is not necessarily to predict. Models in themselves are mental constructs. By developing computational models, one is forced to make one's assumptions explicit and in the process learn how imagineering really takes place. So it is more than prediction – we can learn and create through modelling. Eventually, the only way to predict is to be the first to create, and therefore the first to model.

CONCLUSION

In this chapter I set out to develop a conceptual framework that would enhance economists' understanding of invention, innovation and entrepreneurship (abbreviated as imagineering) at the level of the individual. I showed that the study of cognition will enable us to open the black box of imagineering, and that this cognitive approach is useful and important to economics. Since Adam Smith, economists and management scientists have had ideas of what happens inside the black box of imagineering cognition, and these ideas were integrated in a conceptual framework (Figure 2.4). The insights of the various economic approaches to imagineering (inducement, evolutionary, path dependence and combinatorial) were shown to be complementary to the conceptual framework and incorporated into a more comprehensive framework (Figure 2.5). Different computer scientists and economists have already modelled all aspects of this framework, and therefore it should not be impossible for economists to start integrating imagineering into their economic models.

REFERENCES

Ahmad, S. (1966), 'On the theory of induced invention', *The Economic Journal*, **76** (302), 344–57.

Ames, E. (1961), 'Research, invention, development and innovation', *The American Economic Review*, **51** (3), 370–81.

Ardichvili, A. and R. N. Cardozo (2000), 'A model of the entrepreneurial opportunity recognition process', *Journal of Enterprising Culture*, **8** (2), 103–19.

Argyris, C. (1980), 'Making the undiscussable and its undiscussability discussable', *Public Administration Review*, **May/June**, 205–13.

Arthur, W. B. (2000), 'Cognition: The black box of economics', in Colander, D (ed.), *The Complexity Vision and the Teaching of Economics*. Cheltenham, UK and Lyme, USA: Edward Elgar, pp. 51–62.

Barreto, H. (1989), *The Entrepreneur in Microeconomic Theory: disappearance and explanation*. London: Routledge.

Bartlett, F. C. (1958), 'Adventurous thinking' reprinted in P. E. Vernon (ed.) (1970), *Creativity*. Harmondsworth: Penguin Books, pp. 98–106.

Beattie, R. (1999), *The Creative Entrepreneur: a study of the entrepreneur's creative process. Frontiers of entrepreneurial research*. Wellesley, MA: Babson College, Centre for Entrepreneurial Studies.

Boden, M. (1994), 'Creativity and computers', in T. Dartnall (ed.), *Artificial Intelligence and Creativity: an interdisciplinary approach*. Dordrecht: Kluwer Academic Publishers.

Da Silveira, G. and N. Slack (2001), 'Exploring the trade-off concept', *International Journal of Operations & Production Management*, **21** (7), 949–61.

De Bono, E. (1969), *Mechanism of the Mind*. London: Penguin.

De Bono, E. (1992), *Serious Creativity*. London: HarperCollins.

Denzau, A. T. and D. C. North (1994), 'Shared mental models: Ideologies and institutions', *Kyklos*, **47** (1), 3–31.

Domb, E. and H. W. Dettmer (1999), 'Breakthrough innovation in conflict resolution: Marrying TRIZ and the thinking process', Goal Systems International Working Paper, available at www.goalsys.com accessed 3 June 2002.

Dosi, G. (1982), 'Technological paradigms and technological trajectories', *Research Policy*, **11**, 147–62.

Dosi, G. (1988), 'Sources, procedures and microeconomic effects of innovation', *Journal of Economic Literature*, **26** (3), 1120–71.

Drucker, P. F. (1985), *Innovation and Entrepreneurship: practice and principles*. Oxford: Butterworth-Heinemann.

Foster, R. N. (1986), *Innovation: the attacker's advantage*. London: Pan Books.

Fleming, L. (2001), 'Recombinant uncertainty in technological search', *Management Science*, **47** (1), 117–32.

Grebel, T. (2002), 'Entrepreneurship: A new perspective'. Unpublished doctoral dissertation. University of Augsburg, Germany.

Griliches, Z. (1957), 'Hybrid corn: An exploration in the economics of technical change', *Econometrica*, **25**, 501–22.

Goldratt, E. and J. Cox (1992), *The Goal: a process of ongoing improvement*, 2nd edition. Great Barrington, MA: North River Press.

Gorman, M. E and W. B. Carlson (1990), 'Interpreting invention as a cognitive process: The case of Alexander Graham Bell, Thomas Edison, and the telephone', *Science, Technology and Human Values*, **15** (2), 131–64.

Hamberg, D. (1963), 'Invention in the industrial research laboratory', *The Journal of Political Economy*, **71** (2), 95–115.

Hampden-Turner, C. (1990), *Charting the Corporate Mind: from dilemma to strategy*. Oxford: Blackwell.

Hayek, F. A. (1945), 'The use of knowledge in society', *American Economic Review*, **35** (4), 519–30.

Hayek, F. A. (1976), *The Sensory Order: an inquiry into the foundations of theoretical psychology*, Chicago: University of Chicago Press.

Hench, T. J. and W. R. Sandberg (2000), '*As the fog cleared, something changed*': *opportunity recognition as a dynamic self-organizing process. Frontiers of Entrepreneurial Research*. Wellesley, MA: Babson College, Centre for Entrepreneurial Studies.

Hills, G. E. and R. C. Shrader (1998), *Successful Entrepreneur's Insights into Opportunity Recognition. Frontiers of Entrepreneurial Research*. Wellesley, MA: Babson College, Centre for Entrepreneurial Studies.

Hills, G. E., Shrader, R. C. and Lumpkin, G. T. (1999), *Opportunity Recognition as a Creative Process. Frontiers of Entrepreneurial Research*. Wellesley, MA: Babson College, Centre for Entrepreneurial Studies.

Holland, J. H., K. J. Holyoak, R. E. Nisbett and P. R. Thagard (1986), *Induction: processes of inference, learning, and discovery*. Cambridge: MIT Press.

Holton, G. (1979), 'Constructing a theory: Einstein's model', *American Scholar*, **48**, Summer, 309–40.

Johannessen, J-A., B. Olsen and G. T. Lumpkin (2001), 'Innovation and newness: What is new, how new, and new to whom?', *European Journal of Innovation Management*, **4** (1), 20–31.

Kline, S. J. (1995), *Conceptual Foundations of Multidisciplinary Thinking*. Stanford, CA: Stanford University Press

Koen, P. A. and P. Kohli (1998), *Idea Generation: who comes up with the most profitable products? Frontiers of Entrepreneurial Research*. Wellesley, MA: Babson College, Centre for Entrepreneurial Studies.

Langlois, R. N. (1987), 'Schumpeter and the obsolescence of the entrepreneur'. Paper presented at the History of Economics Society Annual Meeting, Boston.

Leibenstein, H. (1979), 'A branch of economics is missing: Micro-micro theory', *Journal of Economic Literature*, **17** (12), 477–502.

Lewis, M. K and P. D. Mizen (2000), *Monetary Economics*. Oxford: Oxford University Press.

Loasby, B. J. (2001a), 'Cognition, imagination and institutions in demand creation', *Journal of Evolutionary Economics*, **11** (1), 7–21.

Loasby, B. J. (2001b), 'Time, knowledge and evolutionary dynamics: Why connections matter', *Journal of Evolutionary Economics*, **11** (1), 393–412.

Magee, G. B. (2000), 'Rethinking invention: Cognition and the economics of technological creativity'. Working paper, Department of Economics, University of Melbourne.

Maldonado, T. (2001), 'Taking eyeglasses seriously', *Design Issues*, **17** (4), 32–43.
Markman, G. D., D. B. Balkin and R. A. Baron (2002), 'Inventors and new venture formation: The effects of general self-efficacy and regretful thinking', *Entrepreneurship Theory and Practice*, **27** (2), 149–65.
Maclaurin, W. R. (1953), 'The sequence from invention to innovation and its relation to economic growth', *The Quarterly Journal of Economics*, **67** (1), 97–111.
Mitchell, R. K., L. Busenitz, T. Lant, P. P. McDougall, E. A. Morse and J. B. Smith (2002), 'Toward a theory of entrepreneurial cognition: Rethinking the people side of entrepreneurial research', *Entrepreneurship Theory and Practice*, **27** (2), 93–104.
Mokyr, J. (1990), *The Lever of Riches: technological creativity and economic progress*. Oxford: Oxford University Press.
Nelson, R. R. and S. G. Winter (1982), *An Evolutionary Theory of Economic Change*. Cambridge: Cambridge University Press.
Neubauer, F and A. G. Lank (1998), *The Family Business: its governance for sustainability*. Macmillan, London.
Nonaka, I., R. Toyama and A. Nagata (2000), 'A firm as a knowledge-creating entity: A new perspective on the theory of the firm', *Industrial and Corporate Change*, **9** (1), 1–20.
Nonaka, I. and R. Toyama (2002), 'A firm as a dialectical being: Towards a dynamic theory of the firm', *Industrial and Corporate Change*, **11** (5), 995–1009.
Poincaré, H. (1924), 'Mathematical creation', reprinted in P. E. Vernon (ed.) (1970), *Creativity*. Harmondsworth: Penguin Books, pp. 77–188.
Potts, J. (2000), *The New Evolutionary Economics: complexity, competence and adaptive behaviour*. Cheltenham, UK and Lyme, USA: Edward Elgar.
Prince, G. M. (1970), *The Practice of Creativity: a manual for dynamic group problem solving*. New York: Harper & Row.
Prince, G. M. (1975), 'Creativity, self and power', in I. A. Taylor and J. W. Getzels (eds), *Perspectives in Creativity*. Chicago: Aldine Publishing.
Proctor, T. (1998), 'Innovations in time: What can we learn from history?' *Creativity and Innovation Management*, **7** (4), 204–11.
Redelinghuys, C. (2000), 'Proposed criteria for the detection of invention in engineering design', *Journal of Engineering Design*, **11** (3), 265–82.
Rizzello, S. (1999), *The Economics of the Mind*. Cheltenham, UK and Lyme, USA: Edward Elgar.
Rosenberg, N. (1974), 'Science, invention and economic growth', *The Economic Journal*, **84** (333), 90–108.
Ruttan, V. W. (1997), 'Induced innovation, evolutionary theory and path dependence: Sources of technical change', *The Economic Journal*, **107** (444), 1520–29.
Sarett, L. H. (1983), 'Research and innovation', *Proceedings of the National Academy of Sciences of the United States of America*, **80** (14), 4572–74.
Savransky, S. D. (2000), *Engineering of Creativity: introduction to TRIZ methodology of inventive problem solving*. Boca Raton: CRC Press.
Scheinkopf, L. J. (1999), *Thinking for a Change: putting the TOC thinking processes to use*. Boca Raton: St Lucie Press.
Schmookler, J. (1966), *Invention and Economic Growth*. Cambridge: Harvard University Press.
Schumpeter, J. A. (1912), *The Theory of Economic Development*. Cambridge, MA: Harvard University Press.
Scott, M. F. (1989), *A New View of Economic Growth*. Oxford: Clarendon Press.

Shackle, G. (1972), *Epistemics and Economics: a critique of economic doctrines*. Cambridge: Cambridge University Press.

Simon, H. A. (1983), 'Discovery, invention, and development: Human creative thinking', *Proceedings of the National Academy of Sciences of the United States of America*, **80** (14), 4569–71.

Sinnott, E. W. (1959), 'The creativeness of life', reprinted in P. E. Vernon (ed.) (1970), *Creativity*. Harmondsworth: Penguin Books, pp. 107–15.

Terninko, J., A. Zusman, and B. Zlotin, (1998), *Systematic Innovation: an introduction to TRIZ*. Boca Raton: St Lucie Press.

Thomson, R. (1987), 'Learning by selling and invention: The case of the sewing machine', *The Journal of Economic History*, **47** (2), 433–45.

Townes, C. H. (1983), 'Science, technology and invention: Their progress and interactions', *Proceedings of the National Academy of Sciences of the United States of America*, **80** (24), 7679–83.

Von Krogh, G., P. Erat and M. Macus (2000), 'Exploring the link between dominant logic and company performance', *Creativity and Innovation Management*, **9** (2), 82–93.

Weber, R. J. and A. M. Llorente (1993), 'Natural paths to invention: Reinventing the wheel', *Current Psychology*, **12** (1), 66–81.

Weitzman, M. L. (1996), 'Hybridizing growth theory', *The American Economic Review*, **86** (2), 207–12.

3. Learning from disaster

**Robin Cowan, Emmanuelle Fauchart,
Dominique Foray and Philip Gunby**

INTRODUCTION

In 1979 a partial melt-down of the reactor core at Three Mile Island was the worst nuclear power accident to that time. Between June 1985 and January 1987, six people suffered massive radiation overdoses during treatment using the Therac-25 machine. In the summer of 1991, ten million subscribers in the United States lost telephone service for durations ranging from ten minutes to six hours. In 1996, after ten years of development and a $500 million investment, the first Ariane 5 rocket exploded shortly after takeoff. In each of these cases, technological failure occurred. Loss of life, loss of huge investments, or loss of consumer services, caused 'disasters' in a broad sense.

Disasters, however, have the power to change things and are thus opportunities to motivate improvements. For example, the Bhopal chemical disaster changed the way the chemical industry organizes chemical stocks and storage, as well as safety standards and safety procedures (Fabiani and Theys, 1986), resulting in increased safety records. Three Mile Island prompted changes in the US nuclear industry – in equipment, safety practices and regulation – resulting in increased reliability (David *et al.*, 1996).

The purpose of this chapter is to investigate the learning that can be generated by such disasters, and to understand the economic aspects of 'learning from disaster', that is whether economic factors may affect whether learning from disaster takes place, which type and to which extent learning takes place, and whether this learning may benefit beyond the actors that produced it.

There is a wide literature in social sciences on learning in organizations vulnerable to technological risk and more particularly on: the behaviour of organizations using risky technologies and their vulnerability to disasters (Mitroff *et al.*, 1989); the changes that disasters bring about (Fabiani and Theys, 1986; Jasanoff, 1994); the lesser or greater ability of organization to change after a disaster (Vaughan, 1996; Stead and Smallman, 1998; Koorneef, 2000); the reasons why organizations have not learned before the disaster occurred (Stead and Smallman, 1999; Carroll, 1998); or on the forms of organizational learning (Edmonson and Moingeon, 1996; Toft and Reynolds, 1997; Turner and Pidgeon, 1997). Yet, this large literature generally studies organizations rather than learning itself as an independent category of analysis. In this chapter we wish to turn the question on its head and ask not what does our learning tell us about Bhopal, but rather what does Bophal or Therac-25 tell us about learning.

From the point of view of the economics of knowledge, a disaster is an opportunity to produce knowledge, to reduce the probability of future disasters (see for instance Kletz (1993) for a counterfactual analysis of how knowledge generated after previous incidents could have prevented further accidents if the actors had been aware of it) and to improve the performance of technological systems in general (see David *et al.* (1996) for an econometric account of improved technological performance after Three Mile Island). The opportunity lies in the fact that a disaster is usually the outcome of some kind of ignorance about the technology, and can be seen as an 'unplanned experiment' producing data about the system concerned. The issue is then to profit from this costly and rare experiment and, thus, to generate cognitive, technological, and organizational benefits from it.

Yet, our hypothesis is that learning from disaster is likely constrained due to the fact that:

1. technological disasters are likely unplanned events, thus harder to interpret and to infer understanding from; and
2. they are likely to occur in the course of 'doing' or 'using', thus entering in conflict with the normal course of activity.

Our first objective is therefore to identify the characteristics of disasters as unplanned events in the course of doing that may affect the learning from disaster. Our second objective will be to test whether those factors have affected the learning in a real world disaster, the Therac-25 case, of the name of a radiation therapy machine that caused fatalities due to software failure to administer the right radiation doses. This case has been chosen because it has the broad range of relevant characteristics for our testing. A related objective will then be to show how, in this particular case, the constraints on the learning from disaster have been shaped by the incentives of the actors as well as by the institutional environment.

The chapter is organized as follows. In the next section we develop the framework to identify the constraints and context that affect processes of learning from disaster. A detailed case study of the Therac-25 episode will, then, be presented in the third section. The fourth section will test the relevance of those constraints and context on the occurrence and diffusion of learning in the case of the Therac-25 disaster and will derive implications relative to the 'situated' nature of those constraints.

FRAMEWORK: DISASTER AS AN UNPLANNED KNOWLEDGE EXPERIMENT

This framework combines the economics of learning-by-doing (to which learning-from-disaster can be viewed as a particular case) and the economics of disaster (as an event whose context and structure are likely to affect its value as a knowledge experiment): considering a disaster as a knowledge experiment, it is likely to create learning opportunities and externalities; raising issues of private and social optimality. The detailed features of any disaster creates the context in which these issues have to be addressed.

On the Economics of Technological Learning

Learning from disaster is a form of learning-by-doing and further, shares many properties (in terms of the sources and effects of learning) with learning-by-using. Our discussion about structural similarities between learning by doing/using and learning from disaster opens the possibility to transfer some of the most recent advances in the literature on learning-by-doing to our problem.

From learning-by-doing/using to learning from disaster

Learning-by-doing is a form of learning that takes place at the manufacturing (and/or use) stage after the product has been designed (that is after the learning in the R&D stages has been completed). It leads to a variety of productivity improvements, often individually small but cumulatively very large, that stem directly from the production process. Learning-by-doing or using is explicitly not a part of the R&D process, and receives no direct expenditures. Rosenberg (1982) documents several cases of learning-by-using and emphasizes that using a product (and presumably, by extension, engaging in a process) generates problems. This invokes problem-solving capacities, and learning occurs. In this regard the link to learning from disasters is clear. A disaster is a 'problem' that occurs in the course of doing or using, and its occurrence invokes some problem solving.

We can be more specific, however, and discuss three aspects of learning-by-doing that share similarities with the process of learning from disaster:

First, the learning aspect is a joint product of 'doing': any activity involving the production of a good (or the provision of a service) can generate learning and hence knowledge: 'the motivation for engaging in the activity is the physical output, but there is an additional gain, which may be relatively small, in information which reduces the cost of further production' (Arrow (1962)) (by contrast, the classical R&D situation is one in which the actual output is of negligible importance and the motivation lies in the information to be gained).

Second, there is more than simply 'learning by repetition'. One can observe, as part of the production (or use) process the existence of explicitly cognitive learning-by-doing: when faced with a certain kind of problem generated by 'doing' or 'using', people undertake experiments in order to find a better strategy or a better design. Crucial here are the feedback loops back to the development stage, hopefully leading to better and better designs. The locus of the learning process is, however, not the R&D lab but the manufacturing plant or usage site. In other words, explicitly cognitive learning-by doing consists of 'on line' experiments. Those experiments are:

- either totally unplanned or planned but weakly controlled (because experiments are 'on line');
- constrained by the need to keep the production process active.

Third, feedback from the knowledge acquired towards the improvement of designs and organizations can take two main forms: *adaptive or creative learning* (Haas, 1990). Adaptation is the simpler response to a problem. It consists in trying out a new method for achieving the same goal and is characterized by an incremental, trial and error approach to problem-solving. Neither the goals of the organization nor its theories about the technological world are re-examined in the light of new knowledge. Creative learning is a more profound change and requires accepting new knowledge that changes prevailing ideas about the purpose of the organization, its definition of the problem, or the theories that guide its actions.

Learning from disaster as an extreme form of learning-by-doing/using

Why is it possible to consider learning from disaster as an extreme type of learning-by-doing/using and what is at stake? Let us return to the three aspects of learning-by-doing that we just discussed.

First, because disasters take place in the context of use of a technology, they are obviously not an event designed to facilitate learning. The basic motivation at work is production or use, not the knowledge produced, as is the case with any learning-by-doing or using. However, disasters constitute an extreme disturbance of normal activity. In this they are at an extreme of the opportunities to learn.

Second, learning from disaster is explicitly cognitive. This learning arises not from the mere repetition of actions but through the abilities of organizations to understand the 'experiment' and to select strategies to cope with the problems revealed by the experiment. However, the problems (the experiment) generated are always unplanned: learning from disaster is neither the result of a planned and controlled experiment (like simulation or real experiments that can be undertaken at the R&D stage) nor the result of a planned but weakly controlled experiment (like in some cases of learning-by-using). None of the events – Challenger, TWA 800, Bhopal, TMI – was deliberate. By implication, of course, they were not controlled. Thus it is the most challenging experiment for an organization.

The value of learning from disaster depends crucially upon the feedback loops from information collected back to the design stage. However, this rests upon strong technological and organizational conditions: the existence or creation of systems to collect the data as well as to create the linkages and feedbacks from the information collected to the creation of new practices and new designs.

Finally, these feedbacks can take both adaptive *or* creative forms. For instance, adaptive learning would consist in adding a protective equipment to a plant in order to decrease the potential consequences of a problem. An example in the case of TMI would be the improvement of signals to operators or any improvement in warning systems. By contrast, creative learning consists in challenging the existing design and redesigning of the technology. An example would be the reflection about unmanned flights that was prompted by the disaster of the Challenger Space Shuttle and that motivated thinking about the redesign of space flights.

Learning from disaster can, thus, be considered analytically as a particular, and in many ways, extreme category of learning-by-doing/using. It is a totally unplanned experiment, meaning that both the constraints and the economic opportunity to learn are greater. Disasters represent a unique opportunity to take advantage of a rare and costly 'experiment'.

Maximizing learning opportunities and externalities
As a knowledge experiment, any 'event' during production and use of a technology creates learning opportunities and externalities. Economic issues to be addressed deal thus with the private and social optimality of learning. Four aspects of knowledge contribute to the ease or difficulty with which learning takes place and knowledge is created and diffused.

The dispersion of information The greater the number and diversity of learning processes for a given technology the higher the potential for increase in the performance of that technology. For instance multiple experiments, if properly documented and compared, can lead to the selection of the best strategy (the best design) among a number of options (Cowan, 1991).

Thus, multiple learning processes are likely to increase the probability of finding the best design for future activities. However a condition to make this possible is that the information or knowledge generated by those learning processes does not remain dispersed (that is it does not remain within local, disconnected contexts). Learning is typically facilitated when a critical mass of information and the necessary human capital are gathered or agglomerated. This agglomeration facilitates comparison and contrasting different experiences or results of experiments. On the other side, the dispersion of knowledge makes it difficult to agglomerate information from the available learning processes in order to make comparisons and evaluations. Such difficulties become extreme when firms believe it profitable to have 'non-disclosure' strategic behaviour (see below).

Knowledge is constrained   Because learning-by-doing is a joint product, the main microeconomic issue deals with the tension or the conflict between the 'doing' aspect (that is the main motivation) and the 'learning' aspect: doing creates opportunities to learn (through the accumulation of experiences), but its context also creates constraints and limitations as it can conflict with the normal performance that has to be achieved. One cannot undertake a very large number of trials (as can be done at the R&D stage) simply because the main motivation is to manufacture the good or to provide the service. The feedback from experience to inferred understanding is, therefore, severely constrained. Advances in knowledge that are empirically grounded upon inferences from trial-and-error are limited when they are restricted both in the number of trials they can undertake, and by the states of the world they can consider (David, 1998).

Such limitations are very extreme in the context of learning from disaster: the feedback from disaster to inferred understanding is even more limited; in most cases, there will be only one experiment. A disaster is a unique sequence of events that cannot be reproduced (even if the data are not properly collected)!

In general, an experiment is an exploration of some part of the state space of a technology. But the unplanned aspect of the experiment related to a disaster is that the technology exits the normal operating region, and does so in a way that is 'blind': where, in what part of the system the data and the information will be searched and collected is unknown *ex ante*. In other words, what is tested, what is the object of the experimental probe has not been decided in any systematic way. If there is any learning occurring from a disaster, this is a 'learning by accident' (Schelling, 1996).

Information gathering and absorptive capacity   Here there are two aspects. Above all, for an experiment to be profitable in terms of knowledge production, the information or facts that it produces in principle must be captured to be analysed and diagnosed. Instrumentation of a system, which aims to capture facts produced by unexpected events, constitutes an important aspect of system design. The example that comes to mind immediately are the black boxes and voice recorders installed in aircraft, and the general principle here is the recording of data, states of the system or interactions with operators while the technology operates even under normal conditions. But of course disasters occur precisely when the technology operates outside normal conditions so the instruments must be prepared for extreme values.

Gathering information is not enough, however. The information and data so gathered must be changed into knowledge. This clearly involves both human and physical capital, and the ability to do so effectively is a form of absorptive capacity (Cohen and Levinthal, 1990). It is not typically possible to create this 'on the fly', so any agency involved in learning from disaster must have made previous investments in this sort of capital. This can be made in-house, through having a cadre of trained engineers, scientists or technicians; or it can be done using external resources, through having the social capital needed to find and (temporarily) co-opt this capital to produce the knowledge desired, following a disaster.

Knowledge is partially localized   The extent to which knowledge is public or private, general or specific, held locally or widely diffused, has a large impact on the extent to which the learning from a disaster increases welfare. A large body of literature argues that learning-by-doing is at least partially localized: learning that improves one technology may have little (or no) effect on other technologies (Atkinson and Stiglitz, 1969). When this is the case, and if it applies as well to learning from disaster, then the process of learning is essentially a private one, and will have only a minimal impact on social welfare.

However, the degree of standardization and maturation of technology can mitigate this effect, as we discuss more fully below. The product life-cycle literature argues that as a product or technology matures, a dominant design tends to emerge. This is a form of standardization in which functions and technological details become common to all artefacts of the technology or product. Once this has taken place, it becomes much easier to generalize what is learned beyond the particular installation involved, at least to other installations of the same technology.[1] For instance, the learning produced after TMI was immediately applicable to all plants operating with PWR reactors like the TMI plant and was actually implemented. In that respect, from the point of view of the economics of knowledge, mature, relatively standardized technologies have good properties in terms of diffusion of knowledge since they entail a high degree of standardization. Further, the learning from TMI was also applicable, with some adaptation, to plants operating with BWR reactors (boiling-water reactor), another type of light-water reactor. In other cases, knowledge must be much more generic for being useful. Cases of immature technologies provide opposite effects: learning is extremely localized (implying no effect on other technologies) and, thus, positive externalities are limited. In the latter case, increasing the social value of the knowledge produced through learning-by-doing (and learning from disaster) involves, therefore, some costly process (of making knowledge more general and more widely disseminated).

Knowledge is not persistent Evidence in the psychological literature show that if the practising of a task by an individual is interrupted forgetting occurs. A small number of economic studies have examined the effect of an interruption in production on learning. Hirsch (1952) found that when performance was resumed after an interruption it was lower than the level achieved prior to the interruption.

Argote *et al.* (1990) use a data base on the construction of the same type of ship (Liberty Ship) in 16 different shipyards during the Second World War. A large number were produced – 2708. A standard design was adopted and produced with minor variation in all the yards. Argote *et al.* discovered a remarkable lack of learning persistence: the knowledge derived from learning by doing quickly loses its value and that from a stock of knowledge available at the beginning of a year, only 3.2 per cent would remain one year later. Thus, if the stock of knowledge is not replenished by continuing production, it depreciates rapidly. This very weak memory is due to three factors: high turnover (people leave), technological change (depreciation of existing knowledge); and failure of human memory (people forget). These three factors are reinforced by the absence of systems of memorization/codification of the knowledge acquired.

A synthetic view
Four economic issues seem to be very important in determining the magnitude of the learning benefits and externalities generated by a disaster:

1. knowledge dispersion (which is of particular importance when the same kind of disaster occurs in different places) makes it very important to agglomerate information and knowledge to take advantage of the possibility to compare and analyse multiple experiments;
2. knowledge constraints raise the issue of the ability to collect information and data from unpredictable events and to build feedback loops from these data to re-engineering and re-design processes;

3. the partially local character of knowledge raises the issue of deriving
    generic knowledge from a single situated learning process;
4. the weak persistence raises the issue of building organizational memo-
    ries.

The last two issues are actually critical when we consider the problem of
increasing the social return of learning from disaster. Social returns depend
upon knowledge spillovers taking place across many agents, and persisting
over time, both of which support the building and expansion of a 'knowledge infrastructure' for an industry or a sector.

A further element of complication is that disasters are not all similar in
their structure and context. In the following sub-section, we will discuss
significant characteristics of disasters that may affect the nature and
amount of learning.

On Technologies, Experiments and Information

The following features of disasters are likely to affect the processes of information agglomeration, and knowledge production and diffusion.

Technological maturity

The maturity of the technological system (covering in a very broad sense
technologies, human skills, organizations, degree of standardization) is a
key variable of the economics of technological disaster.

First, it influences the diffusion and spillover process. There are three
factors here. First, one feature of mature technological systems is considerable standardization across installations. Dominant designs exist and
variety has been dramatically reduced, so what is learned from or about one
installation is likely to be applicable to many. (See Note 1 for reference on
dominant designs.) Once the origin of a disaster has been identified, the
existence of a common body of knowledge (related to the existence of
a common problem-solving heuristic) is likely to facilitate collective learning and rapid diffusion of the solution towards all companies using the
same dominant design. Further, the issue of a firm's learning capacities can
be alleviated, since if many firms use the same design, their learning capacities can be employed and can under conditions of co-operation in the
learning process, compensate for weaknesses in the capacities of the firm
suffering the disaster. We should add a cautionary note here, though. The
presence of a dominant design implies the presence of a dominant
problem-solving heuristic. This can create a barrier to solution if a problem
is not well-addressed in the dominant heuristic. Thus while mature systems
offer the opportunity for significant generalization beyond the installation,

they can also make learning difficult if the problem lies outside the scope of the dominant heuristic.

Second, standardized components and subsystems are manufactured by specialized suppliers who are related to many similar installations. This kind of industrial structure may provide a useful network for diffusing the knowledge produced as a result of one local accident.

Finally, mature systems tend to be associated with institutions and organizations which, as part of their structures, have in place procedures designed for learning and knowledge diffusion. Codification and storage of knowledge contribute to rapid diffusion and an extensive ability to broaden what is learned through relating it to general, existing archives.

Centralized versus decentralized experiments
As said in the previous section, a disaster is in many cases a unique experiment; meaning that the learning potential is constrained by the fact that there is no possibility to reproduce trials. 'A disaster' represents a particular (possibly complex) failing of a technology. However, the fact that some disasters occur in various places and times (for example the Ford Pinto exploding gas tank; or the Therac-25 radiation burns problem) can be treated as an opportunity to take advantage of multiple experiments. When they are managed explicitly, multiple experiments are designed to collect particular information, the same at each site. Unplanned multiple experiments, if properly 'controlled and investigated' can make it easier to identify empirical irregularities, anomalies and problem areas deserving further investigation, correction and elaboration. However, the potential offered by multiple occurrences is not easily exploited in contexts in which users are dispersed and serious information asymmetry exists between the producer (who knows about all events) and users (who only know about the particular event they have experienced). Here again the key lies in information agglomeration.[2]

Interim Summary

In this section we have developed a framework to address the economic issues of learning from disaster. Taking learning from disaster as a particular case of learning by doing, we have identified four aspects of knowledge that affect the learning process and its ability to generate benefits and externalities. Moreover, the fact that a disaster is a very particular kind of experiment (always unplanned and blind, most often not reproducible) makes the process even more difficult than the standard learning process. Finally, the very features of a disaster (the degree of maturity of the technologies, whether it consists in centralized or decentralized events) play a role in shaping the learning process. We turn now to the detailed analysis of the case of a medical device controlled by software, the Therac-25 radiation treatment machine,[3] which caused several deaths in the early 1980s due to a software failure. The exposition of that case will introduce the discussion about the kind of incentives and socio-economic institutions that can be relied upon to produce and diffuse knowledge in an efficient manner given the particular kind of experiment considered here.

AN ILLUSTRATIVE CASE: THE THERAC-25 DISASTER

Therac-25 is a case of disaster caused by radical ignorance and thus having the potential to create large learning opportunities. The context of this event was that of an immature technology and it was characterized by multiple decentralized occurrences. These various features make the issues of economic incentives and institutions that can be relied upon to generate learning and maximize externalities particularly complex and challenging.

Background

In 1982, Atomic Energy Canada Limited (AECL) introduced a computer-controlled radiation therapy machine, the Therac-25. This superseded the Therac-20, a mechanically-controlled machine. Over the next two years it was used thousands of times without incident.[4] But between June 1985 and January 1987 six people suffered massive overdoses of radiation while undergoing treatment with the Therac-25. Three people died, and three others suffered major physical injuries. These were the first deaths attributed to treatment with a therapeutic radiation machine.[5] The faults at the core of these accidents were eventually corrected, and the machines have operated without incident ever since. Further, the general performance of the machine was improved as a result of these experiences with it. More importantly, however, this event created large amounts of both local and general knowledge about embedded software, software re-use, and quality assurance practices in software engineering. All of these go beyond the Therac-25 machine, applying to the entire software industry and in fact to safety-critical systems in general. Indeed, the Therac-25 episode is considered one of the paradigm cases from which software engineers learn about 'good practice' in North America. The episode also illustrates the role of the interaction between industry and regulatory bodies in learning from disasters. The US Food and Drug Administration (FDA) and the Canadian Radiation Protection Bureau (CRPB) were both involved and played important roles. Finally, the episode can also be used to illustrate how the incentives of different agents affect the learning that takes place after a technology fails.

The Therac-25 is a linear beam accelerator used to treat cancerous tumours, and unlike other radiation therapy machines of that era it could be programmed to fire both accelerated electrons and X-ray photons.[6] The Therac-25 was based on its two direct predecessors, the Therac-6 and the Therac-20. Relative to the Therac-20, the Therac-25 incorporated several innovations that made the machine more flexible and able to treat a wider variety of tumours. In addition to these hardware innovations, it introduced innovations to the control system, largely in the machine's embedded software. Both the Therac-6 and -20 included software, but neither was dependent on it for control. In the Therac-25 version, though, many of the hardware mechanisms of the Therac-6 and the Therac-20 were replaced with software functions. Positioning the patient, setting type and amount of radiation, checking patient position, machine position and settings, shutting down the machine in case of malfunction or bad settings were all now software-controlled. It is important to note that this software was not written from scratch. Following the common belief that software re-use not only speeds up development but also improves reliability, much of the control software developed for the earlier generation machines was re-used. Software re-use was thought to be good engineering practice, since old software has been tested, not only in development, but also in its application. This was thought to improve its reliability.[7]

AECL performed a safety analysis on the machine in March 1983, but appears only to have examined the hardware, and failure rates were given for hardware alone.[8] The AECL report on this analysis appears to assume that software does not degrade, and that computer errors are caused by failures in hardware or by interference from background radiation.

Overview of the Events and Context

The Therac-25 disaster includes six separate incidents. In each case, a patient received a massive radiation overdose, but the machine operator was unaware that this had happened (and in some cases insisted that it could not have happened) and the medical staff did not diagnose it until some time after it had taken place.[9]

When AECL was notified about the possible problems with the machines, in the early cases it was unable to produce doses to match the circumstances of the accidents. Once the cause had been found, however, the events were indeed reproducible. In our schema, the technical cause of the accidents was that the machine entered a part of the state space that was not considered in its design. In essence, experienced operators made a mistake in data entry, but corrected it quickly enough that the machine, having logged the original input, failed to log the correction. Normally mistakes would not have been a problem, as the machine was designed to catch errors, but in this case the sub-routine which set the parameters operated on the incorrect input, while the checking sub-routine, called slightly later, operated on the corrected input. This could only happen with an experienced operator who was able to make corrections quickly: between the time the setting was made and the time the checking was done by the software. It seems likely that this scenario never entered the minds of the designers as a possibility.

1. The first incident took place in Georgia in June 1985. A patient received a massive overdose during the course of treatment. When the patient asked about the cause of his intense, unusual pain, he was assured by the technician that the machine could not produce incorrect radiation dosages. The technician was of the opinion that the machine had operated normally. The resident physicist was somewhat more sceptical, however, and thought a radiation overdose seemed a likely explanation of the patient's symptoms. The event was reported neither to AECL nor to the FDA nor the CPRB. It was considered a fluke by the user.

2. The second incident took place in Hamilton, Ontario, the following month, again involving a massive overdose. Both vendor and regulators were notified, and AECL investigated. It was unable to locate the source of the overdose, but did discover some problems with a mechanical part unrelated to the incident. Here, local, specific learning took place regarding the mechanical control of the turntable. It applied to all installations of the Therac-25, and so was generic in that restricted sense. But it did not have to do with the overdose incidents. Again, the accident was treated as a one-off fluke, and the conceptual model of how the machine worked, used both by AECL engineers and the operators, remained unchanged.

3. In December 1985 in Yakima, Washington, a third overdose occurred. AECL was notified, but denied that such a thing was inherent in the machine, and the event was again treated as a fluke. No learning occurred.

4. In March 1986, in Tyler, Texas, the fourth overdose took place. Again, AECL was notified, but its technicians were again unable to reproduce the result, and were puzzled by it. Their investigation indicated that the machine was functioning normally and should have delivered the right dose. Again their conclusion was, 'One-off'. Interestingly, when asked by

the hospital, AECL responded that it knew of no other similar incidents. If AECL is treated as a monolith this response seems false. The patient in the Marietta, Georgia, incident instigated a lawsuit in which AECL was named. The corporation should have been informed before the first Tyler accident. If AECL is not treated as a monolith, however, it is possible that the technician stating that he knew of no other incidents could have been speaking ingenuously. Whatever the internal workings of AECL over this matter, it is true that up to this point each user was of the opinion that his experiences were unique to him. As a result, there was no pooling of experience, information or expertise in an attempt either to keep informed or specifically to understand the events.

5.   The fifth incident changed this, as it occurred in the same facility, in Tyler, Texas, with the same operator, only 21 days later. Through the efforts of the resident physicist, the immediate cause of the overdose was found. His suspicions had been raised by the previous incident, and he had made inquiries of his colleagues at other institutions. He was willing to entertain the idea that the machine was producing this effect in a deterministic way, and had no prejudices regarding what the source could or couldn't be (or if he did, he was willing to overlook them). Interestingly, his approach to the problem seems to have been highly empirical – he asked the operator to repeat her actions as accurately as she could. By working with the operator in this way he was able to reproduce the event. The absence of a strongly held theory of the machine's operating conditions, environment or user interactions, permitted him to take the machine into a region of its operating space that was not considered by others investigating the events.

Two things are key here. First is the agglomeration of information. With two events occurring in a single venue, and under the 'intellectual authority' of one person, here the resident physicist, enough information was assembled in one place to convince some actor that the events should be linked and jointly investigated to determine the cause. Two occurrences of roughly the same event made the 'fluke' explanation too improbable to be credible. There must be a deterministic cause. Prior to the second accident in Tyler, accidents had occurred at geographically distant locations, and information had not been agglomerated, certainly among the users.

Thus, each user thought his experience was unique. Whether or not AECL had agglomerated the information internally is unclear. Its response to the users' experiences was to confirm their uniqueness. Whether this was deliberate obfuscation on the part of AECL, or whether internal communications within the firm were not what they might have been is a matter of speculation. With the second event at

Tyler, however, information agglomeration did take place, and the cause was quickly found. The second key in this episode was that the investigator, here again the physicist, was not tied rigidly to beliefs about the machine's performance. He did not have strong views on state spaces, neither what they looked like nor the likelihood of visiting different regions of them. Those who develop complex systems must, in the course of development, form precisely such strong beliefs. If they did not, development would be impossible. Thus the presence of an 'outsider' was probably crucial.

The results of the investigation were reported to AECL and eventually to the FDA. Furthermore, the incident was picked up by the media and entered the public realm. The fact that the matter gained public prominence and also the fact that the information provided in the report to the FDA was highly detailed regarding the causes of the events meant that it clearly had to act. It did so, forcing AECL to accept that a problem existed and that a solution must be found and published. At this point we see an interesting change in the behaviour of AECL. After users of the Therac-25 had been informed about the problems editing inputs, and an immediate, short-term fix had been disseminated (it involved disabling one of the editing keys on the keyboard – removing the key cap and putting insulating electrical tape on the contacts!), AECL continued to work on a more permanent solution. The events were now public however, and, seemingly in response to the problems with the Therac-25, a user's group had formed.

6. When the next mishap occurred, for a second time in Yakima, in January 1987, all Therac-25 users were immediately informed, and a solution was quickly found. Again it was a software fault. The accident was of a different type than those in Tyler, and a different part of the software was the cause, but none the less, the source was quickly isolated and a solution quickly found. Response to the second incident in Yakima was different from responses to previous incidents. It was immediately publicly acknowledged, which created very big incentives for a convincing solution to be found. The existence of the user group, and the presence of FDA and CRPB scrutiny made it impossible to keep the diffusion of information circumscribed. The credibility of the machine, and of AECL, was at stake. Second, having discovered that the software was fallible, the model and problem-solving heuristic in which AECL engineers had been entrenched, namely that the software was robust and the problems were more likely to occur in hardware, had been lost. Search for a solution was not restricted to particular parts of the system (that is to say to hardware components), but took place throughout the technology complex (and indeed, given the dis-

coveries in Tyler, probably focused on software, in contrast to previous investigations which had severely down-played that part of the technology).

This broadening of scope in the search for the cause was central in the speed of solution, and could only exist after the engineers had changed their basic understanding of how different parts of the technology interacted, and, perhaps more importantly, on what had been learned about the robustness of the software that was inherited from the previous generations of the machine. Both of these things – the change in views about interaction, and the reliability of re-used code – have since been generalized into software engineering textbooks.

INCENTIVES AND INSTITUTIONS

The previous section has described the events characterizing the Therac-25 disaster as well as the context in which it took place. This disaster consisted in multiple decentralized 'experiments', experienced by users of a rather immature technology – at least in its software controlled dimension; and therefore the context for learning was rather unfavourable due to:

1. the multiplicity and decentralized nature of the experiments;
2. the multiplicity of local conditions;
3. the differences in opinions and consequences of the problems.

Thus, while the problem was systemic, the context in which it arose rather complicated the opportunity to learn since:

1. the information was dispersed; and
2. data were not readily available.

We will now show how the private incentives of the entities involved and the institutional environment affected those constraints and shaped the learning that occurred from the Therac-25 disaster.

On the Dispersion of Information

When a disaster consists of several dispersed events, as in the Therac-25 case, information is generated in several different locations, and its agglomeration can be an important factor contributing to the speed and extent of learning. But for this to be effective, there must be rapid distribution of information among the installations and to the central co-ordinator, who, in the Therac case, was the vendor of the machine, namely AECL. Part of the difficulty in the Therac case is that initially, the actors were unaware even that there could be a systemic problem rather than simply a one-off fluke, confined to that locale. It is no coincidence that the first breakthrough in finding the cause of the accidents came at a facility that experienced two of them in close succession.

What is made clear by the case is that for information agglomeration to take place:

First, agents must know they have useful information. The case shows that the dispersion of users and the possible different contexts in which they use the technology can have a further consequence: the producer itself does not 'see' the failure. Users in hospitals were first told by the vendor that the incident was unique and was probably the result of a fault in use. Implied was that users had nothing to learn, and no valuable knowledge to impart. But beyond this, for agglomeration to take place, it must be possible to connect the events intellectually. That is, the reports must be made in such a way, using language and descriptions that make it possible to see the connections between them. Here, when the event is dispersed, and each one 'relatively small' it is easy to create reports in which symptomatic regularities are not identified. The actor at the centre may itself not know that information about 'the same thing' is being produced.

Second, agents must have incentives to diffuse or collect information and this is related to how their assets are affected by the making sense of the information. From the point of view of the vendor, who often plays the key role in both collecting and distributing information, incentives to conceal information increase if the vendor has a weak market position, since negative information creates a risk that market share will be lost to competitors, particularly if the turnover of the technological artefacts is rapid. Similarly, incentives (to conceal) are relatively strong if information is asymmetric – if the users are dispersed and report individually to the producer. In this case, a bandwagon away from that vendor (or technology) cannot form since information is centrally controlled and not diffused to potential buyers. More than just hiding the information, firms might have the temptation to deny the failure. The economic environment of AECL may have motivated the suppression of negative information. Even though users were replacing their Cobalt-60 machines with microwave linacs, and the Therac-25 was supposed to offer powerful new features and be very cost effective, by 1985 it had in fact only garnered 0.6 per cent of the market for radiation therapy machines and 0.9 per cent of the sales of microwave linacs in the United States. AECL had thus a new and unproven technology and it was trying to build sales. It had a natural incentive to suppress negative information about its product.[10]

This incentive was only increased by the ability of injured patients to sue for damages. In most cases the victims of the accidents launched lawsuits against parties involved, including AECL.[11] For AECL to admit that the machine had defects would have negative consequences in any lawsuit. This may help explain the reluctance of AECL, especially its quality assurance manager, to divulge information about problems.[12]

Incentives work not only at the level of the firm, but also at the level of individuals. Here there are two sorts whose incentives may be important: the clinical physicists, who were users both of radiation therapy in general and the Therac-25 in particular; and the engineers of AECL who were builders/producers of Therac-25. These individuals had human capital assets that would be affected in different ways depending on the source of the problems.

Hospital or clinic physicists were committed to radiation therapy technology and not to the Therac-25. Their main interest was to protect the reputation of radiation therapy. Thus they had incentives to check whether it was the Therac-25 or radiation therapy in general that was at fault. The physicists did uncover the faults and were instrumental in forming the user groups. Unlike the clinic physicists, AECL engineers and technicians were tied directly to the Therac-25 itself. Their natural interest was to protect the reputation of the machine and consequently their goal was to show that it was not the source of the problem. The general reluctance to disclose information to users is consistent with this interpretation.

Moreover, the asymmetry of capacities in terms of testing procedures, which are usually specific assets, might indeed help the firm to hide the failure: when no other organization or institutions can reproduce the failure at low cost, the firm certainly has a strategic advantage when it has to respond to authorities or complainants.

And, finally, there must be mechanisms or structures through which the information agglomeration can happen. From the Therac-25 case we see that professional associations, user groups and regulatory bodies can play a role in collecting and agglomerating the information needed to diagnose and learn about failures. We should also note that the disaster with Therac-25 did not involve the machine's producer in the events themselves. The events involved only the users directly, and their input was vital in solving the problem and fostering the more general learning that followed.

On the Inherent Limitation of the Learning Process

Our case study clearly illustrates the critical dimension of gathering the relevant data on the technology in order to be able to produce new knowledge after the disaster. The professional employees of the users, here the physicists, can take credit for a great deal of the localized learning that occurred. They were able to replicate the faults on at least two occasions and in doing so provided the key information regarding where the fault lay, and provided data that led directly to improvements in the Therac-25. Most significantly here was that these data challenged the conceptual model used by the AECL engineers and forced them to re-think not only details of how the machine worked (what happens when the machine is run by an experienced, fast, operator) but also where faults more generally could lie. Having been forced out of their conceptual model, the AECL technicians were able to address not only the original but also subsequent problems.

Once data have been gathered, the issue of producing knowledge out of it arises, and this relates further to the contents of the learning. To profit from the 'experiment' implies discovering elements that had previously been ignored, either consciously or through ignorance. But further, the goal is to infer wider implications from local knowledge, that is to say, to go beyond the immediate lessons that can be derived from the disaster. Here 'wider implications' is considered broadly to include questions of maintenance, management and control, technology and organization. The temptation should be high in the first instance just to fix the problem.

In the case of Therac-25, the pressure of regulatory bodies and users that conduced the firm to draw wider implications than the narrow consequences, concerning in particular user-machine interfaces and testing procedures (see Table 3.1). The pressure of the regulatory bodies and users made it clear that producing more knowledge would have some positive returns for the firm. In other words, not producing that knowledge would have altered the reputation and confidence of the users and would have induced further costs in managing the relation with the regulation agency and other institutions such that the survival of the Therac-25 would have been threatened. Then, the institutional environment of the firm clearly played a positive role in pushing the firm to produce more knowledge.

On the Diffusion of Knowledge and Informational Spillovers

Once some learning has occurred then there is the issue of its diffusion. Typically the same factors that affect the amount of learning in the first place also affect the diffusion of the learning. For example, a mature technology which is well codified, embodied in systems standardized across installations, is supported by standardized components built by specialist suppliers, and is operated by skilled employees who have undergone a common training regime, will tend to favour a greater diffusion of learning from a disaster and at a faster rate than when the technology is immature since the learning is almost immediately applicable by others.

Table 3.1   The Therac-25 case

Place	Date	Those Notified	Outcome with Respect to the Therac-25
1. Marietta, Georgia	25 June 1985	Lawsuit filed against AECL by patient.	No changes
2. Hamilton, Ontario	26 July 1985	AECL, CRPB, FDA	Changes to microswitch
3. Yakima, Washington	Dec. 1985	AECL	No changes
4. Tyler, Texas	21 Mar. 1986	AECL	No changes
5. Tyler, Texas	11 Apr. 1986	AECL, State of Texas Health Dept, FDA, Users	Major changes to computer hardware and software, computer-user interface, and manuals. Changes to software testing practices. User group formed.
6. Yakima, Washington	17 Jan. 1987	AECL, FDA, Users	Detailed instructions about how to avoid fault. Added to software changes proposed after Tyler incident.

In the case of Therac-25 there were three possible types of potential learning:

1. learning specific to the design, production and operation of the Therac-25 system;
2. learning about treatment procedures, radiation therapy machines in general, and the training, use, and monitoring of radiation therapy technicians and hospital physicists; and
3. generic learning, such as about software design, engineering practices, medical treatment procedures and the training of medical personnel, and regulatory principles.

Specific learning occurred as the Therac-25 eventually was fixed and could be used without the same faults occurring. The scope for the diffusion of this learning though is limited by the very nature of the knowledge gained and so it is the diffusion of the other two types of possible learning to which attention is now paid. Consider a specific example of learning from the

Therac-25 disaster, about software reuse, a case of generic learning.[13] McIlroy in his invited address at the 1968 and 1969 North Atlantic Treaty Organisation conferences on software engineering claimed that software reuse was the way to ensure high quality software.[14] This belief became widespread throughout the software engineering community over the years following the NATO conferences, and was the underlying theme in special issues on software reuse in the journals *IEEE Transactions on Software Engineering* (in 1984) and *IEEE Software* (in 1987).[15] This view had also permeated various government organizations, an example being the Center for Programming Science and Technology, part of the United States National Bureau of Standards.[16]

The Therac-25 disasters gave a lesson to the software engineering industry that in fact software reuse was not the panacea it was made out to be, since the disaster directly involved and implicated software code reused from earlier versions of the radiation therapy machine. This lesson appears to have diffused widely and can be found in monographs such as Leveson (1995) and van Vliet (2000), articles such as Hatton (1997), government bodies such as the Software Safety Group, part of the Ames Research Center at the National Aeronautics and Space Administration, and in course material in computer science courses in various countries.[17]

Learning about software reuse diffused widely and quickly among the software engineering community. Software engineering, while immature compared to the other branches of engineering was still sufficiently well developed for many of its practices and knowledge to have been at least partially codified, reflected by the significant number of professional journals devoted to the subject area. There also existed a sufficient mass of software engineers who were repositories of the then existing software engineering stock of knowledge and a sufficient number of professional bodies existed that were devoted to software engineering and who helped to agglomerate information and lower the costs of its diffusion. Furthermore, software reuse itself was undergoing codification as shown by the two special journal issues, with standardization of the definitions of concepts and terms, and documentation and quantitative analysis being undertaken about the practice of software reuse and its effects. Importantly, though, there was no one dominant 'model' of software reuse, and hence the industry was open to new unexpected knowledge about software reuse. As a result, when the Therac-25 disaster occurred, and learning about software reuse resulted, the environment was conducive to the diffusion of the learning.

Examples of other areas in which learning occurred from the Therac-25 disaster and then diffused are: the use and control of ionizing radiation in medicine (Orton, 1995);[18] the regulation of software in medical devices

(Forsstrom, 1997) and in the production of medical products (Wyn, 1996); and the development of methods and tools relating to the testing of radiotherapy equipment (Thomas, 1994). Furthermore, at the time of the Therac-25 disaster only manufacturers of medical equipment had to report incidents and anomalies associated with their equipment to the United States FDA, whereas by 1990 the FDA explicitly required that users, such as hospitals and treatment centres, also had to report such incidents (to the manufacturers in the first instance, and failing this, the FDA).[19]

Each of these examples of learning diffused to a lesser or wider extent depending on the factors characterizing the specific situation. For example, learning about hardware safety and measurement controls for ionizing radiation in medical devices seems to have diffused widely because the physical technology of radiation therapy was a mature technology, was well codified, and was common to the manufacturers of the radiation therapy machines. On the contrary, learning about the use of software to control radiation therapy machines and to provide much of the functionality of these machines diffused to a lesser extent. This is not surprising since AECL seems to have been a pioneer in this development, so the technology was not standardized or codified, and furthermore, with the disaster, AECL dropped the linear accelerator technology and the unit of AECL that produced radiation therapy machines was sold to another firm, so the knowledge it had acquired was unlikely to have been persistent.

Remedies to Learning Failures

As we have intended to show, learning from disasters is not an automatic process. Complex incentives of agents; technological standardization; the nature of knowledge all add complications to what is, typically, a welfare improving activity. Consequently, both public and private agents and institutions can affect the type of learning that takes place and the benefits that accrue to it.

Private institutions
The 'organizational density' (Perrow, 1999) that surrounds the organization that suffers the disaster can affect positively learning from disaster. Then, the number and diversity of external organizations that have stakes in a disaster, for example unions, user groups, associations of victims, insurance companies, universities and research institutes, technical and professional press affect learning in its different phases. The higher that density, the higher the pressure for finding the causes of the disaster and to learn from it. Especially in the USA, judiciary pursuits greatly contribute to making disasters public and motivating inquiries into the causes of the disasters to

assigning responsibilities. Consumer associations often take part in those complaints and voluntarily make their information public. In addition, the media plays a central role in making a disaster visible by publicizing information about it. Publicity of a disaster is usually a crucial step towards learning from it. Insurance companies are also carriers of public information when they report injuries to public agencies. Technical and professional press motivate learning by diffusing information and moreover by conducting their own tests and analysis of suspected defects. User groups or associations are also carriers of information about failures and they also sometimes undertake their own research about problems. Finally, associations of professional engineers greatly motivate the sharing of information and knowledge and also provide in some cases research assistance for understanding disasters.

Public intervention

Private remedies can be inoperant or insufficient for promoting learning from disaster. Failures to capture learning benefits and externalities can remain (for instance, if the organizational density is weak) or can be inefficiently internalized by market mechanisms (for instance, if competition plays an ambivalent role). In those cases, public intervention is a remedy to the lack of learning. Public intervention takes place through regulatory agencies, public authorities, public commissions of investigation and so on. It can augment learning by different types of interventions. In practice, public intervention after a disaster is mostly of an 'enforcement' type.

First, the mere presence of a regulatory body or other type of public authority whose mission is to set regulations for an industry can be sufficient to motivate the production and diffusion of learning from disaster by firms. A disaster usually entails huge costs for the firm that suffers it and publicizing a disaster and the subsequent learning can drive the adoption of a tougher regulation applicable to all competitors in the industry. Thus, while being presented as a 'moral' action (the firm intends to prevent disasters elsewhere in the industry by diffusing its learning and act in a socially positive way), the firm in fact intends that all competitors have also to bear some costs that follow from its disaster (Kletz, 1993). Another effect, in some sense contrary to the previous one, of the presence of a regulatory body can be that firms prefer to co-operate among themselves rather than keeping their proprietary knowledge, in order to develop some common capacity to face the actions and expertise of the regulator. In that case, competition against the regulator overwhelms competition among firms and generates shared production of knowledge on issues involving catastrophic risks.

Second, public intervention can force firms to incorporate data collecting devices in order to be able to capture new data on the system.

Third, public intervention can force firms to disclose information and to search and reveal an explanation for the disaster, as happened in the case of Therac 25, when the FDA forced AECL to dispatch information to all users and to report incidents.

Fourth, public authorities can also force firms to learn more than they would otherwise have learnt. Public intervention can force firms to learn about technological redesign rather than just fixing the problem by adding protective devices, or it can force firms to derive wider implications than just the immediate lessons of the disaster. This is what happened in the case of Therac-25, where the FDA had to prompt AECL to search further for effective solutions. The presence of a regulatory agency as well as the eventual constituency of user groups played a positive role on information agglomeration and further dispatching. Prior to this case, users were not supposed to report incidents to the FDA. Since Therac-25 they must do it.

Fifth, public funding of research as well as co-operative agreements between firms and public research labs can promote the production of generic knowledge and its further diffusion. Public funds can also finance large test facilities that no private agent or single firm could fund, as is the case in the nuclear industry. Public intervention can also promote the institutionalization of information and knowledge sharing mechanisms.

CONCLUSION

This chapter provides a framework with which to analyse learning from technological failures from an economic point of view. Our purpose has been to examine technological disasters as (unplanned) experiments that open opportunities for learning to take place. In this respect learning is the production of new knowledge in the course of the use of the technology. What is learned from a disaster, then, is knowledge that has not been produced during the conception of the technology, either because it was deemed too costly or simply through not knowing that this knowledge could be produced.

While a disaster represents a unique learning opportunity in which certain types of knowledge, typically difficult to obtain, can be learned, learning after a disaster is not a spontaneous process. As the case study has emphasized, many factors affect this type of learning. Most have to do with the institutional mechanisms that create incentives for the actors involved. Incentive structures not only concern the production of private knowledge to improve the reliability and robustness of the system that failed but also the diffusion of this knowledge to the rest of the industry and beyond and its memorization over time so that the industry as a whole may benefit from such 'knowledge infrastructure'.

Here, history matters in two senses: first, the full realization of private and social benefits deriving from learning from disaster depends greatly on the degree of maturity and standardization of technology and on the creation of institutions capable of generating some kind of collective actions at the level of industry. Standardization and collective institutions like industrial association are both features of the historical process of industry evolution. History matters in a second sense: previous disasters that have been 'useful' in fixing some classes of problems and redesigning technological systems may create a common knowledge about the value of creating the proper conditions to maximize learning. In new emerging fields, in which technologies are not yet standardized and there is a lack of common knowledge about the value of collective learning, the issue of creating the proper incentives and institutions to generate collective actions is a critical challenge.

However, even in a very well-structured and regulated environment, some competitive features may impede the private and social process of learning: the immediate environment of the firm or organization affected by the disaster may have conflicting effects on willingness to learn. Information about a disaster might prove competitively adverse, as publicity about problems or failures affect users' willingness to trust the technology. At the same time, an active, public response can also act as good publicity. What the case has shown is that conflicting immediate effects can to some degree be controlled when the right institutional mechanisms exist. Compulsory implementation of data collecting instrumentation, or compulsory problem-reporting to a regulatory agency, for instance, can counteract the influence of adverse factors like the use of information as a competitive weapon.

The testing of our framework is based in this chapter on a single case. Obviously further testing will be needed in order to evaluate the relevance of the constraints that we consider are important as well as the relevance of incentive and institutional issues in affecting the force of those constraints on the occurrence of learning from disaster, both in its production and diffusion aspects. The comparison of different disasters will thus be a natural follow-up of this study. First it will allow the testing of relevance of this framework in understanding which learning disasters are susceptible to motivate; and second to study whether there are other important constraints on disasters as 'knowledge experiments' or other issues affecting the force of those constraints in shaping the extent of learning from disaster that we would have neglected so far.

ACKNOWLEDGEMENTS

This research was funded by the program 'Risques collectifs et situations de crise' of the French Centre National de la Recherche Scientifique, Paris. Its support is gratefully acknowledged.

NOTES

1. See Abernathy and Clark (1985), Abernathy and Utterback (1978), or Utterback and Abernathy (1975) on product life cycles and dominant designs.
2. The dispersion of occurrences does provide one advantage under some circumstances. If the disaster is taking place in an unusual part of the state space in which the technology operates, it may be better to avoid a centralized approach to the problem. Centralized investigation runs the risk of imposing too much structure, learned from 'normal operation' on an investigation which may be focused on very unusual structures and events. When that is so, it may be advantageous to have a wide variety of approaches to the investigation.
3. Detailed treatment of the Therac-25 disasters can be found in Leveson (1995) and Leveson and Turner (1993). Additional information can be found in *Computer*, (1993), **26**(9), p. 109; *Computer* **26**(10), pp. 4–5); *Batra et al.* (1990) *Communications of the ACM*, **33**(12), p. 138; Joyce (1987); Plummer (1986); and Thompson (1987).
4. By 1986 there were 1144 radiotherapy facilities in the United States employing about 2000 radiation therapy machines in total. These machines were used to treat about 600 000 patients each year. If the average of 306 patients per year used the Therac-25 machines then it would have treated between 3366 patients and 13 464 patients, depending precisely when the 11 machines were sold. See Karzmank *et al.* (1993, Appendix B).
5. Joyce (1987, p. 6).
6. Of the 2000 radiotherapy machines employed in the United States in 1986, 1200 were microwave linacs, of which the Therac-25 was an example. The trend in the United States at the time was the replacement of the Cobalt-60 machines by microwave linacs. See Karzmank *et al.* (1993, p. 287 and Appendix B).
7. See Yourdon (1993, p. 35 and Chapter 9) and Hatton (1997, p. 51).
8. Leveson (1995, p. 520).
9. A radiation treatment typically involves in the neighbourhood of 200 rads. The accidents involved doses in excess of 15 000 rads. It is estimated that a dose of 500 rads to the entire body is fatal 50 per cent of the time.
10. However, in a competitive industry, one might expect that the competition of AECL would have publicized the problems with the machine. There were 13 producers of radiation therapy machines in the world in 1985: AECL, ATC and Varian in North America; BBC, CGR-MeV, Scanitronix and Siemens in Western Europe; the Russian government; the Chinese government; and Mitsubishi, NEC and Toshiba in Japan (Karzmank *et al.* (1993, p. 290)). This competition appears not to have had any effect in publicizing the information. This may be explained by the fact that the source of the problem lay in the software. Without access to the source code, which AECL refused to release, it was not possible to investigate the software directly. This feature of the technology reduced dramatically the ability of 'outsiders' to search for the causes of the disaster.
11. For details of the legal implications of software defects and of the lawsuits stemming from the Therac-25 disaster, see Joyce (1987).
12. Indeed, Orton (1995, p. 675) says 'It is vitally important that we learn from these experiences but, unfortunately, very few have found their way into the referenceable literature, probably because of malpractice fears or legal restrictions. It is hard enough that

these errors are made in the first place, but the real tragedy is that our ability to learn from them is hampered by our litigious society.'

13. Karlsson (1995, p. 3) defines software reuse as '. . . the process of creating software systems from existing software assets, rather than building software systems from scratch.'
14. Naur, Randell, and Buxton (1976, pp. 88–95).
15. As an example consider Lenz *et al.* (1987, p. 34) who state that 'Software reusability has attracted increasing attention over the past few years and is now a major interest. It promises substantial quality and productivity improvements.'
16. Wong (1986).
17. See slides on software reuse incorporating the Therac-25 disaster for a presentation by D. Kulkarni titled 'How to reuse safely', Software Safety Group, NASA Ames Research Center: 27 pp. Online. Available: http://ic.arc.nasa.gov/ic/projects/safety-maint/ presentation.pdf, 12 July, 2002. Examples of course material are: a sample of a writing exercise from course 6.033: Computer System Engineering – Spring 2001, Department of Electrical Engineering and Computer Science, Massachusetts Institute of Technology ((2001), Spring: 4 pars. Online. Available: http://web.mit.edu/6.033/2001/wwwdocs/ reports/r 01-wchan.html. 12 July, 2002); and lecture notes from course CP 114: Bad Software, Winter 2002, Department of Physics and Computing, Wilfed Laurier University ((2002), Winter: 3 pars. Online. Available: http://sauron.wlu.ca/scripts/ lpsiis.dll/physcomp/cp 114_bad_software.htm. 12 July, 2002).
18. See also the presentation given to PHYS 107: Introductory Physics, Queen's University, (2002), 1 April,: 30 pp. Online. Available: http://physics.queensu.ca/~phys 107/ radiation.ppt. 17 July, 2002.
19. See United States Food and Drug Administration (1996).

REFERENCES

Abernathy, W. J. and J. M. Utterback (1978), 'Patterns of industrial restructuring', *Technology Review*, **80**(7), 1–9.

Abernathy, W. J. and K. B. Clark (1985), 'Innovation: mapping the winds of creative destruction', *Research Policy*, **14**, 3–22.

Argote, L., S. Bechman and D. Epple (1990), 'The persistence and transfer of learning in industrial settings', *Management Science*, **36**(2), 140–54.

Arrow, K. (1962), 'The economic implications of learning by doing', *Review of Economic Studies*, **29**, 155–73.

Arthur, B. (1989), 'Competing technologies, increasing returns, and lock-in by historical events', *Economic Journal*, **99**(394),116–31.

Atkinson, A. B. and J. Stiglitz (1969), 'A new view of technical change', *Economic Journal*, **79**(315), 573–8.

Batra, D., J. A. Hoffer and R. P. Bostrom (1990) 'Comparing representations with relational and EER Models, *Communications of the ACM*, **33**(12), 126–39.

Bikchandani, S., D. Hirshleifer, and I. Welch (1998), 'Learning from the behaviour of others: conformity, fads, and informational cascades', *Journal of Economic Perspectives*, **12**(3),151–70.

Carroll, J. S. (1998), 'Organizational learning activities in high-hazard industries: the logics underlying self-analysis', *Journal of Management Studies*, **36**(6), 699–717.

Choi, J. (1996), 'Standardisation and experimentation: ex ante vs. ex post standardisation', *European Journal of Political Economy*, **12**(2), 273–90.

Cohen, W. M., and D. A. Levinthal (1990), 'Absorptive capacities: a new perspective on learning and innovation', *Administrative Science Quarterly*, **35**, 128–52.

Computer (1993), 'Medical Systems', *Computer*, **26**(9), 109.

Computer (1993), 'Therac-25', *Computer,* **26**(10), 4–6

Cowan, R. (1991), 'Tortoises and hares: choices among technologies of unknown merit', *Economic Journal*, **101**(407), 801–14.

Cowan, R. and D. Foray (1997), 'The economics of codification and the diffusion of knowledge', *Industrial and Corporate Change*, **6**(3), 595–622.

David, P. A. (1998), 'Path dependence and varieties of learning in the evolution of technological practice', in J. Ziman (ed.), *Technological Innovation as an Evolutionary Process*, Cambridge: Cambridge University Press.

David, P. and S. Greenstein (1990), 'The economics of compatibility standards: an introduction to recent research', *Economics of Innovation and New Technology*, **1**(1–2), 3–42.

David, P. A., R. Maude-Griffin and G. Rothwell (1996), 'Learning by accident?: reductions in the risk of unplanned outages in us nuclear plants after Three Mile Island', *Journal of Risk and Uncertainty*, **13**, 175–98.

Edmonson, A. and B. Moingeon (1996), 'When to learn how and when to learn why: appropriate organizational learning processes as a source of competitive advantage', in Moingeon B. and A. Edmondson (eds) (1996), *Organizational Learning and Competitive Advantage*, London: Sage, pp. 17–37.

Fabiani, J. L. and J. Theys (1986), *La société vulnérable*, Paris: Presses de l'ENS.

Food and Drug Administration (1996), *Medical Device Reporting for User Facilities*, Rockville, Maryland.

Forsstrom, J. (1997), 'Why certification of medical software would be useful?', *International Journal of Medical Informatics*, **47**, 143–52.

General Accounting Office (1996), 'Aviation acquisition: a comprehensive strategy is needed for cultural change at FAA, Report to the Chairman, Subcommittee on Transportation and Related Agencies, Committee on Appropriations, House of Representatives, August, Washington DC.

Haas, E. B. (1990), *When Knowledge is Power : Three Models of Change in International Organizations*, Berkeley: University of California Press.

Hatton, L. (1997), 'Software failures: follies and fallacies', *IEE Review*, **43**, 49–52.

Hirsch, W. Z. (1952), 'Manufacturing progress functions', *The Review of Economics and Statistics*, **XXXIV**, 143–55.

Jasanoff, S. (ed.) (1994), *Learning From Disaster: Risk Management After Bhopal*, Philadelphia, PA: University of Pennsylvania Press.

Joyce, E. (1987), 'Software bugs: a matter of life and liability', *Datamation*, **33**, 88–92.

Karlsson, E. (ed.) (1995), *Software Reuse: A Holistic Approach*, Chichester: Wiley & Sons.

Karzmank, C., C. Nunan, and E. Tanabe (1993), *Medical Electron Accelerators*, New York: McGraw-Hill.

Kirby, A. (1988), 'Trade Associations as Information Exchange Mechanisms', *Rand Journal of Economics*, **19**(1), 138–46.

Kletz, T. (1993), *Lessons from Disaster: How Organizations Have No Memory and Accidents Recur*, Institution of Chemical Engineers.

Koorneef, F. (2000), *Organisational Learning from Small Scale Incidents*, Delft: University Press Delft.

Koorneef, F. and A. R. Hale (2001), 'How organizations may learn from operational surprises', Proceedings of the 5th International Conference on Technology, Policy and Innovation, Delft, June.

Leland, H. (1979), 'Quacks, lemons, and licensing: a theory of minimum quality assurance standards', *Journal of Political Economy*, **87**, 1328–46.

Lenz, M., H. Schmid and P. Wolf (1987), 'Software reuse through building blocks', *IEEE Software*, **4**(4), 34–42.

Leveson, N. (1995), *Safeware: System Safety and Computers*, Reading, MA: Addison–Wesley.

Leveson, N. and C. Turner (1993), 'An investigation of the Therac-25 accidents', *Computer*, **26**(7), 18–41.

Mitroff, I. I., T. C., Pauchant, M. Finney and C. Pearson (1989), 'Do some organizations cause their own crises? The cultural profiles of crisis-prone versus crisis-prepared organizations', *Industrial Crisis Quarterly*, **3**(1), 269–83.

Naur, P., B. Randell, and J. Burton. (eds) (1976), *Software Engineering: Concepts and Techniques*, Proceedings of the NATO Conferences, New York. Petrocelli/Charter.

OECD (1993), *Achieving Nuclear Safety*, Paris: Nuclear Energy Agency.

Orton, C. (1995), 'Uses of therapeutic x rays in medicine', *Health Physics*, **69**(5), 662–76.

Perrow, C. (1999), *Organisations à hauts risques et 'normal accidents'*, Séminaire du Programme 'Risques Collectifs et Situations de Crise', Actes de la 14ème séance, CNRS.

Pisano, G. (1996), 'Learning-before-doing in the development of new process technology', *Research Policy*, **25**(7), 1097–119.

Plummer, W. (1986), 'A computer glitch turns miracle machine into monster for three cancer patients', *People Weekly*, **26**, 48–50.

Rosenberg, N. (1982), *Inside the Black Box*, Cambridge: Cambridge University Press.

Schelling, T. (1996), 'Research by accident', *Technological Forecasting and Social Change*, **53**(1): 15–20.

Shapiro, C. (1983), 'Premiums for high quality products as returns to reputation', *Quarterly Journal of Economics*, **98**(4), 659–79.

Stanley, S. (1986), *Air Disasters*, London: Ian Allan.

Stead, E. and C. Smallman (1999), 'Understanding business failure: learning and unlearning lessons from industrial crisis', *Journal of Contingencies and Crisis Management*, **7**(1), 1–18.

Tassey, G. (2000), 'Standardization in technology-based markets', *Research Policy*, **29**(4–5), 587–602.

Thomas, M. (1994), 'The story of the Therac-25 in LOTOS', *High Integrity Systems Journal*, **1**(1), 3–15.

Thomke, S., E. von Hippel and R. Franke (1998), 'Modes of experimentation: an innovation process – and competitive – variable', *Research Policy*, **27**(3), 317–34.

Thompson, R. (1987), 'Faulty therapy machines cause radiation overdose', *FDA Consumer*, **21**(10), 37–8.

Toft, B. and S. Reynolds (1997), *Learning from Disasters: A Management Approach*, Leicester: Perpetuity Press Ltd.

Turner, B. A. and N. F. Pidgeon (1997), *Man-Made Disasters*, (2nd edn) London, Butterworth-Heinemann.

United States House of Representatives (1997), 'Allegations of cost overruns and delays in the FAA's wide area augmentation system (WAAS)', Report of the Subcommittee on Aviation, 1 October, Washington DC.

Utterback, J. M. and W. J. Abernathy (1975), 'A dynamic model of process and product innovation', *OMEGA*, **3**(6), 639–56.

Vaughan, D. (1996), *The Challenger Launch Decision*, Chicago: The University of Chicago Press.

Van Vliet, H. (2000), *Software Engineering: Principles and Practice*, (2nd edn) New York: Wiley & Sons.

von Hippel, E. (1988), *Sources of Innovation*, Oxford: Oxford University Press.

von Hippel, E. and M. Tyre (1995), 'How learning by doing is done: problem identification in novel process equipment', *Research Policy*, **24**(1), 1–12.

Wong, W. (1986), *Management Guide to Software Reuse*, NBS Special Publication; 500–155, United States National Bureau of Standards. Gaithersburg, MD. National Bureau of Standards.

Wyn, S. (1996), 'Regulatory requirements for computerised systems in pharmaceutical manufacture', *Software Engineering Journal*, **11**(2), 88–94.

Young, A. (1993), 'Invention and bounded learning by doing', *Journal of Political Economy*, **101**(3), 443–72.

Yourdon, E. (1993), *Decline and Fall of the American Programmer*, Englewood Cliffs, NJ: Yourdon Press.

APPENDIX: THERAC-25 DISASTER TIMELINE

1985

3 June	Marietta, Georgia, overdose. Later in the month, Tim Still calls AECL and asks if overdose by Therac-25 is possible.
26 July	Hamilton, Ontario, Canada, overdose. AECL notified and determines microswitch failure was the cause.
September	AECL makes changes to microswitch. Independent consultant recommends potentiometer on the turntable.
16 September	AECL sends letter to users of Therac-25 claiming an improvement in safety of 10 000 000%.
October	Georgia patient files lawsuit against AECL and hospital.
8 November	Letter from CRPB to AECL asking for additional hardware interlocks and software changes.
13 November	Lawsuit filed against the Kennestone Regional Oncology Center, Marietta, AECL, and a servicing company, by the patient overdosed on 3 June.
December	Yakima, Washington, overdose.

1986

January	Attorney for Hamilton clinic requests potentiometer be installed on turntable.
31 January	Letter from Yakima to AECL reporting overdose possibility.
24 February	Letter from AECL to Yakima saying overdose was impossible and no other accidents had occurred.
21 March	Tyler, Texas, overdose. AECL notified. AECL claims overdose impossible and no other accidents had occurred previously. AECL suggests hospital might have an electrical problem.
7 April	Tyler machine put back into service after no electrical problem could be found.
11 April	Second Tyler overdose. AECL again notified. Software problem found.
15 April	AECL files accident report with FDA.
2 May	FDA declares Therac-25 defective. Asks for CAP and proper re-notification of Therac-25 users.
13 June	First version of CAP sent to FDA.
23 July	FDA responds and asks for more information.
August	First Therac-25 users group meeting.
19 August	AECL sends letter to FDA claiming that in March it had received notice of a lawsuit filed by the patient at Marietta.
26 September	AECL sends FDA additional information.
30 October	FDA requests more information.
12 November	AECL submits revision of CAP.

December	Therac-20 users notified of a software bug.
11 December	FDA requests further changes to CAP.
22 December	AECL submits second revisions of CAP.

1987

17 January	Second overdose at Yakima.
26 January	AECL sends FDA its revised plan.
February	Hamilton clinic investigates first accident and concludes there was an overdose.
3 February	AECL announces changes to Therac-25.
6 February	FDA contacts Canada's Health and Welfare and advises that the FDA recommends that all Therac-25s be shut down until permanent modifications are made. Canadian authorities concur and agree to co-ordinate with FDA.
10 February	FDA sends notice of adverse findings to AECL, declaring Therac-25 defective under US law and asking AECL to notify customers that it should not be used for routine therapy. Health Protection Branch of Canada takes the same action. This lasts until August 1987.
March	Second Therac-25 user group meeting.
5 March	AECL sends third revision of CAP to FDA.
9 April	FDA responds to CAP and asks for additional information.
1 May	AECL sends fourth revision of CAP to FDA.
26 May	FDA approves CAP subject to final testing and safety analysis.
5 June	AECL sends final test plan and draft safety analysis to FDA.
July	Third Therac-25 users group meeting.
21 July	Fifth and final version of CAP sent to FDA.

1988

| 29 January | Interim safety analysis report issued. |
| 3 November | Final safety analysis report issued. |

Source: Leveson and Turner (1993).

PART II

Studies of Knowledge-based Industries

4. The value of knowledge integration in biotechnology

Lionel Nesta

INTRODUCTION

Little is known about the valuation by shareholders of intangible assets, although previous work has repeatedly revealed some statistical relationships between some measures of related diversification and some measures of performance (Rumelt, 1974; Scott, 1993). In this chapter, I concentrate on intangible assets by adding to the scale of the research effort and to the patent stock of a firm a measure of knowledge integration, defined as the way in which different components of the knowledge base of a firm are combined in a complementary manner. Using a sample of biotechnology firms, defined as active in biotechnology research and able to obtain future revenue from their subsequent innovation, I bring new evidence regarding the extent to which the coherence of the knowledge base is a discriminating determinant of the firms' market valuation.

In the following section, a simple model of firm market valuation is elaborated. I then provide details of the dataset and of the metrics used to measure knowledge capital and knowledge integration. These proxies are then introduced as regressors for the market value of biotechnology-related firms, together with firm profitability and R&D intensity. I comment the main results and conclude in the final section.

A SIMPLE MODEL OF MARKET VALUATION

Questions relating to the market valuation of firms have gained momentum in the past two decades, providing growing evidence that intangible capital has become a very important determinant of firms' market value. This is consistent with the fact that, since the 1950s, intangible capital has overtaken physical capital (Abramowitz and David, 1996; Kendrick, 1994). In particular, this progression of intangible capital becomes understandable as we move towards the so-called knowledge-based economy.

Amongst the main components of intangible capital studied there are R&D stocks, patent stocks, advertising (Griliches, 1981; Pakes, 1985; Jaffe, 1986; Cockburn and Griliches, 1988; Connolly and Hirschey, 1988; Hall, 1993; Hall *et al.*, 2000). Other authors have pointed to the importance of focus in firm diversification (Wernerfelt and Montgomery, 1988; Scott and Pascoe, 1987), structure performance relationship (Smirlock *et al.*, 1984) and degree of unionization (Salinger, 1984). Each of these studies focuses on a subset of the potential components of intangible capital and on relatively short periods of time. However, our understanding of the components and valuation of the firms' intangible capital remains very partial and imperfect.

I concentrate on the following intuition: two firms with equivalent knowledge stocks might have a different market value depending on their differential ability to combine different pieces of knowledge coherently, that is, depending on their degree of knowledge integration. That a firm is not a collection of unrelated activities has been demonstrated by the concept of coherence of the firm, as proposed by Teece, *et al.* (1994). These authors argue that the non-random organization of activities has its very roots in the firm's competencies. When entering into new business lines, firms move into activities with similar scientific and technical competencies and common complementary assets. Thus, diversification strategy is not a free game; hazardous and aggressive diversification may threaten the overall coherence of the firm and even its viability. Diversification inherently calls for some sort of integration, to increase the coherence of the firm's activities and the underlying knowledge base.

I argue that knowledge integration is likely to be a particularly important aspect of a firm's activities in knowledge intensive sectors. I expect the market valuation of the firm to depend on a few particular aspects: knowledge integration, knowledge capital, R&D investment and profit. Like Griliches (1981), Salinger (1984) and Jaffe (1986), I start from a simple representation of the firm's market value V, where the latter is a linear function of sum of the current value of the firm's conventional assets C and the current value of its intangible resources IR:

$$V_{nt} = q_{nt} \cdot C_{nt} \cdot K_{nt}^{\gamma} \cdot I_{nt}^{\tau} \tag{1}$$

where $n \in \{1, \ldots, N\}$, and $t \in \{1, \ldots, T\}$ denote firm and time respectively, I is a quantitative measure of knowledge integration, K is a measure of the firm's knowledge stock. Equation (1) says that the relative value of a unit of knowledge may vary a great deal depending on how knowledge is integrated within the firm. Contrary to the literature, I assume that all variables

C, K and I enter multiplicatively rather than additively. Equation (1) implies that a given degree of knowledge integration spreads over each unit of capital and of the knowledge stock. Alternatively, an additional unit of knowledge will also spread over all units of capital, given knowledge integration. The firm's tangible and intangible assets are valued at price q as follows:

$$q_{nt} = A \cdot \Pi_{nt}^{\beta} \cdot R_{nt}^{\lambda} \cdot \exp(u_{nt}) \tag{2}$$

where A is a constant, Π and R are respectively firm's profit and firm's research intensity. In Equation (1) stock variables are entered while Equation (2) introduces flow variables, which reflect current profitability and R&D investments. The disturbance term u_{nt} is decomposed into individual and annual disturbance terms plus a random error term, which is assumed to be normally distributed with zero mean and constant variance. Substituting Equation (2) into Equation (1), dividing through by C_{nt} and taking logs yields

$$v_{nt} - c_{nt} = a + \gamma \cdot k_{nt} + \tau \cdot i_{nt} + \beta \cdot \pi_{nt} + \lambda \cdot r_{nt} + u_{nt} \tag{3}$$

where the dependent variable $(v - c)$ is equivalent to (the log of) Tobin's q (V/C), and the terms γ, τ, β and λ are the parameters to be estimated. Note that the β and λ parameters grasp the elasticity of the dependent variable with respect to the firm's current profit π and research intensity r. While the representation, interpretation and measure of the firm's conventional assets are relatively straightforward, the representation of the firm's intangible resources deserves more attention.

DATA AND MEASUREMENTS

The variable called either coherence or knowledge integration constitutes the main addition of this paper to previous knowledge. Thus, I expose its underlying logic in greater detail than for the other variables.

The measure of knowledge integration is based on the degree of technological relatedness within the firm. Relatedness has been investigated in several publications (Sherer, 1982; Jaffe, 1986, amongst others). In this chapter, I use the survivor measure of relatedness developed by Teece *et al.* (1994). Their measure is based on the idea that economic competition leads to the disappearance of relatively inefficient combinations of businesses. But, instead of applying it to industry SIC codes, I apply it to technologies (Breschi, *et al.*, 2003). Thus, I assume that the frequency with which two technology classes are jointly assigned to the same patent documents may be thought of as the strength of their technological relationship, or relatedness.

The analytical framework departs from the square symmetrical matrix obtained as follows. Let the technological universe consist of K patent applications. Let $P_{ik} = 1$ if patent k is assigned to technology i, $i = \{1,...,n\}$, 0 otherwise. The total number of patents assigned to technology i is thus $O_i = \Sigma_k P_{ik}$. Now let $P_{jk} = 1$ if patent k is assigned to technology j, 0 otherwise. Again, the total number of patents assigned to technology j is $O_j = \Sigma_k P_{jk}$. Since two technologies may co-occur within the same patent document, then $O_i \cap O_j \neq \emptyset$ and thus the number J_{ij} of observed joint occurrences of technologies i and j is $\Sigma_k P_{ik} P_{jk}$. Applying the latter to all possible pairs, I then produce the square matrix Ω ($n*n$) whose generic cell is the observed number of joint occurrences J_{ij}.

$$\Omega = \begin{bmatrix} J_{11} \cdots J_{i1} \cdots J_{n1} \\ \vdots \quad \ddots \quad \vdots \\ J_{1j} \quad J_{ii} \quad J_{nj} \\ \vdots \quad \ddots \quad \vdots \\ J_{1n} \cdots J_{in} \cdots J_{nn} \end{bmatrix} \tag{4}$$

This count of joint occurrences is used to construct our measure of relatedness, relating it to its expected value μ_{ij} under the hypothesis of random joint occurrence. Given this scheme, I consider the number x_{ij} of patents assigned to both technology i and j as a hypergeometric random variable of mean and variance (Population K, special members O_i, and sample size O_j):

$$\mu_{ij} = E(X_{ij} = x) = \frac{O_i O_j}{K} \tag{5}$$

$$\sigma_{ij}^2 = \mu_{ij} \left(\frac{K - O_i}{K} \right) \left(\frac{K - O_j}{K - 1} \right) \tag{6}$$

If the actual number J_{ij} of co-occurrences observed between two technologies i and j greatly exceeds the expected value μ_{ij} of random technological co-occurrence, then the two technologies are highly related: there must be a strong, non-casual relationship between the two technology classes. Inversely, when $J_{ij} < \mu_{ij}$, then technology classes i and j are poorly related. Hence, the measure of relatedness is defined as:

$$\tau_{ij} = \frac{J_{ij} - \mu_{ij}}{\sigma_{ij}} \tag{7}$$

The relatedness square matrix Ω' with elements τ_{ij} has been computed for each year between 1981 and 1997. Calculations depart from all biotechnology patent applications assessed in the Derwent Biotechnology Abstracts (DBA). Today, more than 90 000 patents are reported in the DBA, from 1965 to 1999, covering 40 intellectual property authorities. Over the period, the number of patent applications has increased almost every year. Because three years are needed for inventory purposes, and the curve drops precipitously after 1997, the analysis will be exclusively concerned with the period before 1997, and will thus be based on 80 163 patents. Each patent is described by its year of approval and by a vector of 30 technology classes, taking value 1 if a technology occurs in the patent, 0 if otherwise. For example, if technologies A and B occur within patent P, P can be described by the 30 dimensional vector $I = \{1,1,0...0\}$.[1] The matrix Ω' is symmetrical, with 435 possible linkages between pairs of technologies. It is of importance that it displays the outcome of a large diversity of actors, differing in type (universities, research institutes or firms), country and size. Thus, the matrix Ω' provides us with some sort of objectified biotechnological relatedness, being the outcome of the interactions of a wide variety of actors.

The measure of coherence is based on the degree of technological relatedness within the biotechnology firm. I use a sample of biotechnology firms, defined as active in biotechnology research and able to obtain future revenue from their subsequent innovation. These biotechnology firms belong to three main industries, namely the pharmaceutical, chemical and the agrofood industries, but are also seen as dedicated biotechnology firms (DBFs). DBFs were created to explicitly explore and develop new biotechnology products and services and thus are newer and smaller than traditional industries. Biotechnology is one of the technologies that emerged at the end of the 1970s and that have created enormous expectations of future economic development in several industrial sectors, the three mentioned above being the earliest to benefit (Saviotti, 1998). The period that I study, the 1980s and most of the 1990s, covers the early emergence of a set of new technologies, including biotechnology, to the stock market bubble of the 1990s.

Similar to Teece, *et al.* (1994), the weighted average relatedness WAR_i of technology i with respect to all other technologies within the firm is defined as: the degree to which technology i is related to all other technologies present within the firm, weighted by patent count p_j. It is thus a measure of the expected relatedness of technology i with respect to any given technologies randomly chosen within the firm. WAR_i may be either positive or negative, the former (latter) indicating that technology i is closely (weakly) related to all other technologies within the firm. For a firm developing competencies in a number of – say five – technological DBA classes, five corresponding measures of WAR_i are computed. Consequently, the coherence of the firm's knowledge base is defined as the weighted average of the WAR_i measures:

$$I = \sum_{i=1}^{30}[WAR_i \times f_i] \quad \text{where} \quad WAR_i = \frac{\sum_{i\neq j}\tau_{ij}p_j}{\sum_{i\neq j}p_j} \quad \text{and} \quad f_i = \frac{p_i}{\sum_i p_i} \quad (8)$$

Equation (8) estimates the average relatedness of any technology randomly chosen within the firm with respect to any other technology. As in the previous cases, this measure can be either negative or positive, the latter indicating that the firm's technologies are globally well related, while a negative value shows a poor average relatedness amongst the technologies in which the firm has developed competencies. Firms with a higher degree of knowledge relatedness are supposedly more integrated. I posit that the more integrated knowledge bases are also more coherent because they can better exploit the synergies, that is the complementarities, between the technologies.

In order to reduce the noise induced by changes in technological strategy, patent counts p_j are summed for the previous five years. This compensates for the fact that learning processes are time-consuming, due to certain rigidities in firms' technological competencies. Most knowledge capital measures apply a similar correction by summing past R&D expenditures over time. Note that Equation (7) involves two elements that might affect I. As already mentioned, relatedness is determined by the interactions of all actors for a given year, while patent count p_j clearly follows the firms' internal learning strategies. Therefore, a disconnection exists between the objectified biotechnological relatedness and the firm's knowledge base. Changes in technological relatedness might cause corresponding changes, that is increase or a decrease, in the firm's coherence, even in the absence of any change in the firm's technological portfolio. This convincingly illustrates the fact that firms are embedded in a technological environment that they marginally affect, whereas they are considerably affected by it.

The measure of coherence of the knowledge base developed is derived from the procedure used by Teece *et al.* (1994). While this procedure is formally similar to theirs, it differs in that it applies to the knowledge base rather than to outputs, and to the interpretation of the meaning of coherence. Teece *et al.* defined coherence as relatedness. I argue that both similar and complementary components of the knowledge base are related, but that we are more likely to find complementary than similar pieces of knowledge in a firm's knowledge base. I expect a firm's competitive advantage in a knowledge intensive sector to rely on its ability to integrate different but complementary pieces of knowledge. This means not only choosing pieces of knowledge that are complementary in the sense of being jointly required to produce the firm's overall output, but also combining them effectively. The construction of a coherent knowledge base depends both on choosing the right pieces of knowledge and on integrating them effectively. Thus I use the terms coherence and knowledge integration interchangeably.

Besides knowledge integration, I measure knowledge capital K as the cumulated stock of past patent applications, using a 15 per cent depreciation rate. Obviously, patents are a noisy measure of knowledge capital for the distribution of the value of patented knowledge is highly skewed: only a small fraction of all patents capture most of the returns from knowledge appropriation. A solution would be to use citation-weighted patent counts. Hall, *et al.* (2000) show that citation-weighted patent counts are more highly correlated with the firm's stock market value than mere patent counts. While I acknowledge the advantage of such a measure, the citation-weighted count is not applicable in our case. Most citation databases come from legal authorities such as the USA, the World or the European patent offices. The Derwent database covers 40 patent authorities so that the gathering of citation-weighted patent counts would be almost impossible. Consequently, I use a simple patent count to proxy the firm's knowledge capital, bearing in mind that this rudimentary metric is likely to bias downward its potential impact on the firm's market value.

Conventional wisdom suggests that patent-based and R&D-based figures are alternative measures of the firm's knowledge capital. I assume that each provides us with complementary information. Patent applications equate with past successes in R&D, while current research efforts supposedly predict future inventions. Thus I associate the former with the revealed knowledge capital while the latter informs us about the intensity of use of this knowledge capital. I will consistently use measures of R&D intensity, rather than mere R&D figures, to indicate the intensity of exploitation of the knowledge capital. Finally, data on the firms' research and development expenditures RD, operating income Π, market capitalization V and real assets C were collected from Worldscope Global Researcher (WGR), which provides financial information on public companies since 1989. All variables have been deflated in constant 1990 US dollars.

Descriptive statistics of the variables are found in Table 4.1 The empirical model (3) is estimated using a sample of 99 firms active in biotechnology. These firms were chosen on the basis of both patent activity and data

Table 4.1   Descriptive statistics (Pooled sample: 1989–97)

Variable	Obs	Mean	Std. Dev.	Min	Max
Market capitalization	842	8 986 073.0	13 400 000.0	9 836.7	99 500 000.0
Total assets	842	6 503 285.0	8 078 725.0	4 422.2	46 900 000.0
Operating income	842	625 825.0	927 905.2	−426 524.9	4 510 622.0
Research and development	842	307 655.5	380 118.4	858.5	1 918 850.0
Knowledge capital	842	40.5	54.5	0.0	333.1
Knowledge integration	842	3.0	5.5	−6.0	35.1

Notes: All financial variables are expressed in thousands of 1990 US dollars.

availability. The sample is composed of 33 pharmaceutical firms, of which 17 are large chemical firms and 12 are active in agro-food industries.[2] These industries have all benefited from biotechnology at different levels and for different purposes. However, for all these industries biotechnology has been a radical technological opportunity, the exploitation of which should be shown to be related to their innovative performance. Our sample also includes 22 firms categorized as DBFs, that is firms that were created on the basis of their distinctive competencies in biotechnology. In fact, the technological discontinuity induced by biotechnology created favourable conditions for the entry of these new actors into the competition (Kenney, 1986; Orsenigo, 1989; Grabowski and Vernon, 1994; Saviotti, 1998). Yet, the consequent rise in the number of DBFs has not led to the expected replacement of incumbents. For example, whilst large pharmaceutical firms invested heavily in building in-house research capabilities in biotechnology, DBFs found it very difficult to integrate complementary assets such as distribution channels, production facilities, and so on. Consequently, successful integration for DBFs has been the exception rather than the rule. In our case, the DBFs chosen represent a particular sample of the entire DBF population. Because firms were chosen on the basis of availability of data between 1989 and 1997, all DBFs here are publicly held. Thus, they are generally the older DBFs – established before the mid-1980s. Following integrative strategies, some now considerably more than 1000 employees. The final database is an unbalanced panel indexed by firm and by year with 709 effective observations.

RESULTS

I estimate Equation (3) using six different econometric specifications, in order to test the robustness of the relationship between (the log of) Tobin's q and the four explanatory variables: (the log of) knowledge capital (k), (the log of) knowledge integration (i), (the log of) profit (π) and (the log of) R&D intensity (r). The results are presented in Table 4.2.

Table 4.2 Market value and knowledge integration: 1989–1997

	OLS (1)	Within (2)	Between (3)	AR1 (4)	GMM-1 (5)	GMM-2 (6)
Operating income						
	0.298	0.196	0.25	0.087	0.016	0.014
	[0.029]***	[0.060]***	[0.076]***	[0.041]**	[0.096]	[0.027]
Research and development						
	0.247	0.245	0.367	0.276	0.261	0.258
	[0.031]***	[0.059]***	[0.054]***	[0.040]***	[0.066]***	[0.036]***
Knowledge capital						
	0.044	0.019	0.014	0.027	0.04	0.029
	[0.022]**	[0.036]	[0.065]	[0.038]	[0.107]	[0.020]***
Knowledge integration						
	0.361	0.103	0.651	0.146	0.156	0.126
	[0.048]***	[0.055]*	[0.150]***	[0.052]***	[0.114]	[0.033]***
Constant						
	−3.951	−1.771	−3.115	−0.347	0.05	0.052
	[0.472]***	[0.862]**	[2.269]	[0.608]	[0.010]***	[0.005]***
N. Obs.	842	842	842	842	447	447
F-Stat	57.5***	9.4***	13.7***	15.6***		
R^2	0.509	0.133	0.634	0.172		
Wald					132.9***	6920.8***
Sargan					224.8***	89.1
AR1					−4.907***	−2.956***
AR2					−2.008**	−1.256

Notes:
Robust standard errors in brackets.
* significant at 10%; ** significant at 5%; *** significant at 1%.
Dependent Variable: Log of Tobin's q. Estimate – *(p*-values). The full sample has 842 observations. The GMM1 and GMM2 models have 447 observations using three lags. All models include year and sectoral dummy variables with the exception of the within, GMM1 and GMM2. In GMM1 and GMM2, the financial variables are considered endogenous while the variables characterizing the firms' knowledge base are entered as predetermined. Year dummy variables are entered as instruments in the GMM specifications. All standard errors are adjusted for panel heteros kedasticity using White's correction.

Looking firstly at column (1), the ordinary least square specification produces positive and significant parameter estimates for all independent variables. The variables describing firm profitability, R&D intensity and knowledge integration have a higher explanatory power than the variable describing knowledge capital. This is consistent with the fact that patents are a rather noisy measure of knowledge value, due to a great variance in their economic value. Thus the use of patent stocks as a proxy for knowledge capital brings measurement errors that are likely to bias downward the knowledge capital estimate. The positive and significant OLS estimate of knowledge integration conforms to my initial intuition, and suggests that more integrated knowledge bases are associated with higher market capitalization.

The financial variables have a straightforward meaning: a 1 per cent increase in the firm's operating income raises the firm's valuation by 0.298 per cent, whereas a 1 per cent increase in the firm's research intensity yields a 0.247 per cent rise. Knowing that $q = \log(V/C)$, $\beta = (\partial V/V)/(\partial \Pi/\Pi)$ and $\lambda = (\partial V/V)/(\partial R/R)$, I derive the expected effect of a dollar increase in profit and research expenditures on the stock market valuation of firms. I find that at the mean, a \$1 rise in profit produces a \$4.28 increase in the firm's market value, while a \$1 rise in its research spending is valued at \$7.21. These estimates are higher than those of Connolly and Hirschey (1988) who found that an extra dollar of R&D expenditures adds \$3.60 to the firm's excess value[3] and \$2 to its market value. When analysing the value of an additional patent to the firm's knowledge stock, I find that an additional patent in the firm's knowledge stock is valued at \$10 000. Previous estimations indicate that an additional patent is valued at approximately \$200 000 (Connolly and Hirschey, 1988; Griliches, 1981; Hall, *et al.*, 2000) and \$810 000 (Pakes, 1985). This under-valuation reflects partially the variety of industries under scrutiny.

It is difficult to attribute value to knowledge integration, because little is known about investments by firms to improve knowledge integration. A possibility is to regress the dependent variable on the *ranked* values of knowledge integration. The results show that a one-point increase in the *ranked* value of knowledge integration is associated with a \$m32.8 increase in the stock market valuation of the firm. Yet, this remains poorly informative: these preliminary and indicative results suggest that knowledge integration as measured in this chapter is economically valuable, the extent to which this is so remains difficult to assess.

I test for the robustness of the results by using alternative, more conservative specifications. Column (2) introduces the within specification, where all variables are transformed as differences from firm means. The financial variables remain strongly significant, but the knowledge-based variables lose a substantial part of their explanatory power, although knowledge integration remains significant at the 10 per cent level. In column (3), I introduce firm means to test for structural relationships (also called between regressions). Firm profitability and commitment to research remain strongly significant, and satisfactorily, knowledge integration enters the equation being strongly positive and significant. The difference between the lack of significance of the within specification and the strong significance of the between specification suggests that the integration of scientific knowledge by firms is stable overtime: thus processes of technology absorption, integration and exploitation are all the more time consuming. The lack of significance of the knowledge capital variable is at odds with prior results. Although I have experimented for alternative measures (for example technology diversification) and databases (USPTO database), this result remains stable and deserves further investigation on its own. In column (4) I test the presence of spurious correlation by experimenting with an autoregressive model. The introduction of a common factor ρ representing first order autocorrelation produces estimates, which are consistent with previous specifications.

In column (5) and (6), I allow for the endogeneity (or simultaneity within equation) of variables by adopting the GMM specification. Relying on the findings of Arellano and Bond (1991) and Kiviet (1995), I use lagged differences as instruments to wipe out possible simultaneity problems. The Sargan statistics (1958) are used to test the validity of instruments, under the H_0 hypothesis of no asymptotic correlation between the instruments and the perturbation. If the model is correctly specified, the statistic is chi-square distributed. Moreover, the GMM estimator is consistent if there is no second-order serial correlation in the error term of the first-differenced equation. Arellano and Bond propose to test first and second order autocorrelation of the residuals. They note that if the errors are uncorrelated, then the first differenced perturbations shall have negative first-order correlation but no second or higher order correlation. Thus, a test for the validity of the instruments (and the moment restrictions) is a test of second-order serial correlation in these residuals. Table 4.2 reports the estimates from the one- and two-step estimators (respectively GMM1 and GMM2). Testing for the validity of instruments (Sargan test) and second order serial correlation (AR1 and AR2) in column (6) provides evidence of the suitability of our instruments and the validity of the estimates. With the exception of the research intensity variables, all variables lose their significance at once (GMM1), whereas in the two-step estimator (column 6), the knowledge-based variables recover their full significance. The magnitudes of the parameter estimates for firm R&D intensity and knowledge integration corroborate the previous findings. Notably for R&D, the stability of the parameter estimate suggests that for the representative firm of the sample, a $1 increase in its research budget does indeed increase its market value by $7.

Looking at the broad picture from the results provided here, one can be confident in knowledge integration as a relevant candidate for explaining part of the variance in firm market value. This evidence supports the view that the diversification in the firm's knowledge base must exploit the complementarities between the various technologies mastered by firms. This corroborates the findings of Scott (1993) where the author notes that purposive diversification leads to productivity growth. As expected, the stock market valuation of firms does eventually reflect the productive value of their intangible assets and, more particularly, that coherent knowledge bases are considered by shareholders to be economically valuable.

Importantly, these results are a candidate explanation for the 'diversification discount' (Rajan, *et al.*, 2000; Lamont, *et al.*, 2001; Graham, *et al.*, 2002). Diversification comes at costs, stemming from increase in agency costs, sub-optimal choices in investments across divisions, imperfect internal capital market, and so on. An additional but more subtle cost is that diversification is likely to momentarily disrupt knowledge integration at both the plant and conglomerate level, resulting in lower levels of knowledge integration. In turn, firms must devote part of their management focus towards integrating these new sets of activities, competencies and technological knowledge with pre-existing ones.

CONCLUSION

This chapter has dealt with the determinants of the market value of biotechnology firms in the period 1989–97. I found evidence that the degree of knowledge integration within firms is a significant explanatory variable of firms' stock market value. This means that knowledge integration is economically valuable, as our initial intuition suggested. I found additional evidence that the explanatory power of knowledge integration is at least as great as the variable for knowledge stock. While knowledge stock is indeed important, the way firms combine their technology is equally valuable for shareholders.

NOTES

1. Within one patent, a maximum of six technologies may be assigned, which leads to a maximum of 768 211 possible combinations in a 30-dimensional technological space. The list of DBA technologies can be found online at the Derwent Biotechnology Abstract website.
2. Another 15 firms were grouped under the heading 'Miscellaneous' industries.
3. The excess value is defined as the market value of common assets plus book value of debts minus the book value of tangible assets.

REFERENCES

Abramowitz, M. and P. A. David (1996), 'Technical change and the rise of intangible investments: the US economy growth-path in the twentieth century', in D. Foray and B.-A. Lundvall, *Employment and Growth in the Knowledge-Based Economy*, Paris: OECD.

Arellano, M. and S. R. Bond (1991), 'Some tests of specification for panel data: Monte Carlo evidence and an application to unemployment equations', *Review of Economic Studies*, **58**, 277–87.

Breschi, S., F. Lissoni and F. Malerba (2003), 'Knowledge-relatedness in firm technological diversification' *Research Policy*, **32**(1), 69–87.

Cockburn, I. and Z. Griliches (1988), 'Industry effects and appropriability measures in the stock market's valuation of R&D and patents', *American Economic Review*, **78**(2), 419–23.

Connolly, R. A. and M. Hirschey (1988), 'Market value and patents: a Bayesian approach', *Economics Letters*, **27** (1), 83–7.

Graham, J. R., M. L. Lemmon and J. G. Wolf (2002), 'Does corporate diversification destroy value?', *Journal of Finance*, **57**, 695–720.

Grabowski, H. G. and J. M. Vernon (1994), 'Innovation and structural change in pharmaceuticals and biotechnology', *Industrial and Corporate Change*, **3**(2), 435–49.

Griliches, Z. (1981), 'Market value, R&D, and patents', *Economics Letters*, **7**(2), 183–7.

Hall, B. H. (1993), 'The Stock Market's valuation of R&D investment during the 1980s', *American Economic Review*, **83**(2), 259–64.

Hall, B. H., A. D. Jaffe and M. Trajtenberg (2000), 'Market value and patent citations: a first look', Economics Department Working Paper E00-277, University of California.

Jaffe, A. D. (1986), 'Technological opportunity and spillovers of R&D: evidence from firms patents, profits and market values', *American Economic Review*, **76**, 984–1001.

Kendrick, J. W. (1994) 'Total capital and economic growth', *Atlantic Economic Journal*, **22**(1), 1–18.

Kenney, M. (1986), *Biotechnology: The University-Industry Complex*, New Haven, CT: Yale University Press.

Kiviet, J. F. (1995), 'On bias, inconsistency, and efficiency of various estimators in dynamic panel data models', *Journal of Econometrics*, **68**(1), 53–78.

Lamont, O. A. and C. Polk (2001), 'The diversification discount: cash flows versus returns', *Journal of Finance*, **56**, 1693–721.

Orsenigo, L. (1989), *The Emergence of Biotechnology*, New York: Palgrave Macmillan, St Martin's Press.

Pakes, A. (1985), 'On patents, R & D, and the Stock Market rate of return', *The Journal of Political Economy*, **93**(2), 390–409.

Rajan, R., H. Servaes and L. Zingales (2000), 'The cost of diversity: the diversification discount and inefficient investment', *Journal of Finance*, **55**, 35–80.

Rumelt, R. P. (1974), *Strategy, structure, and Economic Performance*, Boston, MA: Harvard Business School Press.

Sargan, J. D. (1958), 'The estimation of economic relationships using instrumental variables', *Econometrica*, **26**,329–38.

Salinger, M. A. (1984), 'Tobin's q, unionization, and the concentration-profits relationship', *The RAND Journal of Economics*, **15**(2), 159–70.

Saviotti, P. P. (1998), 'Industrial structure and the dynamics of knowledge generation in biotechnology', in J. Senker (ed.), *Biotechnology and the Competitive Advantage*, Cheltenham, UK: Edward Elgar, pp. 19–43.

Scott, J. T. (1993), *Purposive Diversification and Economic Performance*, Cambridge, New York and Melbourne: Cambridge University Press.

Scott, J. T. and G. Pascoe (1987), 'Purposive diversification of R and D in manufacturing', *Journal of Industrial Economics*, **36**(2), 193–205.

Sherer, F. M., (1982), 'Using linked patent and R&D data to measure interindustry technology flows', *Review of Economics and Statistics*, **64**, 627–34.

Smirlock M., T. Gilligan and W. Marshall (1984), 'Tobin's q and the structure-performance relationship: reply', *American Economic Review*, **76**(5), 1211–13.

Teece, D. J., R. Rumelt, G. Dosi and S. Winter (1994), 'Understanding corporate coherence: theory and evidence', *Journal of Economic Behavior and Organisation*, **22**, 1–30.

Wernerfelt B. and C. A. Montgomery (1988), 'Tobin's q and the importance of focus in firm performance', *American Economic Review*, **78**(1), 246–50.

5. The anchor tenant hypothesis revisited: computer software clusters in North America

Norhene Chabchoub and Jorge Niosi

INTRODUCTION

The software industry is now a large component of the North American economy, and is becoming a major contributor to the production and exports of some industrial and developing countries, including such diverse nations as the United States and India. The software industry includes several major segments: telecommunication software, computer software, as well as programs for numerically controlled machines, robots, and games. Within the computer software segment, two major types of companies are to be found: computer hardware/software producers, such as IBM, Apple, Sun Microsystems and Dell, and independent software producers such as Microsoft, Oracle, Computer Associates in the United States and, SAP in Germany, in Canada, ATI and Cognos.

The development of the computer software industry has gone through several stages (Hoch *et al.*, 1999). The first one, starting in the 1950s, was the development of custom-made products for several thousand government and corporate users of large mainframes, most of them manufactured by IBM, and located in North America and Western Europe. By 1967, the United States hosted some 2800 professional software service firms. In the second stage, during the 1960s, several thousand new companies emerged, producing packaged software for the now more frequent mainframes. The third stage, started in 1969, was characterized by customized enterprise solutions; SAP of Germany was one of the first firms of this type. The fourth phase was that of the personal computer, and it began with the launching of the IBM PC in 1981. Once again, the new packaged software industry for PCs was located in North America. The fifth era was that of Netscape, Internet and the browser, and it commenced in 1994 in Silicon Valley. In the early 2000s, the packaged software industry for the personal computer dominates all segments of the industry and most large producers are located in the United States, Western Europe, followed by Canada, and Japan. This industry hosts thousands of companies, but computer hardware and independent software producers compete in an oligopolistic market dominated by such corporations as IBM, Microsoft, Apple, Dell and Hewlett Packard. In 2002, the world market for packaged software reached $US 200 billion, against $77 billion in 1994. North America represented close to 50 per cent of the production and the market for such type of software, but Western Europe hosts some of the largest producers of telecommunication software, while Japanese producers dominate the game segment of the software market. Another indicator of the size of the software industry is the total market capitalization of the software editors. As of 22 April 2003, independent software companies were the seventh largest North American industrial group in terms of market capitalization, worth $US 540 billion, ahead of computer hardware ($US 250 billion) and computer services ($US 237 billion). Microsoft was the largest ICT public corporation by market capitalization, and IBM was second.

SOFTWARE PATENTS

An increasing number of ICT companies are patenting software. The Foundation For a Free Information infrastructure, based in Munich, analysed the European Patent Office (EPO) Database and showed that, between 1976 and early 2003, there were 74 517 software patent applications (including computer, telecommunications and other types of software) in the EPO. Close to 80 per cent (or 60 000) of these applications were accepted. Some 44 per cent of the applications came from the United States, 29 per cent from Japan, 22 per cent from European based companies, and 2 per cent from those companies based in Canada. The rest of the world represented 3 per cent (Foundation For a Free Information Infrastructure, 2003). There are no similar figures for US software patents, and it would be difficult to create such a figure, because there are no reliable national or international codes for software patents. Our study analysed the patents of computer hardware and software firms, identified through keywords and company industrial (NAICS) codes and found that, since 1976, computer software had received not less than 22 000 patents in the USPTO, out of which some 18 600 were granted to publicly quoted firms located in North America. This figure is perfectly compatible with the EPO ones, and is the basis of our study. Our data were collected from USPTO, and sources of publicly quoted software companies.

SOFTWARE CLUSTERS AND THE ANCHOR HYPOTHESIS

Studies on high technology clusters and regional systems of innovation are numerous (Porter, 2000, 2001; Clark *et al.*, 2000; Cooke and Morgan, 1998; de la Mothe and Paquet, 1998; Fornahl and Brenner, 2003; Martin and Sunley, 2003). Those on software clusters are much less common (but see Arora *et al.*, 2001; Baptista and Swann, 1998; Cottrell, 2002; Giarratana and Torrisi, 2002; Swann, 1998). These few pieces of research tend to agree on a high rate of geographical agglomeration of software companies, and a certain tendency of these agglomerations to specialize into specific types and/or applications. It is also suggested that large corporations tend to be the main attractors or incubators of many other smaller firms. These empirical generalizations tend to support the more recent hypothesis developed by Maryann Feldman (2002), namely the anchor tenant hypothesis. Simply stated, this hypothesis suggests that large high-technology agglomerations tend to be created by the investment of large corporations, in a similar process to the one produced by a large retail corporation in a shopping mall. In a short lapse of time, these corporations promote the creation of a local labour market, the attraction of service firms and infrastructure, and the production of knowledge externalities. By the same token, the anchor tenants attract smaller corporations that thrive on the newly created labour market, on service firms and infrastructure, as well as on the knowledge externalities produced by the anchor.

The anchor hypothesis suggests that the agglomeration is created by the attraction of smaller firms. However, we would like to propose that the gathering of firms around a large corporation may occur through different mechanisms, one of which may be the attraction of footloose firms from other regions, but that other processes may be at stake, such as the incubation of smaller firms (spin-offs) by the anchor, or the creation of local firms (start-ups) by members of the newly formed local labour pool. It may also happen that there is more than one anchor in the region, and that the anchor firm disappears or moves away from the agglomeration, and the cluster develops on the basis of the new firms.

Also, we suggest that, as large corporations display a much higher propensity to patent, and are able to attract personnel from smaller firms, and/or benefit from knowledge spillovers generated by these other occupants of the cluster, in those regions where a large firm was at the origin of the cluster and patents its novelties, there must be other, smaller patenting firms, whatever their specific origins.

Finally, it may happen that a cluster in a large metropolitan area may be formed by the common activity (whether by attraction, by incubation or other underlying process) of several, not just one, anchor tenants. On the basis of the above discussion, we developed the following hypotheses:

Hypothesis 1: Software clusters develop around a tenant, a major company producing and patenting software. This is the original Feldman hypothesis about the formation of clusters.

Hypothesis 2: No cluster would be formed by only one large patenting corporation. In other words, all clusters with at least one major corporation should host other, smaller patenting firms. In other words, even in the smaller metropolitan areas, the presence of a large software laboratory creates a cluster of patenting firms.

Hypothesis 3: The size of the cluster (the number of patenting firms) will depend on the size of the agglomeration. The larger the population of the metropolitan area, the larger will be the potential number of new entrants in the region.

It is worth noting that, contrary to biotechnology innovative regions, software clusters do not necessarily include research universities, government laboratories or other public or quasi-public organizations. Large corporations are, by themselves, able to attract highly skilled labour, and provide them with commercially useful projects and missions. Whether it is in Galway (Ireland) or in Poughkeepsie, large corporations could create their software laboratories through the attraction of competent programmers from different regions and even different countries.

TESTING THE HYPOTHESES

Our database is composed of the 220 public companies operating in North America, having requested and been granted patents in the USPTO. Together they have obtained a total of 19 607 US software patents between 1986 and 2002. Of this total, 331 have been invented in Canada, and the others in the United States. US companies, such as IBM in Toronto, may invent in Canada and Canadian companies, such as Creo, may have invented in the United States. Patents, thus, are classified by location of inventors, not by the country of control of the patenting firm, or on the basis of the head office of the corporation. The USPTO publishes the region where the inventor(s) is located, allowing us to precisely locate the place where the invention is made.

We have organized the patents by year of publication and by region of inventor, as well as by company. Some large companies, such as IBM, Hewlett Packard (HP) and Unisys, have invented software programs in different locations, and obtained patents based on their regional laboratories. Their patents have been distributed in their respective sites.

Computer software patents are strongly concentrated in a small number of firms (Table 5.1). IBM is far ahead at the top of the list, followed by Microsoft, HP, Sun Microsystems and Apple Computers. It is worth noting that half of the largest patentees are at the same time hardware manufacturers and software producers.

Also, software patents are geographically agglomerated in a small number of census metropolitan areas (CMAs) (Table 5.2). In fact, the top 30 CMAs gather 97 per cent of all the software patents of North American public corporations; among them there is only one major Canadian agglomeration (Toronto), and 29 American ones. Silicon Valley is at the very top of the list, as one could imagine, but it is closely followed by Austin (Texas), Boise (Idaho) and Seattle (Washington state). These four major agglomerations concentrate half of North American computer software patents. The size of the agglomeration, in terms of total population, is not related to the number of patents (Figure 5.1), but is related to the number of patenting firms. Thus, some very small agglomerations, such as Poughkeepsie (state of New York) have more patents than Boston, or Washington DC, due to the activity of one major IBM laboratory, and a few other smaller firms. However, these small metropolitan areas are not growing too many patenting firms. This is also the case in smaller CMAs, such as Burlington (Vermont), Eugene

Table 5.1   Economic concentration of patents: top 10 patentees

Company	US patents obtained between 1986 and 2002
IBM	10405
Microsoft	2413
Hewlett-Packard	2300
Sun Microsystems	1023
Apple Computer	616
Unisys	408
Oracle	402
Adaptec	253
Silicon Graphics	230
Dell Computer	223
Total, top ten	18273
Top ten as percentage of all public	93%

Table 5.2   Economic concentration of patents: top 30 agglomerations in North America

Agglomeration	(1) USPAT US Patents 1986–2002	(2) POP Population (000)	(3) PAT. Firms Patenting firms 1996–2002
Silicon Valley, CA	3306	6874	107
Austin, TX	2160	1146	29
Boise, ID	1966	408	13
Seattle, WA	1840	3466	26
Minneapolis-St Paul, MN	1128	2872	18
New York, NJ, L. Island	980	20197	37
T. Research Park, NC	816	1106	4
Miami-F. Lauderdale, FL	766	3711	4
Denver, CO	722	2418	26
Poughkeepsie, NY	565	30	3
Boston, MA	490	5667	49
Syracuse, NY	483	733	5
Portland, OR	304	2181	26
Dallas, TX	288	4910	21
San Diego, CA	255	2821	25
Toronto, ON	241	4500	14
Washington, DC	227	7359	15
Tucson, AR	198	804	4
Los Angeles, CA	177	16037	33
Lexington, KY	158	456	2
Philadelphia, PA	158	5999	18
Hartford, CT	136	1147	11
Chicago, IL	132	8886	17
Eugene, OR	111	315	4
Provo, UT	100	347	7
Detroit, MI	89	5469	9
Pittsburgh, PA	82	2331	7
Burlington, VT	80	166	5
Sacramento, CA	57	1741	12
Atlanta, GA	50	3857	13

Notes:
Pearson correlation coefficient (POP/US Patents): 0.02.
Pearson correlation coefficient (POP/PAT. Firms): 0.43.

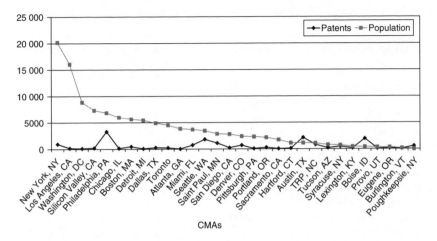

Figure 5.1   Population by CMAs in 2002 and US patents, 1988–2002

(Oregon), or Lexington (Kentucky). Conversely, large cities or agglomerations such as Silicon Valley, New York/New Jersey/Long Island, or Los Angeles, are hosts to many patenting firms.

Anchors tenant firms are present everywhere. In 16 agglomerations, IBM is the anchor tenant, and the first patenting firm. These clusters include Boise (ID), the Minneapolis – St Paul metropolitan area, New York/New Jersey/Long Island (where IBM's central lab is located), Toronto, and the Triangle Research Park in North Carolina (Table 5.3). IBM is also co-tenant in four other clusters, including Silicon Valley, Boston, Hartford (CT) and Denver (CO).

HP is the anchor company in four other localities: San Diego (California), Sacramento (CA), Portland and Eugene (both in Oregon). They are co-tenants in Boston (MA), Silicon Valley (CA) and Philadelphia (PA). Note that these HP localities are all in the Pacific coast, while those in which IBM has launched the patenting game are all distributed across the US and in Canada's largest CMA.

Microsoft is the only tenant in its own turf, Seattle. There is nowhere else in the United States where the largest global independent software company has a similar commanding role. Unisys is the tenant in two large agglomerations, Detroit (MI) and Los Angeles (CA), where it holds a smaller share of the patents. Lexmark is the anchor tenant in Lexington (Kentucky) as Wallace is in Chicago (Illinois) and Novell in Provo (Utah).

In five agglomerations no company was patenting in the first period. They are Atlanta (Georgia), Burlington (Vermont), Pittsburgh (Pennsylvania), Toronto (Ontario) and Tucson (Arizona). In all of them, IBM appeared as

Table 5.3   Anchor firms in each cluster, and share of patents by period

Agglomeration	Anchor	1986–90 (%)	1991–5 (%)	1996–2002 (%)
Silicon Valley, CA	IBM, HP, Apple	84	61	42/59
Austin, TX	IBM	98	90	82
Boise, ID	IBM	99	98	93
Seattle, WA	Microsoft	100	96	95
Minneapolis-St Paul, MN	IBM	62	87	76
New York, NJ, L. Island	IBM	94	95	90
T. Research Park, NC	IBM	100	100	99
Miami-F. Lauderdale, FL	IBM	100	100	94
Denver, CO	HP, IBM	100	97	79
Poughkeepsie, NY	IBM	100	100	99
Boston, MA	DRC, HP, IBM	50	58	34
Syracuse, NY	IBM	0	98	98
Portland, OR	HP	80	87	77
Dallas, TX	IBM	100	97	35
San Diego, CA	HP	62	63	66
Toronto, ON	IBM	NA	66	43
Washington, DC	IBM	100	98	68
Tucson, AR	IBM	NA	100	99
Los Angeles, CA	Unisys	49	20	40
Lexington, KY	Lexmark	0	33	94
Philadelphia, PA	HP, Unisys	100	95	68
Hartford, CT	Gerber Scientific, IBM	67	0	90
Chicago, IL	Wallace	100	91	44
Eugene, OR	HP	100	100	94
Provo, UT	Novell	80	87	91
Detroit, MI	Unisys	100	94	37
Pittsburgh, PA	IBM	NA	92	75
Burlington, VT	IBM	NA	NA	97
Sacramento, CA	HP	100	82	80
Atlanta, GA	IBM	NA	95	24

Notes:
NA = No patents.
DRC = Dynamics Research Corporation.

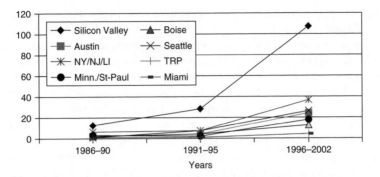

Figure 5.2   Number of patenting firms in larger clusters

a late anchor, or started patenting much later after their original installation. This is the case in Toronto, where IBM lab was founded in 1967 as the first software R&D organization of the American corporation.

Two agglomerations show a changing anchor, a process that mirrors similar processes in shopping malls. They are Boston and Silicon Valley. In the 1986–90, in Boston, Dynamics Research Corporation (DRC) was the original tenant, but it was superseded by HP in the 1991–5 period, then by IBM after 1996. In Silicon Valley, IBM was the dominant patentee in 1986–90, but HP became the most important one in 1991–5 and Apple Computer joined the group in 1996–2002. In this latest period the three corporations were granted hundreds of patents, with IBM as the major one, followed by Apple and HP.

Figure 5.2 shows that the number of patenting firms varies according to the agglomeration. Silicon Valley's cluster grew to over 100 patenting, while places such as Miami and Poughkeepsie only grew four such firms.

CONCLUSION

The anchor tenant hypothesis (Hypothesis 1) is largely confirmed on the basis of our data. In 20 out of 30 agglomerations, one major corporation appears to be settled at the beginning of the patenting spree. In several others, the patenting process started later, and in at least two of them, Boston and Silicon Valley, several major corporations were patenting from the start. However, we discovered clusters where more than one major firm acted as anchors, and others where the anchor has changed over time.

Hypothesis 2 is also confirmed: all clusters have more than one patenting firm, but the number of firms depends on the size (population) of the CMA (Hypothesis 3). However, the number of patents granted to firms in the different agglomerations does not depend on the population of the CMA. Some larger metropolitan areas have obtained comparatively fewer patents than smaller ones. Probably some underlying processes are at stake, such as the human capital of the region, and the efficiency of the local infrastructure and service firms. A large CMA is no guarantee of a large innovative cluster. Further research will try to understand these underlying factors behind the growth of the innovation capabilities in the cluster.

Almost everywhere the share of the tenant in the total number of local patents declines over time, as new entrants claim their share of patents, but in a few cases (mostly in smaller CMAs) the part of the anchor increases or remains constant. Again, further research may discover the causal processes at work.

Our research develops the new anchor tenant hypothesis and suggests that innovation activities are also linked to anchors, not simply the cluster phenomenon as such. The next stage will be to better understand the relative importance of the different processes (attraction, incubation, startup) that create the cluster.

BIBLIOGRAPHY

Arora, A., A. Gambardella and S. Torrisi (2001), 'In the footstep of Silicon Valley? Indian and Irish software in the international division of labour', Stanford, SIEPR Discussion Paper 00–41.

Baptista, R. and G. M. P. Swann (1998), 'Clustering in the UK computer industry: a comparison with the USA', in G. M. P. Swann, M. Prevezer, and D. Stout, (eds), *The Dynamics of Industrial Clustering*, Oxford: Oxford University Press, pp. 106–23.

Clark, G. L., M. Feldman and M. S. Gertler (eds) (2000), *The Oxford Handbook of Economic Geography*, New York: Oxford University Press.

Cooke, P. and K. Morgan (1998), *The Associational Economy. Firms, Regions and Innovation*, Oxford: Oxford University Press.

Cottrell, T. (2002), 'Clusters and trajectories. Does collocation affect product development?' A paper presented to the seminar Clusters in High-Technology, Montreal, November.

De la Mothe, J. and G. Paquet (eds) (1998), *Local and Regional Systems of Innovation*, Boston: Kluwer.

Foundation for a Free Information Infrastructure (2003), Database, www.ffii.org

Feldman, M. (2002), 'The locational dynamics of US biotech industry: Knowledge externalities and the anchor hypothesis', A paper presented to the seminar Clusters in High-Technology, Montreal, November.

Fornahl, D. and T. Brenner (eds) (2003), *Cooperation, Networks and Institutions in Regional Innovation Systems*, Cheltenham, UK: Edward Elgar.

Giarratana, M. and S. Torrisi (2002), 'Emerging clusters in the international production of software: evidence from patents, trademarks and linkages', A paper presented to the seminar Clusters in High-Technology, Montreal, November.

Hoch, D., C. R. Roeding, G. Purkert, and S. K. Lindner (1999), *Secrets of Software Success*, Boston, MA: Harvard Business School Press.

Martin, R. and P. Sunley (2003), 'Deconstructing clusters: chaotic concept or policy panacea', *Journal of Economic Geography*, **31**(1), 5–35.

OCDE (2001), *Innovative Clusters, Drivers of National Innovation Systems*, Paris: OECD.

Porter, M. (2000), 'Locations, clusters and company strategy' in G. L. Clark, M. Feldman and M. S. Gertler (eds), *The Oxford Handbook of Economic Geography*, New York: Oxford University Press, pp. 253–74.

Porter, M. (2001), 'Innovation, location matters', *Sloan Management Review*, **42**(4), 28–36.

Yifei, S. (2000), 'Spatial distribution of patents in China', *Regional Studies*, **34**(5), 441–54.

Swann, G. M. P. (1998), 'Clusters in the US computing industry', in G. M. P. Swann, M. Prevezer and D. Stout (eds), *The Dynamics of Industrial Clustering*, Oxford: Oxford University Press, pp. 77–105.

6. Industry dynamics in the German insurance market

Michael Menhart, Andreas Pyka,
Bernd Ebersberger and Horst Hanusch

INTRODUCTION

Evolutionary models of organizational change have become an increasingly important part of the literature on organizational analysis. Most prominent organization theories explain diversity and change in organizational forms by the process of adaptation through individual organizations. Organizational ecology challenges this approach and argues that adaptation of organizational characteristics occurs at the population level through selective replacement of different organizational forms.[1] The theory attempts to explain long-rung organizational change in industries by analysing founding and mortality events depending on the number of existing organizations, former founding and mortality rates and other population characteristics such as size and age of the organizations.

Empirical research in organizational ecology has mainly focused on analysing founding and mortality rates using life history data of the organizations. We try to extend this approach in our study in a number of ways. In contrast to most empirical studies in organizational ecology, we chose a population of service organizations, the development dynamics of which are rather obvious in the innovative activities of existing organizations than in founding activities. We further discuss the points of contact between the organizational ecology approach and the theory of industry life cycles and extend the analysis to the relationship between innovative activities and population dynamics. The study examines the effects of population density, former events, and organizational size and age structure in the population of property and casualty insurance companies on the number of product innovations generated. We will further develop a concept for an insurance specific industry life cycle with a non-typical maturation and degeneration phase, and discuss to what extent the concept of Maslow's pyramid of needs can have explanatory power regarding the pattern of density dynamics. This study proposes an empirical framework for evaluating the hypotheses generated on the basis of the organizational ecology theory and the insurance specific industry life cycle. We estimate and report specific tests of the innovation rates using the traditional approach of event history analysis based on the negative binomial model.

HISTORICAL DEVELOPMENT OF THE GERMAN INSURANCE MARKET

The global insurance industry experienced a significant growth in the twentieth century. The number of insurance companies increased from about 1300 in the year 1900 to more than 14 000 today. More than a third of the companies are located in Europe.[2] The German insurance market in the year 1999 comprised approximately 2000 companies.[3] In this chapter, we intend to give an overview of the development of the German insurance industry to one of the most important economic sectors of Germany from two perspectives. First, we want to describe the key milestones in the evolution of the insurance sector from its origins against the background of the economic and political developments. Moreover, we will present the history of the German insurance industry in the light of technological inventions and the following insurance specific innovations.

The modern insurance industry in Germany is the result of a development process the roots of which lead back as far as to the origins of the idea of insurance in the antiquity.[4] In the legislative bill of the Babylonian king Hammurabi in the year 1750 BC, one can identify specific rules regarding financial arrangements of salesmen protecting them against losses of their caravans due to robberies. In the economy of the Greek empire around the year 200 BC, owners of merchant vessels could receive a loan before setting sails, which they had to return in case the vessels arrived safely in the harbour. Four hundred years later, the first life insurance was introduced in the Roman Empire. In middle Europe, the first contractual arrangements similar to today's insurance practice can be found in the so-called 'Kapitulare' of the German emperor 'Charlemagne' in the year 779. In this legislative bill, the mutual financial support of craft and trade co-operatives in case of fire accidents is described.

However, these first insurance agreements consisting of the mutual guarantees to support each other in case of an accident or a catastrophe differ significantly from today's insurance practice. The beginning of the modern, profit-oriented insurance industry in Europe dates back to the fourteenth century and has its roots in the Mediterranean countries as well as England and the Netherlands.[5] The essential difference to the ancient predecessors of insurance was the fact that, for the first time, insurance premiums to be paid in advance were included in the contracts. The first arrangements of this nature are documented for the insurance of Italian ships in the second half of the fourteenth century. In the years following, this 'innovation' made its way to England, Spain, the Netherlands and finally to Germany.

The German insurance industry is not only based on the import of the insurance idea via Mediterranean salesmen, but also on two other independent lines of development. In the sixteenth century, craft and trade co-operatives started to offer their insurance products to customers who were not members of their organizations. Apart from that, the first public insurance companies were founded in the seventeenth century by merging the administrations of already existing fire insurance contracts in big cities.[6]

Nevertheless, it was not before the founding of the first joint-stock insurance companies in Germany at the beginning of the nineteenth century that the insurance industry started to grow into a significant economic sector. The idea of insurance gained further acceptance within the society when the era of liberalism led to the founding of several private insurance companies.[7] The industrialization and the increase of the living standards of major parts of society led to the fact, that more and more people had 'something to lose' and therefore also had something that needed to be insured. Insurance contracts were no longer a privilege of the upper class, but a 'product for everyone'. However, the 'final breakthrough' for the German insurance industry came with the first social legislation in the year 1881. The introduction of a public medical insurance in 1883, a public accident insurance in 1884 and a sort of public pension insurance in 1889 did not imply a substitution of private by public insurance institutions, but helped to further spread the idea of insurance within the society, a development from which the private insurance industry profited significantly.[8]

The years between 1850 and 1900 must be seen as the period, in which almost all of the major product innovations were introduced into the German casualty and property insurance market, as can be seen in the Table 6.1.

The industrialization and the development of new technologies also led to new needs of insurance, such as the classes of machine/technology or car insurance. At the same time, the government forced the employers to protect their employees against accidents at work, leading to the introduction of accident insurance. As the potential claims in case of accidents caused by new technologies reached sums not experienced before by the owners of machinery such as railways, the personal liability insurance became increasingly important.

The First World War caused the first major crisis in the German insurance industry. The total international business of reinsurance and transport insurance collapsed. The life and accident insurance companies first invested major parts of their capital into the so-called 'Kriegsanleihen', war

Table 6.1 Year of the introduction of exemplary product innovations in the casualty and property insurance industry[9]

Class of insurance	Germany	UK	France	USA
Hailstorm	1719	1840	1802	1870
Animal	1765	1844	1805	
Accident	1853	1848		1864
Glass	1862	1852	1829	1874
Personal liability	1874	1875	1829	
Water	1886	1854		
Burglary/theft	1895	1846		1878
Credit/loan	1898	1820		1876
Car	1899	1896		
Machine/technology	1900	1872		

bonds issued by the government. Moreover, they had to pay enormous sums due to war casualties, which had been excluded from the insurance contracts before the war, but finally were reintroduced due to public pressure.[10]

Those companies surviving the war were hit by the next fundamental exogenous shock, the period of inflation in the 1920s. At the beginning of this decade, the insurance market experienced a boom caused by the enormous surplus of money created during inflation. Many new insurance companies arose and even firms from the manufacturing industry decided to found own banks and insurance companies. However, only few of them were able to overcome the final devaluation of the money. Thus, this period experienced the most dramatic consolidation in the history of the German insurance industry.

The third fundamental exogenous shock in the first half of the twentieth century was, of course, the regime of the National Socialists respectively the Second World War. In the 1930s, the government tried to centralize the insurance market and forced many small companies to merge. The Second World War deleted not only the capital reserves of the insurance companies, but also their administrations. The medical and life insurance companies again had to pay enormous sums and the car insurance industry completely collapsed due to the destruction of the public infrastructure. The total insurance market of the Eastern regions was withdrawn after 1945, so that many insurance companies moved to the west.

However, just as the whole German economy, the insurance industry soon recovered from this catastrophe and experienced a period of steady and continuous growth after 1950. While the development of this sector was significantly influenced by fundamental exogenous shocks in the first half of the twentieth century, in the last 50 years only two events need to be mentioned in this respect, the German reunification in 1990 and the deregulation of the European insurance market in 1994. The effects of both of these exogenous changes are not comparable to the effects of the crises before the Second World War. The German reunification more or less only led to a single increase in the insurance volume of Germany, which was almost totally captured by the major existing players in the market. European deregulation was first believed to motivate international companies to enter the German insurance market. However, the major effect in reality was the beginning of a price war between the existing companies, as the insurance offerings no longer had to be approved by the public authorities.

Moreover, the twentieth century, in general, and the last 50 years, in particular, did not experience the same amount of fundamental product innovations as the nineteenth century. The major trends of this last epoch of the insurance industry were the diversification of the product portfolios of existing companies as well as the introduction of product modifications such as the combination of several classes of insurance in one contract, or the adjustment of the insurance premiums to meet the individual needs of the customers.

PRODUCT INNOVATIONS IN THE INSURANCE MARKET

Before we can lay the theoretical base for the analysis of the historical development of the German insurance market and the role of product innovations in the evolution of this industry, we first want to define the product created by an insurance company, and discuss the different forms of innovation in this sector. In the existing literature, there is more or less general agreement that the insurance industry belongs to the service sector.[11] However, there is not so much consent on how the product of an insurance company can be defined.[12] Albrecht (1992: 4) sees the insurance product as a transfer of information and conditional payments from the insurance company to the customer and, at the same time, a transfer of risks and a monetary premium vice versa, as shown in Figure 6.1.

The insurance company sells specific information regarding the insured object to the customer. The information consists of the guarantee to pay a monetary equivalent for the object insured in case a defined event (accident, fire, and so on) occurs. The customer pays a certain premium and transfers the risk of having a monetary disadvantage due to potential damage to the insurance company.

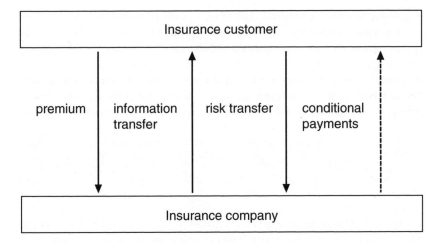

Figure 6.1   Insurance as transfer of risk and information[13]

In order to define the different forms of innovation in the insurance industry, we differentiate between the subject and the object dimension of the product innovation.[14] In the subject dimension, the degree of newness is regarded from the perspective of the customer. If the product is new to the market, it is called market novelty. In case an insurance company introduces a product that has not been in its product portfolio before, but already existed on the market, we call it *internal novelty*.

In the object dimension of an innovation, the degree of newness of an insurance product is measured from the perspective of the company offering it. We will follow the methodology of Vielreicher (1995) to differentiate between product innovations and product modifications. In his model, an insurance product can only be called innovative if it creates a new 'field of insurance'. A field of insurance consists of certain risk factors (for example negligence or fire-raising), insured objects (for example houses or cars) and forms of incidents (fire or accidents). An innovative field of insurance is created when one of those elements is changed completely or if parts of those elements are extracted and offered as an independent product. All other changes in the composition of the field of insurance are considered to be product modifications. Following this methodology, we create the following definitions:

Definition 6.1: A product innovation is called a market novelty, if an insurance company creates a new field of insurance that has not been offered on the market before.

Definition 6.2: A product innovation is called an internal novelty, if an insurance company offers a field of insurance that is new to the company, but already exists on the market.

As the insurance industry is part of the service sector, one of the specific characteristics of the output produced is the difficulty to differentiate between the product and the process component of the good:

> The first analytical problem raised by services is the relatively fuzzy and unstable nature of their product. Indeed a service is a process, a sequence of operations, a formula, a protocol, a mode of organization. It is difficult, in many cases, to locate the boundaries of a service in the same way as those of a good can be fixed.[15]

Services such as those offered by insurance companies are products as well as processes, as they are produced and consumed at the same time. Service companies cannot produce their output in advance and store it in order to sell it in the future. Similarly, customers of service companies cannot buy the goods and store it for later consumption. Therefore, the process of production is an essential part of the product itself. That is why the customers need to participate in the production process. Each service product hat a unique nature. It is produced according to the individual needs and problems of the customer. Customer interaction also plays a crucial role in the sales of service products. Muth (1988: 1586) claims that 80 per cent of people buying a financial product such as an insurance contract insist on having a personal consultation with a representative of the respective company in advance.

Moreover, service goods are immaterial.[16] The customers cannot test the quality of the good to be purchased in advance. Thus, a certain degree of confidence is required in the product to be bought from the service company. This is especially true for insurance products. The product sold by the insurance company is the guarantee to pay a monetary equivalent for the object insured in case a defined event (accident, fire, and so on) occurs. This guarantee is not only immaterial, but the customer can only experience the quality of the product if the insured event actually happens. Therefore, the product has also a very abstract nature. Above all, in case of product innovations, the reputation and the image of the insurance company are essential factors for the success of the product. This is why customers often tend to buy insurance bundles from one company rather than several insurance contracts from different suppliers. Especially if the insurances purchased concern the basis of one's livelihood (for example life insurance, fire insurance and so on), people often stick to the supplier they have trusted before in other classes of insurance.

As service goods such as insurance products are immaterial, it is generally easy for competitors to imitate product innovations:

> The vector of service characteristics . . . is linked to possible functional imitation by all actual or potential competitors (including clients). The service characteristics are indeed highly visible and 'volatile', which makes them easy to imitate. The most convincing examples are to be found in financial and personal insurance services. The specifications of an insurance policy or of a financial product are in the public domain. They are object of firms' marketing and advertising policies (advertising leaflets etc.).'[17]

However, while competitors can copy specific product characteristics quickly, it is far more difficult to reach the same level of reputation and customer acceptance first movers in the insurance market have. Kubli (1988: 87) assumes that it takes approximately six months for a competitor to copy an innovative insurance product. According to Vielreicher (1995: 26) it can take more than five years for an imitator to gain the level of customer confidence needed to succeed in a new insurance class.

Another typical market characteristic of the insurance industry the companies have to keep in mind in the generation of product innovation is the *insurance-specific risk*. It stands for the fatal risk of an insurance company, that payments to be made due to the occurrence of insured events exceed the sum of the premium income and the capital reserves of the companies.[18] The insurance-specific risk comprises two elements, the risk that, by pure chance, the number of insured events is higher than the expected number, and the risk that the calculations of the probability of expected events by the insurance company are wrong. As for product innovations, the insurance companies, in general, only have limited experience in the specific estimations. Therefore the insurance-specific risk is especially high for innovative product offerings. Pearson (1997: 242) further differentiates between the technical uncertainty describing the uncertainty of the insurance companies regarding the optimal product offering and the market uncertainty as a lack of knowledge whether the innovative product will be accepted on the market. In either case, the insurance company can reduce the total insurance-specific risk by diversifying its product portfolio and, hence, spreading the risk over more fields of insurance.

THEORETICAL ISSUES

We chose the organizational ecology theory and the industry life cycle concept as theoretical bases for our analysis of the innovation dynamics in the German insurance market, since both approaches look at the evolution of whole industries and make assumptions about the determinants of the number of market entries. However, while most studies testing the relevance of the industry life cycle concept mainly focused on descriptive pictures of the observed evolution of industries,[19] the analyses based on the organizational ecology approach tried to identify the determinants of the development dynamics based on various statistical models.[20] On top of that, the service sector has so far been widely neglected in life cycle-specific investigations, whereas population ecologists also tested the relevance of their concept in areas such as voluntary social service organizations,[21] investment firms,[22] credit unions[23] or the savings and loan industry.[24]

In this section we will discuss both approaches and finally generate the hypotheses to be tested in the following empirical analysis.

The Organizational Ecology Approach

'Why are there so many different kinds of organizations?' This question asked by Hannan and Freeman (1977: 956) in their well-known essay 'The population ecology of organizations' was the base for the development of the organizational ecology theory, an evolutionary approach trying to explain the long-term development of organizational populations, which has become an increasingly important part of the literature on organizational analysis. The organizational ecology approach differs from other organizational theories on change processes[25] especially in two points. First, it tries to explain the dynamics in the development of whole organizational populations,[26] and second, organizations are structurally inert. In contrast to adaptive theoretical approaches, organizations do not change their structures actively, but superior forms replace them.[27] Organizational change happens through selection processes. The evolution of a population follows a Darwinian concept. The survival chances of organizations depend on the degree to which they meet the demands of the environmental conditions.

Model of density dependence

Based on Hannan's (1986) model of density dependence, the determinants of founding and disbanding rates in organizational populations are analysed in organizational ecology theory.[28] An analogy to biological populations is used to explain evolutionary processes in the so-called concept of the niche. Just as populations of animals live in particular ecological niches, organizational populations also need a specific resource space for survival and reproduction. The resource space of an organizational population comprises elements like raw materials, technologies, customers or personnel. As the resource space of an organizational population is limited, populations cannot grow infinitely.

According to the model of density dependence, the processes of legitimation and competition determine the growth and development dynamics of an organizational population.[29] An organizational form is legitimate, if it is commonly accepted as the normal way of producing a specific organizational outcome. Competition effects are caused by direct competition between the members of an organization and diffuse competition, if organizations do not interact directly but still compete for the same resources. While legitimacy of an organizational form is supposed to increase the founding rate and heighten the survival changes at a decreasing rate, the effects of competition on the founding rate are believed to be negative.[30] All in all, the processes of legitimation and competition lead to a non-monotonic relationship between the density of a population and the founding and disbanding rates. The founding rate follows an inverted U-shaped pattern in dependence of the population density. It first increases to a maximum and then decreases to finally reach a stable, lower level.

Delacroix and Carroll (1983) extended the initial approach of density dependence by analysing the effects of prior founding and disbanding rates on the further development dynamics. They argued, that a high number of prior foundings indicates favourable environmental conditions and leads to more market entries. As in the case of population density, these effects are believed to be non-monotonic and become negative when a certain level is reached.[31] The density dependence model has experienced further extensions and various applications. On top of the analysis of development dynamics between different organizational populations[32] or between specialist and generalist organizations in the resource-partitioning model it was also used to study labour market dynamics.[33]

While the initial concept of structural inertia did not allow for adaptive changes within organizations, some scholars in the community of organization ecology research have claimed that under certain circumstances active change of organizational structures can also be analysed from a population ecology perspective.[34] Especially the parting line between founding events and internal organizational change has been in the focus of the latest studies:

If organization-level analysis routinely treat change and death as competing risks for individual organizations, the rise of network organizational forms makes it necessary for ecologists to model change and foundings as competing risks. (Amburgey and Rao, 1996: 1275)

Particularly corporate organizations can choose between different strategies in entering new markets. They can build a new unit within the existing organization or modify the strategic direction of an existing unit.

Alternatively, they might as well found a new organization, which is separated from the existing business units. The first of those three alternatives can be regarded as a process of diversification by creating an internal product innovation in the way we defined it for the German insurance market on pp. 105–6. In the process of diversification, the organization faces challenges similar to those of entrepreneurs founding a new organization and those of enterprises going through structural changes. They are entering a new market and at the same time they are adjusting the strategic direction of an existing organization. Market entry by way of diversification has been examined in several studies based on the organizational ecology theory. In their analysis of the development dynamics in the US semiconductor industry, Hannan and Freeman (1989) regard both market entry by existing organizations and the founding of new companies as events affected by population density in the same way. Mitchell (1995) argues that diversification activities represent changes in the peripheral structures of organizations, while Havemann (1993b) considers them to affect the core of the organization.

The motivation for diversification activities is mainly based on three elements.[35] The organizations can catch the opportunity to enter an attractive market, they might leave industries in which they cannot achieve the growth rates expected or they might regard their product range as investment portfolio and try to spread the entrepreneurial risk over several product groups. In the organizational ecology theory, the attractiveness of a market is determined by legitimation and competition processes. In accordance to Havemann (1994), we try to transfer the model of density dependence to explain diversification dynamics. We attempt to identify whether the market entries of existing organizations are affected by the same mechanisms that determine the U-shaped pattern of founding rates in dependence of population density.

However, population density is not the only factor to influence organizational change processes. Fligstein (1991) as well as Havemann (1993a) assume, that prior diversification activities in organizational populations might lead to imitation by other members of the population studied. They argue that an increasing number of market entries through diversification will increase the legitimation of this strategy and motivate other companies to imitate this way of market entry. At the same time, organizational ecology theory also believes that organizational size and age might have an impact on the willingness of organizations to go through structural change. Older organizations are believed to have higher structural inertia than younger competitors.[36] According to the liability of newness theorem, they have developed stable structures, internal hierarchies and external relations to key partners in the organization environment. These characteristics increase their survival chances, but at the same time strengthen the resistance to any sort of organizational change. The size of an organization is believed to have a similar effect. According to the liability of smallness theorem, organizations need to build standardized and formal procedures in order to cope with the increasing complexity that is created with increasing size.[37] Once again, those stable processes are supposed to help the organization to survive the selection mechanism in the evolution of the population, but also strengthen the resistance against change processes such as the diversification of the product portfolio.

Development of hypotheses
The core concept of the organizational ecology theory is the model of *density dependence*. As discussed on pp. 108–10, this approach has already been transferred to explain the dynamics of market entries of existing organizations by ways of diversification of their product portfolio in several studies.[38] Following this conceptual procedure, we also develop a hypothesis for the effect of population density on the market entries through internal product innovations. We assume, that the innovation rate shows a curvilinear pattern in dependence of the number of existing insurance companies due to the processes of legitimation and competition.

> *Hypothesis 1:* The number of internal product innovations shows a non-monotonic, inverted U-shaped pattern with rising population density.

As discussed before, neither the organizational ecology theory nor the existing empirical studies can deliver consistent concepts and results on the relationship between the number of previous market entries and the further development of the entry rate. However, as several authors emphasize the importance of imitation processes for diversification activities in organizational populations,[39] we assume that a high number of previous product innovations is regarded as an indicator for positive market entry conditions and will therefore increase future innovation rates.

> *Hypothesis 2:* The number of previous internal product innovations is positively related to future innovation rates.

While the organizational ecology theory and the comments on the specific characteristics of the demand for insurance products on pp. 106–7 both come to the conclusion that old organizations have higher survival chances due to the liability of newness (Hannan and Freeman, 1989) theorem respectively the importance of market reputation and market experience in the insurance sector, there is a significant difference regarding the respective judgements on the probability of market entry in dependence of organizational age. In the insurance industry where market reputation plays a crucial role in successfully entering new markets[40], one would expect older companies to generate product innovations more easily. However, from a population ecology point of view, the structural inertia rises with increasing age and leads to a higher resistance against any kind of organizational change such as the diversification of the product portfolio via internal product innovations.

> *Hypothesis 3:* Organizational age has a negative effect on the rate of internal product innovations.

In an analogy to the arguments presented for Hypothesis 3, the organizational ecology approach also claims that structural inertia rises with organizational size. The larger the organization, the more it relies on formalized and standardized processes and the higher is the resistance to change those routines. Hannan and Freeman (1984: 184ff) claim this to be the main difference between formal organizations and loose coalitions of individuals. The latter can respond quickly to any change of environmental conditions, as long as it is small enough to act without the need to delegate decisions within the organization. Otherwise, formalized processes are needed, which secure its survival through strengthening the reliability and accountability, but increase the inflexibility of the organization.

Once again, the assumption of large organizations having a lower propensity to generate a product innovation is counter-intuitive to what we have learned about the importance of market presence and a large customer network for insurance companies. However, when arguing from an organizational ecology point of view, the effect of structural inertia will outweigh the influence of the specific characteristics of the demand for insurance products. In accordance to Havemann (1994: 154f), who states that especially in populations dominated by a few large firms, market entry for smaller companies becomes more difficult due to increased diffuse competition, we assume a negative relationship between organizational size and the innovation rate in our last hypothesis.

> *Hypothesis 4:* Organizational size has a negative effect on the rate of internal product innovations.

Industry Life Cycles in the Insurance Market

Biological lifecycles describe the development processes of an individual from birth to death. Economic life cycle concepts assume, that in analogy to biological organisms, economic systems also experience typical phases of development in their evolution.[41] In the economic literature, life cycle concepts were used to explain the development patterns of single products, organizations,[42] technologies[43] and whole industries. In the standard model of the life cycle concept, specific characteristics of the unit of analysis such as sales volume, turnover or number of competitors first increase to a maximum, then decrease significantly and finally reach a level of stability, or they are discontinued completely.

Standard model and insurance specific modifications

In the industry life cycle concept, the unit of analysis is either the sales volume of an industry[44] or the number of competitors in the market.[45] If the development of the sales volume is analysed, the industry life cycle is the sum of the life cycles of product generations and single products in the respective industry, as is shown in Figure 6.2.

Similar to the industry life cycle model based on the sales volume of the products, the model regarding the development of the number of companies in the market also assumes an inverted U-shaped pattern.[47] After an increase in the number of competitors to a maximum due to high entry rates, the number of market exits exceeds the entries. Thus, the population density is reduced through a shakeout process and finally stabilizes at a lower level.[48] While there is general consent in the existing literature regarding the general pattern of the industry life cycle, its interpretations, especially regarding the massive market shakeout after the maximum differ significantly.[49] In general, the different concepts assume that there is a shift

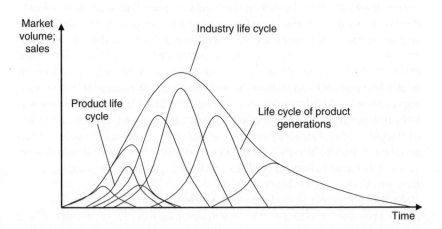

Figure 6.2   Product life cycles and industry life cycle[46]

in the innovative activities from product innovations in the beginning of the life cycle to process innovations in the latter phases, which forces companies not capable of adapting the innovations to leave the market.[50]

However, the existing studies analysing industry life cycles exclusively focus on the consumer goods or the manufacturing industry, while the service sector is neglected completely. Only on the level of product life cycles, a few attempts were made to integrate the specific characteristics of the service industry into the life cycle concepts.[51] The reason for the strong bias of life cycle studies towards the manufacturing industry may lie in the fact that products in these sectors show relatively high death and innovation rates, so that product life cycles can be identified easily. In contrast to most goods in the manufacturing sector, the motivation for the purchase of an insurance product is based on the long-term need for precautions against essential risks in one's livelihood. Farny and Kirsch (1987) therefore claim basic insurance classes such as life or fire insurance to be 'immortal products'.

Another difficulty in modelling the product life cycle in the insurance industry is caused by the specific characteristics of the demand for insurance products. Their life cycles overlap with external factors such as the density of the population, the number of potential risks to be insured or the insurance specific legislation. Besides, as the customer buys many insurance products in bundles, it is hard to identify single product life cycles. Considering this reasoning, Vielreicher (1993) assumes that the product life cycle of an insurance product shows an atypical pattern, as can be seen in Figure 6.3.

In the first three phases, the insurance life cycle is similar to the standard model. After the product introduction, the sales volume increases to a maximum. In the maturation and degeneration phase of the life cycle however, the shape cannot be determined ex ante. The sales volume may decline as in the standard model, it may also show further increases or remain stable. The reasons for this atypical pattern lie in the specific characteristics of the demand for insurance products. First, an insurance product life cycle basically consists of two life cycles, one for the new insurance contracts sold and one for the premium income generated by the existing contracts. Thus, an insurance product can still generate volume, although the insurance companies may not even offer it anymore. On top of that, the 'immortality' of certain insurance lines such as life or fire insurance prevents the product from finally dying out after the maturation phase.[52] Innovative insurance classes mainly supplement the existing products, but they do not substitute them.

As it is not possible to clearly determine the shape of a single life cycle of an insurance product in the maturation and degeneration phase, the pattern of an industry life cycle consisting of the sum of all individual product life cycles cannot be determined either. However, a possible

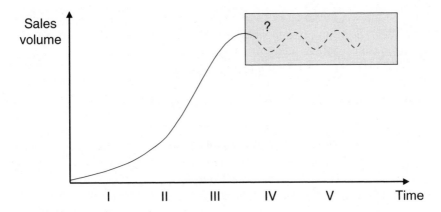

Figure 6.3   Life cycle of an insurance product

explanation of its development can be derived from the specific income elasticity of the demand for insurance products on an aggregate level. In the existing literature, there have been only limited, but controversial discussions regarding the income elasticity of the demand for insurances. Koeniger (2001) claims in his analysis of the UK car industry, that higher income leads to lower demand for car insurance, as high-income households can afford to pay for potential repair costs more easily. Eisenhauer and Halek (1999) as well as Banerjee and Newman (1991) identify a positive relationship between the income level of a household and its risk aversion. Geiger (1992) analyses the demand for personal liability, accident, legal costs, and household insurances in Germany. Following his results, there is a positive effect of household income on the insurance density in the population.

A different approach to the demand for insurance products is based on Maslow's theory of human motivation, according to which there is a hierarchy of needs observable in the goods consumed by the people.[53] Maslow developed a pyramid of needs consisting of five different levels, as is shown in Figure 6.4.

On the lowest level of Maslow's pyramid, there are the basic physical needs such as food, shelter or clothing. The second level describes the need for safety in the sense of protection from all kinds of physical and psychological threats. It stands for the need to feel free from all kinds of anxiety. On top of the safety needs, Maslow sees the need for social contacts and love, the need for esteem in the sense of respect, status and competence and finally the need for self-fulfillment. Maslow's model claims that this hierarchy determines everybody's behaviour. The needs on higher levels only

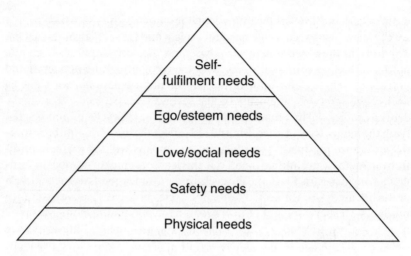

Figure 6.4   Maslow's pyramid of needs[54]

become relevant, if the lower levels are already satisfied.[55] On the other hand, once a higher level is reached, people are supposed to focus their activities completely on the fulfilment of the respective need.

It is quite obvious that the demand for basic insurance products is assumed to be part of the second level of Maslow's hierarchy, the need for safety. The history of the German insurance sector yields several examples supporting this hypothesis. In the early years of the insurance industry, in the middle of the nineteenth century, the purchase of an insurance was a privilege of the upper class. However, once industrialization raised the living standard of major parts of the population, insurances became popular for lower classes as well. On the other hand, immediately after the Second World War, the priority of the population was to satisfy the basic physiological needs. Only after the economy recovered and the basic needs were fulfilled in the beginning of the 1950s did the insurance industry experience a significant upturn.[56]

While the physiological needs of the population can be regarded as being more or less satisfied after the 1950s, this is not necessarily the case for the need for safety. In the last 50 years, almost all classes of insurance in Germany experienced significant growth rates. On the other hand, Geiger (1992) identified that even at the beginning of the 1990s 40 per cent of the private households in West Germany did not have a life insurance and 70 per cent in the Eastern parts did not have an accident insurance.

Moreover, the concept of Maslow's pyramid of needs also helps to explain the further growth of the insurance population after the economic upturn in the 1950s and 1960s. Once the second level of needs is satisfied, people seek for new goals such as the need for esteem and self-actualization.[57] One way to fulfil these needs is the purchase and the consumption of specific products that are supposed to increase the recognition and accelerate the process of self-actualization. If the people nevertheless do not want to neglect the safety requirements of the second level of needs, they might demand additional insurance coverage. Hence, the life cycles of goods satisfying the higher level of needs should also affect the life cycles of the respective insurance products. A car insurance company will for example profit from an increase in national income, if this leads to a higher number of families having two cars. Thus, the life cycles of consumer goods of higher levels in the hierarchy are connected to the life cycles of the respective insurance products. The development of new needs in the population along Maslow's hierarchy does not only induce further growth in the existing insurance classes, it also leads to the generation of innovative insurance products. Classes such as the insurance of journeys, of domestic animals, of art or musical instruments do not satisfy the need for safety regarding essential risks in one's livelihood. They give additional protection in the fulfilment of higher levels of Maslow's hierarchy.

All in all, we have two sources for the derivation of an insurance specific industry life cycle, the pattern of the product life cycle in the insurance industry and the specific characteristics of the demand for insurance according to Maslow's model. Combining those two approaches leads to an industry life cycle, as shown in Figure 6.5.

Similar to the standard model, the industry life cycle of the insurance sector starts with the introduction of the first product innovation. As more and more supplementary insurance classes are added, the industry life cycle measuring the total sales volume increases to a maximum. However, since the shape of the life cycle cannot be determined for neither of the individual products, it is also impossible to see *ex ante*, how the aggregated industry life cycle will develop once a certain maximum is reached. Considering our theses regarding the specific characteristics of the demand for insurances in Maslow's model, we claim, that in this atypical maturation or degeneration phase, the shape of the industry life cycle will be determined by the general economic development.

Based on this model, we can also derive the insurance specific industry life cycle describing the development of the number of competitors in the market. In this respect, the standard model assumes an inverted U-shaped pattern along the life cycle of an industry. The increase in the number of competitors in the first phases of the life cycle also seems to be plausible for the insurance market. After the introduction of the first insurance products, a few companies will dominate the market. As it is fairly easy to

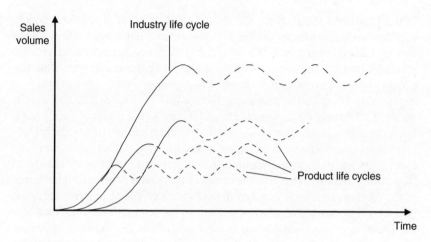

Figure 6.5   Product and industry life cycles in the insurance industry

imitate insurance products,[58] other companies will soon enter the market. Thus, the population density rises up to a certain level.

Once again, the shape of the life cycle in a mature market does not necessarily fulfil the assumptions of the standard model. In the manufacturing industry, various reasons for a market shakeout in the maturation phase are possible, for example the development of a certain technological standard which some companies are unable to imitate. In the insurance industry, the products are immaterial and potential standards can therefore be copied more easily. Moreover, due to the necessity to cope with the insurance-specific risk and the customers' demand for product bundles, insurance companies often have an incentive to diversify their product portfolio and enter new insurance markets, even when they have already reached a mature phase of the life cycle.

Again, the standard reasoning does not yield a satisfying theoretical base for the shape of the life cycle in mature insurance markets. Therefore, we return to the model of Maslow used in the derivation of the insurance-specific product life cycle. The standard model assumes that the number of competitors in the market decreases once a certain level is reached. However, if opposite to the standard development of the sales volume in the life cycle concepts, the insurance markets further grow in the maturation phase, companies still have an incentive to join the market. Therefore, we hypothesize, that in mature insurance markets, the respective industry life cycle measuring the number of competitors cannot be determined *ex ante*, but will mainly be influenced by the general economic and the

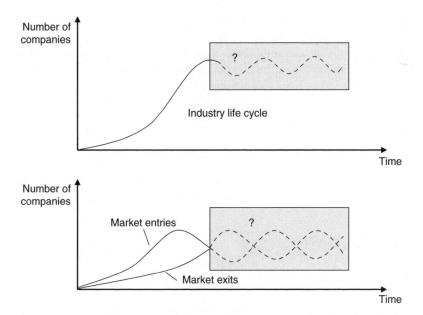

Figure 6.6   Life cycle, market entries and exits in the insurance industry

market development. The respective shape of the life cycle and the dynamics in the market entries are shown in Figure 6.6.

Development of hypotheses

The main difference between the standard model and the insurance specific industry life cycle is the non-typical pattern of the latter in the maturation and degeneration phase. In its derivation on pp. 115–18 we assumed that the development dynamics of a population of insurance companies are not *ex ante* determined but depend on the growth rate of national income. This hypothesis was based on the assumption, that due to its unique income elasticity the demand for insurance products is mainly influenced by the level on Maslow's pyramid of needs the majority of the population has achieved. Hence, the determinants of the development dynamics change as soon as the second level on the pyramid, the need for safety, is reached. We also use this concept to explain the rate of market entries through internal product innovations.

Hypothesis 5: If the industry life cycle shows a non-typical pattern in the maturation and degeneration phase, the rate of market entries is solely determined by the general economic development.

According to these industry life cycle specific hypotheses, the only external variable to be significant in the latter phases of the evolution of the insurance industry is the general market and economic development. All other factors to be taken into consideration in the organizational ecology theory are not supposed to have a significant effect.

Going forward, the empirical analysis of the German insurance population will have to consist of two parts. First, we will regard the general development of the population density to decide whether the years to be included into the analysis represent the non-typical maturation and degeneration phase in the insurance specific industry life cycle. Based on these findings, we will then test, whether the life cycle or the organizational ecology specific hypotheses are better suited to explain the observed innovation dynamics.

DATA AND METHODS

Data

In most of the empirical studies based on the organizational ecology theory, the criterion for the definition of an organizational population is the organizational output produced.[59] Following this approach we will concentrate on casualty and property insurance companies.[60] We will further neglect the many small local insurance companies only active in some regions of Germany.[61] The preferable empirical way to study the development dynamics of a population is to analyse its whole evolution starting at the beginning of the industry. However, due to the limited data availability only a few studies have actually comprised whole life cycles.[62]

A complete picture of the evolution of the German insurance industry can only be drawn by extending the time period under investigation as far as the sixteenth century.[63] Obviously, it is impossible to gather company specific data covering five centuries. Moreover, the development of this sector in the first half of the twentieth century was significantly influenced by fundamental exogenous shocks such as the two World Wars and the period of hyperinflation in the 1920s. In the comments on the historical development of innovation activities in the German insurance market, we have also learned that the vast majority of fundamental market innovations were generated between 1850 and 1900, whereas the innovation activities in the time after the Second World War were dominated by product modifications and internal product innovations. Hence, we will limit our analysis to the time after 1950. All in all, the database for our empirical tests consists of the life histories of 264 casualty and property insurance companies between 1950 and 1998 and comprises 8369 data sets. For each of the companies we have information on the year and the kind of founding and disbanding, organizational changes, the complete product portfolio of the insurance company and the premium income per year and per class of insurance.

The specification of the endogenous variable in the analysis is based on the definition of the internal product innovation on pp. 105–6. An insurance company generates an internal product innovation, when it creates a new class of insurance respectively separates an existing insurance area from a class it has already offered before. In the data set analysed, the population members had the possibility to diversify their product portfolio to the classes of personal liability, car, accident, fire, burglary/theft, glass, storm/ hailstorm, machine/technology, nuclear sites, aviation, transport, credit/ loan, animal, legal cost and other insurances. To test the relevance of the density dependence model for market entries through product innovations in Hypothesis 1 we used the number of existing casualty and property insurance companies to measure population density, and the number of internal product innovations, as defined above, in the year before to capture the effects of previous events on future innovation rates in Hypothesis 2.

In the literature on organizational ecology theory there are several alternatives to control for size effects on the innovation dynamics, as stated in Hypothesis 4. Brüderl and Jungbauer-Gans (1991) chose the number of employees to measure organizational size in their analysis of survival rates of young companies in Bavaria. Barnett and Amburgey (1990) study the effects of organizational size on competition processes in the population of telephone companies in the USA by looking at the total 'mass' of the population defined as the total number of subscribers. Wiedenmayer (1992) uses average industry production of beer to analyse the relationship between organizational size in the population of German breweries and founding rates. A similar way was chosen for this analysis. The exogenous variable to capture the effect of organizational size on the innovation rate equals the average premium income of an insurance company in the population per year.

Just as in the case of organizational size there are also several ways to measure the relationship of organizational age and the founding rates to test Hypothesis 3. Having in mind the long history of the German insurance market, looking at the values of average age in the population might lead to a distorted impression of the age structure due to the high number of very old organizations. Therefore, we will include two age specific variables in the analysis, the share of companies older than 40 years and the share of organizations, which are five years old or younger. Moreover, we will also measure the influence of the age variance in the population to get additional information of the role of rejuvenation processes in the population on innovation activities.

To test for Hypothesis 5 regarding the relationship of economic development and the innovation dynamics we will measure the effect of the growth rates of premium income on the number of product innovations. At first sight, the national income would be the perfect determinant to test the relevance of our assumptions based on Maslow's pyramid of needs. However, the premium income and the national income show a correlation of $r^2 = 0.97$. Moreover, choosing the premium income as exogenous variable additionally allows to control for capacity constraints in the development of the market (Wiedenmayer, 1992).

Methods

In modelling the innovation process in the population of insurance companies, we define the population as the unit of analysis and treat internal product innovations as events in a count process.[64] The most common method to specify this process implies the use of a Poisson model.[65] The basic form of the Poisson process assumes, that the arrival rate of the events is a time independent constant. Let $B_t = b$ be the cumulative sum of product innovations generated at t. Then the arrival rate λ_t denotes the conditional probability to reach $b+1$. The arrival rate is specified as[66]

$$\lambda_t = \lim_{\Delta t \to 0} \frac{\Pr(B_{t+\Delta t} - B_t = 1 | B_t = b)}{\Delta t} = \lambda \tag{1}$$

The conditional probability that the number of product innovations generated in the population rises from b to $b+1$ within the infinitesimally small time period $[t, t + \Delta_t]$ equals the constant λ. The arrival rate is independent from t or any other exogenous determinants. However, it is possible to include the time dependence and the effects of potential covariates x_{tj} by specifying λ_t as

$$\lambda_t = e^{\sum_{j=1}^{p} \beta_j x_{tj}} \tag{2}$$

Under the assumption of a Poisson distribution of the random variable B_t the coefficients β_j can be estimated in a Poisson regression with

$$\Pr(B_t = b) = \frac{e^{-\lambda_t} \lambda^b}{b!} \tag{3}$$

The Poisson regression has become the conventional method for event data analysis on population level. However, it implies some severe restrictions.

The Poisson model is based on the assumption that the conditional mean and the variance of the random variable are equal:[67]

$$E(B_t) = \text{Var}(B_t) = \lambda_t \tag{4}$$

In the case of overdispersion, when the variance exceeds the mean, this can cause misleadingly small standard errors of the estimated coefficients. Thus, coefficients might become falsely significant.[68] Therefore, we base our analysis on the negative binomial model, a modified version of the Poisson model that takes the possibility of overdispersion into account.[69] The negative binomial model assumes, that λ itself is a random variable, denoted by λ':[70]

$$\lambda' = \lambda u \tag{5}$$

Just as specified in Equation (2) for the standard model of the Poisson regression, the parameter λ is determined by the values of the exogenous variables x_i. Additionally, λ' is affected by the random term u, which is independent from x_i. Under the assumption, λ' has a gamma distribution $\Gamma(\alpha, \alpha/\lambda)$ with conditional mean λ and variance λ^2/α, the density function of the negative binomial model with Γ as gamma function and $\alpha, \lambda \in \Re^+$ respectively $b \in \aleph$ can be written as[71]

$$\Pr(B_t = b | \alpha, \lambda) = \frac{\Gamma(\alpha + b)}{\Gamma(\alpha)\Gamma(b + 1)} \left(\frac{\alpha}{\lambda + a} \right)^\alpha \left(\frac{\lambda}{\lambda + a} \right)^b \tag{6}$$

For the conditional mean and the variance, it follows

$$E(B_t | \alpha, \lambda) = \lambda \tag{7}$$

$$\text{Var}(B_t | \alpha, \lambda) = \lambda + \lambda^2/\alpha \tag{8}$$

Since $\alpha, \lambda \in \Re^+$, the variance always exceeds the conditional mean. Hence, the negative binomial model allows for the possibility of overdispersion. The step to the negative binomial regression is taken by specifying λ according to Equation (2) with $\alpha = 1/\sigma^2$. For $\sigma \to 0$ the negative binomial model converges into the Poisson model. The estimates of the parameters β_j are derived by maximizing the respective log-likelihood function.

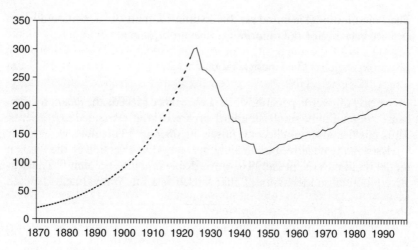

Figure 6.7   Population density of German casualty and property insurance companies[72]

FINDINGS

As discussed on pp. 111–20, the empirical analysis of the development and the innovation dynamics in the German insurance market comprises two parts. First, we want to identify whether the time period between 1950 and 1998 can be regarded as non-typical maturation or degeneration phase in the insurance specific industry life cycle. Second, we will test the hypotheses on the determinants of the innovation rates in the population of German casualty and property insurance companies based on the negative binomial model.

Population Dynamics in the German Insurance Market

Figure 6.7 shows the development of the population density in the German casualty and property insurance market between 1870 and 1998.

The number of insurance companies in Germany increased significantly between 1870 and the mid-1920s, before it was heavily reduced during a market shakeout between 1926 and 1949. From 1950 to the mid-1990s, the population showed a continuous density growth. However, we have to take into account, that the pattern of the population density until the year 1923 in Figure 6.7 is only estimated, not based on actual values. To the knowledge of the authors, there is no consistent documentation of the population entries and exits for the time period before.[73] Despite this restriction, we can find several indicators in the history of the German service sector and the insurance industry supporting the estimated pattern of the population density before 1923.[74] The tertiary sector globally gained importance in the second half of the nineteenth century (Fourastié, 1969). This phenomenon also holds true for the economic dynamics in Germany between 1870 and 1925 (Pyka *et al.*, 2004). As we can see in Figure 6.8, the development of sectoral employment shows a shift from the primary to the tertiary sector.

Besides, the industrial revolution generated new objects to be insured and the social legislation by Bismarck in the year 1870 supported the distribution of the insurance idea in Germany. At the same time, several new classes of insurance arose and the idea of a profit-oriented insurance industry was finally established and accepted within the economy and society. Hence, the pattern of the population density between 1870 and 1923 as shown in Figure 6.7 seems plausible.

In accordance to the standard model of the industry life cycle, a shake-out period began immediately after the density maximum was reached in the year 1925 with 303 insurance companies, which steadily reduced the number of organizations to 117 in 1948. However, we have to take into account, that this development was significantly influenced by fundamental exogenous political and economic shocks. The hyperinflation in Germany in the 1920s first caused an increase in foundings in the insurance industry, but soon led to a wave of mergers and disbandings. Political decisions to centralize the insurance industry by the NS-regime, the economic collapse of Germany in the Second World War and the loss of the East German areas further intensified the market consolidation. Nevertheless, we can also find indicators for the evolution of a mature market in

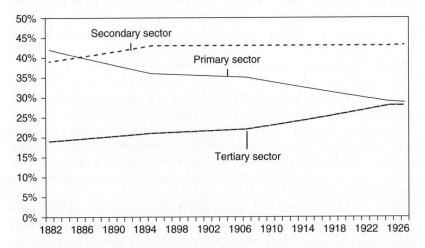

Figure 6.8   Development of sectoral employment in Germany, 1882–1926[75]

alignment with the predictions of the industry life cycle. In accordance with Abernathy und Utterback (1978) assuming that the first half of the industry life cycle is dominated by product innovations while in mature and degenerated markets process innovations are more important, in the time between 1870 and 1930 the Germany insurance industry generated most of the fundamental product innovations which still play a major role today. In the time after, the insurance market was characterized by product modifications and process refinements respectively extensions of the product portfolios.

Having in mind these considerations and remembering the long history of the German insurance industry, it seems valid to claim that the period between 1950 and 1998 can be seen as a phase of maturation and degeneration in the insurance specific industry life cycle. In contrast to the pattern of the standard model, the number of market participants after 1950 did not decline, but rose continuously until the mid-1990s. As we hypothesized in deriving the insurance specific industry life cycle, we see a non-typical development in the maturation and degeneration phase. On pp. 115–18, we claim that the development dynamics of the population of insurance companies in the maturation and degeneration phase is determined by the growth rate of national income. Following the concept of the Maslow's pyramid of needs an increase in national income should lead to a higher demand for safety in the society, a development from which the insurance sector can profit more than other branches.

Under the assumption, that right after the Second World War the satisfaction of the basic needs of the people dominated their behaviour and that only after the economic recovery in the 1950s parts of the people managed to climb from the first to the second level of needs, the concept of Maslow does have some explanatory power regarding the development dynamics of the population of insurance companies. As we can see in Figure 6.9, the premium income and the GDP show a similar pattern between 1950 and 1998. However, the premium income grew stronger than the GDP. Obviously, the branch of casualty and property insurance profited to a high degree from the economic recovery in Germany after the Second World War. At the same time, we know from Figure 6.7 that the number of insurance companies between 1950 and 1998 grew almost continuously. All these observations support the hypothesis, that in this mature market, the economic growth and the development dynamics of the insurance population are strongly correlated.

Only the years after 1994 show a slight decline in population density despite an increasing GDP. However, we have to take into account, that this period was influenced by the European deregulation in the insurance industry in 1994, which led to a price war resulting in a high number of mergers

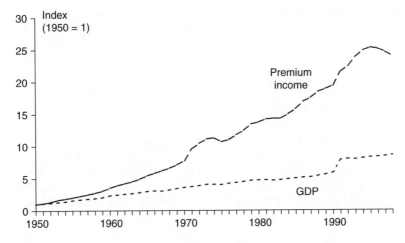

Figure 6.9   Index of premium income and GDP in Germany[76]

and acquisitions, which mainly affected the population of small and local companies, but also had an impact on the density in our population of Germany-wide active organizations.[77]

To sum up, the analysis of the density development in the population of the casualty and property insurance companies in Germany yielded two major results. First, the time period between 1950 and 1998 can be regarded as a non-typical maturation and degeneration phase as assumed in the derivation of the insurance specific industry life cycle. Second, the development of the population density in those years is strongly related to the growth of the national income as forecasted, based on the concept of Maslow's pyramid of needs.

Innovation Dynamics in the German Insurance Market

The analysis of the innovation dynamics in the population of German casualty and property insurance companies focuses on the development of the number of internal product innovations between 1950 and 1998, which can be seen in Figure 6.10.

In total, we observed 683 such events between 1950 and 1998. After a continuous increase in the number of internal product innovations between 1950 and 1956, the innovation rate reached its maximum between 1957 and 1964 with approximately 25 to 30 market entries per year. In the following years, the trend line of the innovation rate decreased, while the yearly numbers showed cyclical fluctuations. The pattern of the innovation rate immediately after the Second World War is consistent with the expectations

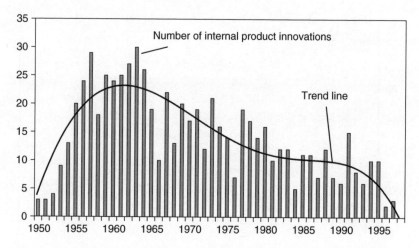

Figure 6.10   Number of internal product innovations, 1950–1998[78]

considering the historical development of the insurance industry in Germany. Until the mid-1950s, the insurance companies had to restore their infrastructure and assure that normal business in the existing classes of insurance was re-established (see pp. 103–4). Diversification through internal product innovations was not yet a dominant strategic option. Only after the legal and economic base for further growth in the insurance industry was given again, the recovery of the insurance industry also resulted in an increasing propensity to diversify the product portfolios. However, for the remainder of the time period under investigation, historical facts cannot suffice to explain the pattern of the innovation rate. Therefore we turn our attention to the negative binomial regression estimating the effects of population density, prior innovation rates, organization age and size as well as the growth rate of the premium income on the number of product innovations. Table 6.2 shows the regression results.

We conduct the empirical test of the hypotheses described on pp. 111–20 based on 7 models. In model 1, we only look at the effect of population density on the innovation rate, models 2 to 4 add gradually the other potential determinants. Models 5 to 7 give separate analyses for the influence of the age specific exogenous variables. The quality of the models is measured by the respective R^2. The effects of all determinants on the innovation rate are estimated with a one-year time lag. The results in Table 6.2 show that except in model 7 adding more explanatory variables generally increases the quality of the estimation.

In Hypothesis 5 we predicted that if the industry life cycle shows a non-typical pattern in the maturation and degeneration phase, the rate of

Table 6.2 Results of the negative binomial regression, 1950–1998[79]

Covariates	Model 1	Model 2	Model 3	Model 4	Model 5	Model 6	Model 7
Constant	-10.4228**	-2.8732	-7.0371**	-8.2716**	-9.1910**	-4.6975	-43.4961**
	(2.6767)	(2.6611)	(2.9730)	(3.0738)	(3.0028)	(3.0594)	(16.2818)
Density	$+0.1742$**	$+0.0731$**	$+0.1114$**	$+0.1226$**	$+0.1612$**	$+0.0666$**	-0.0649
	(0.0329)	(0.0342)	(0.0358)	(0.0365)	(0.0408)	(0.0378)	(0.0868)
Density^2	-0.0006**	-0.0003**	-0.0003**	-0.0003**	-0.0004**	$-8.1*10^{-5}$	$+0.0002$
	(0.0001)	(0.0001)	(0.0001)	(0.0001)	(0.0001)	(0.0001)	(0.0002)
Prior innovations		$+0.0263$**	$+0.0189$**	$+0.0187$**	$+0.0179$**	$+0.0129$**	$+0.0048$
		(0.0088)	(0.0086)	(0.0085)	(0.0080)	(0.0079)	(0.0114)
ø Premium income			$-6.9*10^{-6}$**	$-6.9*10^{-6}$**	$-6.4*10^{-6}$**	$-9.9*10^{-6}$**	$-6.3*10^{-6}$**
			$(2.4*10^{-6})$	$(2.3*10^{-6})$	$(2.2*10^{-6})$	$(2.4*10^{-6})$	$(2.6*10^{-6})$
Growth rate premium income				$+1.9826$*	$+1.9462$*	$+1.4632$	-2.0401
				(1.1537)	(1.0577)	(1.0208)	(0.9006)
% Organizations > 40 years					-3.0724**		
					(1.5607)		
% Organizations ≤ 5 years						$+6.8937$**	
						(2.0853)	
Age variance							$+0.0408$**
							(0.0159)
Age variance^2							$-7.9*10^{-6}$**
							$(3.2*10^{-6})$
R^2	0.47	0.60	0.63	0.62	0.69	0.69	0.54
Lags	1	1	1	1	1	1	1

129

market entries is solely determined by the general economic development, which is captured through the growth rate of the premium income. The regression results only partly support this assumption. As predicted, models 4 and 5 yield significant and positive coefficients for the variable growth rate of the premium income, but an exclusive determination of the innovation rate could not be identified. All the other exogenous variables tested simultaneously showed a significant influence as well.

Model 7 is the only one not delivering significant coefficients for the effects of population density and the respective squared values.[80] Hence, we can confirm Hypothesis 1 forecasting an inverted U-shaped pattern of the innovation rate in dependence of the population density. Following the results of the negative binomial regression, the model of density dependence commonly used to explain founding and death rates in organizational populations is also transferable to the innovation dynamics in the population of German casualty and property insurance companies.

However, we have to be careful in also copying the interpretation underlying the model of density dependence in the case of founding and disbanding dynamics. In the original concept of Hannan (1986), the level of legitimation of an organizational form rises with the number of population members and leads to higher founding rates further increasing population density, so that more intense competition reduces the rate of organizational foundings and causes more disbandings. In our case, the occurrence of the event 'internal product innovation' does not change the density of the population. We look at the entry of already existing organizations into the diverse sub-markets of the industry. Hence, legitimation processes do not affect the rate of acceptance of a specific organizational form, but of the diversification of the product portfolio as a commonly accepted strategic direction.

At the same time, increasing competition within the population can have positive and negative effects on the rate of internal product innovations generated. A higher number of competitors forces the existing organizations to search for ways to differentiate from the remainder of the population. One way for differentiation is the generation of an internal product innovation. On the other hand, the probability of success of an internal product innovation will be higher, the less other companies have already seized the market and developed a market reputation that cannot be easily copied by new entrants. The inverted U-shaped pattern of the innovation rate according to the results of the negative binomial regression indicates, that up to a certain density, the positive effects of legitimation of the diversification strategy and innovation due to the need to differentiate have dominated the innovative behaviour of the population members, before negative competition effects reduced the number of innovations generated.

Similarly, the results regarding Hypothesis 2 assuming a positive effect of prior innovations on the future rates, can be confirmed in all tests of the negative binomial regression except model 7. Obviously, a high innovation rate was interpreted as an indicator for favourable environmental conditions for market entries and led to an imitation of the diversification strategy in the following year, while decreasing innovation rates also diminished the future propensity of population members to generate product innovations. However, the database showed that there is no such thing as the typical 'pioneer' company in terms of diversification in certain sub-branches. The first organizations to diversify into the several classes of insurance between 1950 and 1998 built a very heterogeneous group consisting of small and large, young and old companies. The only consistent trend observable was that almost all 'pioneers' already had diversified into other classes of insurance before. Obviously, the specialist companies first waited until the probability of success of diversifying in a specific class was clear and then imitated the 'pioneers'.

While the small companies were not the first to follow a diversification strategy, Hypothesis 4 assuming a negative relationship between organizational size and the innovation rate still was confirmed in the negative binomial regression. The variable 'average premium income' yielded significant negative coefficients in all models tested. This result seems to be counterintuitive having in mind the specific characteristics of the demand for insurance products discussed on pp. 115–17, which tend to favour companies with large sales organizations and a broad market presence in the process of implementation of a product innovation. However, large organizations often already have satisfied their diversification needs. On average, the 20 largest companies in the population offered products in 11.7 classes of insurance, whereas the 20 smallest organizations only were active in 3.5 classes. Apart from the lower need of large organizations for further diversification, they also can choose between different alternatives to enter a new market. Instead of creating an internal product innovation they might as well buy a smaller competitor that already acts in the market of interest.

Similar arguments can be brought forward in explaining the effect of organizational age on the innovation rate. The importance of the market reputation of an insurance company when entering a new market[81] would lead to the assumption that older organizations would generate a higher number of product innovations. However, the coefficients of the share of over 40 old companies yields a significantly negative value, whereas the percentage of organizations which are 5 years old or younger obviously have a significantly positive influence on the innovation rate. The relationship of the innovation rate and the age variance follows a inverted U-shaped pattern, similar to the effects identified for the population

density. Hence, Hypothesis 3 is generally supported in the negative binomial regression.[82] Once again, the higher structural inertia of the older
insurance companies can have several reasons. They might have gone
through diversification processes in younger years,[83] or they might be spe-
cialists from their founding on and traditionally do not intend to diversify
their product portfolio.[84]

CONCLUSION

Although the long-term evolution of industries has been on the agenda
of economics since the early twentieth century (Schumpeter, Kuznets,
Clark) this tradition was almost neglected since the mid-1950s when industrial economics became embedded in the so-called Structure-Conduct-
Performance-Paradigm. However, since the 1980s a branch of literature
emerges dealing again with the phenomenon of long term developments
driven by technology dynamics and innovation. On the one hand, population ecology is transferring concepts of evolutionary biology on sector
development. On the other hand, the so-called theory of industry life cycles
is focusing on cyclical phenomena during the period between the emergence and maturation of industries.

This chapter is an attempt to transfer basic ideas of both theories to the
service industries, in particular the insurance market and to test hypotheses
concerning the origins and mechanisms of the dynamics observable there.
It is shown that a one-to-one application of these theories which were constructed having in mind manufacturing industries is not possible. However,
referring to the special features relevant for service industries and in particular insurance industries allows the derivation of modified hypothesis
concerning the observed industry dynamics which empirically can be
tested. The patterns of market entry, exit and innovation observed in the
German insurance industry follow predictions made by both theoretical
approaches.

NOTES

1. Carroll (1997).
2. Surminsky (2000a, p. 112).
3. Bundesaufsichtsamt für das Versicherungswesen (2000, p. 8).
4. Koch (1988, p. 4ff.).
5. Wandel (1998, p. 59).
6. Koch (1988, p. 6) and Wandel (1998, p. 59f.).
7. Schieren (1990, p. 21).
8. Borscheid (1990, p. 12).

9. Arps (1965), Borscheid (1988), Koch (1988), Borscheid (1990), and Pearson (1997: 239). For the empty cells in the table, the year is not known. For the classes of fire, storm and transport insurance the exact date of introduction is not known.
10. Wandel (1998: 63f.).
11. Farny (1971), Haller (1982) or Vielreicher (1995).
12. Farny (1979), Müller (1981).
13. Following Albrecht (1992).
14. Widmer (1986).
15. Gallouij (2002: xv).
16. Hipp (2000: 19f.) Gallouij (2002: xv).
17. Gallouij (2002: 128).
18. Albrecht (1992).
19. While at least parts of the theoretical concepts regarding the product life cycle approach deal with the service industry (Farny and Kirsch, 1987, Barras, 1986a, or Barras, 1986b), this sector has not been investigated from an industry life cycle specific point of view yet.
20. Hannan and Freeman (1989).
21. Singh *et al.* (1991).
22. Messallam (1998).
23. Barron *et al.* (1994).
24. Havemann (1994).
25. Carroll (1997) gives a summary of the other main approaches.
26. Wiedenmayer *et al.* (1995).
27. Tucker *et al.* (1990).
28. The base for the population point of view in this approach is the so-called principle of isomorphism, first developed by Hawley (1968) in his human ecology approach. According to the principle of isomorphism, organizations that face the same environmental conditions will take similar forms and build an organizational population.
29. Carroll (1993).
30. Hannan and Freeman (1989).
31. However this hypothesis has received mixed evidence in empirical tests. While Barnett and Amburgey (1990) identify a continuously negative relationship, Staber (1989a) finds support for a positive, but monotonic influence of prior on future founding rates.
32. Wiedenmayer (1992), Barnett (1990) or Delacroix and Solt (1988).
33. Windzio (2001) or Havemann (1995).
34. Kelly and Amburgey (1991), Amburgey and Rao (1996).
35. Fligstein (1991).
36 Aldrich and Auster (1986).
37. Kelly and Amburgey (1991).
38. Havemann (1992).
39. Fligstein (1991), Havemann (1993b).
40. See pp. 106–7.
41. Cathomen (1996).
42. Höft (1992).
43. Perez and Soete (1988).
44. Höft (1992).
45. Klepper and Graddy (1990) and Klepper and Simons (1997).
46. Ford and Ryan (1981: 120).
47. Gort and Klepper (1982).
48. Klepper (1997).
49. Utterback and Suárez (1993), Jovanovic and MacDonald (1994) or Klepper (1996).
50. Utterback and Abernathy (1975) and Abernathy and Utterback (1978).
51. Barras (1986a) or Barras (1986b).
52. In the history of the German insurance market, only a few exotic insurance lines such as the 'rain insurance' or the 'riot insurance' died out in the evolution of the industry. See Borscheid (1990).
53. Maslow (1977).

54. Brösse (1999: 26).
55. Hagerty (1999).
56. Borscheid (1990) or Surminsky (2000e).
57. Maslow (1977: 85ff).
58. See p. 107.
59. Hannan *et al.* (1995), Swaminathan (1995), Barron *et al.* (1994) or Messallam (1998).
60. Other classes of insurance such as life and health insurance as well as the complete sector of reinsurance companies are excluded of the analysis despite accounting for approximately 70 per cent of the total premium income generated. However, the products offered in those four classes are either fundamentally different from each other (a life insurance company offering capital investment products can hardly be compared with a company selling products in the area of fire or car insurance) or are significantly influenced by the development of public institutions (the evolution dynamics of the private health insurance market fundamentally depends on the development of the public health insurance agencies).
61. Although this will potentially lead to a loss of information as these thousands of small companies may interact with the population of the non-local players via processes of diffuse competition, this restriction still seems reasonable due to their marginal economic importance.
62. Exceptions are represented by the studies of the evolution of the telephone industry from the nineteenth century on in various states in the USA by Barnett (1990) and Barnett and Carroll (1987) or the empirical investigations on the population of automobile producers in the USA by Klepper (1997) and Klepper and Simons (1997).
63. See the historical overview of the evolution of the German insurance market on pp. 101–4.
64. Cox and Oakes (1984). Analysing the innovation dynamics on the level of the population in contrast to identifying organization specific determinants of the innovation activities is necessary due to the fact that multiple events can occur within one period and that we only can rely on yearly data. Moreover, our key interest lies in the innovation dynamics of the whole population, not in the company specific success factors and prerequisites for successfully implementing a product innovation. See Carroll *et al.* (1993).
65. Hannan and Freeman (1989).
66. Wiedenmayer (1992: 94).
67. Winkelmann (1994: 25ff).
68. Cameron and Trivedi (1986: 31).
69. Carroll *et al.* (1993: 173).
70. Winkelmann (1994: 112).
71. Winkelmann (1994: 113ff).
72. The figure only shows casualty and property insurance companies active in all parts of Germany. Small local population members are not included.
73. The key source for this analysis, Neumanns 'Jahrbuch für das Versicherungswesen im Deutschen Reiche' goes back to the year 1903, but only catches parts of the whole classes of insurance in the casualty and property business.
74. However, it is very likely, that the steady increase of the population density shown in Figure 6.7 was interrupted during and immediately after the First World War. See pp. 102–3.
75. Source: Fourastié (1969: 112).
76. Statistisches Bundesamt (2001: 654ff.).
77. Between 1994 and 1998 companies merging consisted above others of the 'DBV Deutsche Beamtenversicherungsgesellschaft', the 'Winterthur Lebensversicherung AG' and the 'Delfin Lebensversicherung AG' (1998), the 'Itzehoer Versicherungsverein' with the 'Schleswig-Holsteinische Brandgilde' (1997) or the 'INTERUNFALL Internationale Unfall- und Schadenversicherungs-Gesellschaft AG' with the 'Erste Allgemeine Versicherungs-AG München' (1994). Companies acquired in this period comprised the 'Gerling Rechtsschutz Versicherungs-AG' (1998), the 'Bruderhilfe

Rechtsschutzversicherung' (1998), the 'Deutsche Versicherungs-AG' (1998), the 'TELLIT Direct Versicherung AG' (1998), the 'Württembergische Rechtsschutz-versicherung AG' (1997), the 'Magdeburger Versicherung AG' (1996), the 'Badenia Glasversicherungsverein AG.' (1995), the 'Gebäudeversicherung Baden AG' (1995), the 'Elektra Versicherungs-AG' (1994), the 'Hamburger Phönix Gaedesche Versicherungs-AG' (1994) and the 'Skandia Sachversicherung AG' (1994).

78. Source: Own estimation. The trend line represents a polynom of fifth degree with $R^2 = 0.73$ ab.
79. * $p < 10$ per cent, ** $p < 5$ per cent.
80. Model 6 shows a significant value for the effect of density, the coefficient for density^2 however, is insignificant.
81. See pp. 106–7.
82. An increase in the age variance indicates a trend of rejuvenation in the population. The effect of this variable on the innovation rate is non-monotonic. The number of internal product innovation rises until a certain value of age variance, after which the negative effect dominates. The first part of this effect is consistent with the results of the other age specific exogenous variables. But if the population consists mainly of very old and very young companies and the age variance therefore exceeds a certain value, then the competitive advantages of old and experienced companies obviously play a major role and the market entry of younger competitors via product innovations becomes more difficult.
83. Organizations that are five years old or younger offer products in 3.8 classes on average, companies older than 40 years 6.8 classes.
84. Such specialist organizations are for example the 'Gartenbau-Versicherung VVaG' in Berlin (founded in 1847), the 'Kölnische Hagel-Versicherungs-Gesellschaft' (1853), the 'Union Actien-Gesellschaft' in Hamburg (1857), the 'Pfälzische Viehversicherung VaG' in Ludwigshafen (1849) or the 'Union, Allgemeine Deutsche Hagel-Versicherungs-Gesellschaft' in Hamburg (1853).

REFERENCES

Abernathy, W. J. and J. M. Utterback (1978), 'Patterns of industrial innovation', *Technology Review*, **80**, 41–7.

Albrecht, P. (1992), *Zur Risikotransformationstheorie der Versicherung: Grundlagen und ökonomische Konsequenzen, Veröffentlichungen des Instituts für Versicherung-swissenschaft der Universität Mannheim*, Bd. 40, Karlsruhe, Verlag Versicherung-swirtschaft e.V.

Aldrich, H. E. and E. R. Auster (1986), 'Even dwarfs started small: liabilities of age and size and their strategic implications', *Research in Organizational Behavior*, **8**, 165–98.

Amburgey, T. L. and H. Rao (1996), 'Organizational ecology: past, present, and future directions', *Academy of Management Journal*, **39**, 1265–86.

Arps, L. (1965), *Auf Sicheren Pfeilern: Deutsche Versicherungswirtschaft vor 1914*, Göttingen, Vandenhoeck & Ruprecht.

Banerjee, A. V. and A. F. Newman (1991), 'Risk-bearing and the theory of income distribution', *The Review of Economic Studies*, **58**, 211–35.

Barnett, W. P. (1990), 'The organizational ecology of a technological system', *Administrative Science Quarterly*, **35**, 31–60.

Barnett, W. P. and T. L. Amburgey (1990), 'Do larger organizations generate stronger competition?', in J. V. Singh, (Ed.), *Organizational Evolution: New Directions*, Newbury Park: Sage Publications, 78–102.

Barnett, W. P. and G. R. Carroll (1987), 'Competition and mutualism among early telephone companies', *Administrative Science Quarterly*, **32**, 400–21.

Barras, R. (1986a), 'Towards a theory of innovation in services', *Research Policy*, **15**, 161–73.

Barras, R. (1986b), 'A comparison of embodied technical change in services and manufacturing industry', *Applied Economics*, **18**, 941–58.

Barron, D. E., E. West and M. T. Hannan (1994), 'A time to grow and a time to die: growth and mortality of credit unions in New York City, 1914–1990', *American Journal of Sociology*, **100**, 381–421.

Borscheid, P. (1988), 'Kurze Geschichte der Individual- und Sozialversicherung in Deutschland', in P. Borscheid and A. Drees (Eds); *Versicherungsstatistik Deutschlands 1750–1985*, Scripta Mercaturae Verlag, 3–49.

Borscheid, P. (1990), *100 Jahre Allianz*, München: Allianz Aktiengesellschaft Holding.

Brösse, U. (1999), *Einführung in die Volkswirtschaftslehre – Mikroökonomie, 3. Auflage*, München: R. Oldenbourg Verlag.

Brüderl, J. and M. Jungbauer-Gans (1991), 'Überlebenschancen neugegründeter Betriebe: Empirische Befunde auf Basis der Gewerbemeldungen in Oberbayern im Zeitraum 1980–1988', *Die Betriebswirtschaft*, 499–510.

Bundesaufsichtsamt für das Versicherungswesen (Hrsg.) (1976–2002), *Geschäftsbericht – Jahre 1975–2001*, Berlin/Bonn: Teile A und B.

Cameron, A. C. and P. K. Trivedi (1986), 'Econometric models based on count data: comparisons and applications of some estimators and tests', *Journal of Applied Econometrics*, **1**, 29–53.

Carroll, G. R. (1993), 'A sociological view on why firms differ', *Strategic Management Journal*, **14**, 237–49.

Carroll, G. R. (1997), 'Long-term evolutionary change in organizational populations: theory, models and empirical findings in industrial demography', *Industrial and Corporate Change*, **6**, 119–43.

Carroll, G. R., P. Preisendoerfer A, Swaminathan, and G. Wiedenmayer (1993), 'Brewery und brauerei: the organizational ecology of brewing', *Organization Studies*, **14**(2), 155–88.

Cathomen, I. (1996), *Der Lebenszyklus von Interorganisationssystemen*, Lohmar, Köln: Verlag Josef Eul.

Cox, D. R. and D. Oakes (1984), *Analysis of Survival Data*, London: Chapman and Hall.

Dean, J. (1950), 'Pricing policies for new products', *Harvard Business Review*, **28**, 81–94.

Delacroix, J. and G. R. Carroll (1983), 'Organizational foundings: an ecological study of the newspaper industries in Argentina and Ireland', *Administrative Science Quarterly*, **28**, 274–91.

Delacroix, J. and M. E. Solt (1988), 'Niche formation and foundings in the California wine industry' – 1941–84, in G. R. Carroll, (Ed.), *Ecological Models of Organizations*, Cambridge, Ballinger Publishing Company, 53–70.

Eisenhauer, J. G. and M. Halek (1999), 'Prudence, risk aversion and the demand for life insurance', *Applied Economics Letters*, **6**, 239–42.

Farny, D. (1971), *Absatz und Absatzpolitik des Versicherungsunternehmens*, Karlsruhe.

Farny, D. (1979), 'Versicherungsbetriebe(n), Produktion', in W. Kern, (Ed.), *Handwörterbuch der Produktionswirtschaft*, Stuttgart, C. E. Poeschel Verlag, pp. 2138–45.

Farny, D. (1994), 'Künftige Konzernstrukturen deutscher Versicherer', in U. Hübner, and E. Helten and P. Albrecht (Eds.), *Recht und Ökonomie der Versicherung, Festschrift für Egon Lorenz*, Karlsruhe: Verlag Versicherungswirtschaft e.V., 281–93.

Farny, D. and W. Kirsch (1987), 'Strategische Unternehmenspolitik von Versicherungsunternehmen', *Zeitschrift für die gesamte Versicherungswissenschaft*, **76**, 369–401.

Fligstein, N. (1991), 'The structural transformation of American industry: the causes of diversification in the largest firms, 1919–1979', in W. W. Powell, and P. J. DiMaggio (Eds.), *The New Institutionalism in Organizational Dynamics*, Chicago and London: The University of Chicago Press, 311–36.

Ford, D. and C. Ryan (1981), 'Taking technology to market', *Harvard Business Review*, **59**, 117–26.

Fourastié, J. (1969), *Die große Hoffnung des zwanzigsten Jahrhunderts (deutsche Übersetzung der 1963 unter dem Titel 'Le grand espoir du XXe siècle' veröffentlichten Erstausgabe)*, 2. Auflage, Köln: Bund-Verlag.

Gallouij, F. (2002), *Innovation in the Service Economy: The New Wealth of Nations*, Cheltenham, UK and Northampton, US: Edward Elgar.

Geiger, H. (1992), *Die Versicherungsdichte ist nicht nur vom Wohlstand abhängig, Der Langfristige Kredit*, 21, Frankfurt/Main: Verlag Helmut Richardi, 49–52.

Gort, M. and S. Klepper (1982), 'Time paths in the diffusion of product innovations', *The Economic Journal*, **92**, 630–53.

Hagerty, M. R. (1999), Testing Maslow's hierarchy of needs: national quality-of-life across time, *Social Indicators Research*, **46**, 249–71.

Haller, M. (1982), 'Risiko- und Versicherungsprobleme des privaten Haushalts – aus Sicht der Privatversicherung', *Zeitschrift für die gesamte Versicherungswissenschaft*, **71**, 383–437.

Hannan, M. T. (1986), 'Competitive and institutional processes in organizational ecology', Technical Report 86-13, Department of Sociology, Cornell University, Ithaca, and University of California, Berkeley.

Hannan, M. T, G. R. Carroll, G. R. Dundon and J. C. Torres (1995), 'Organizational evolution in a multinational context: entries of automobile manufacturers in Belgium, France, Germany, and Italy', *American Sociological Review*, **60**, 509–28.

Hannan, M. T. and J. Freeman (1977), 'The population ecology of organizations', *American Journal of Sociology*, **82**, 929–64.

Hannan, M. T. and J. Freeman (1984), 'Structural inertia and organizational change', *American Sociological Review*, **49**, 149–64.

Hannan, M. T. and J. Freeman (1989), *Organizational Ecology*, Cambridge and London: Harvard University Press.

Havemann, H. A. (1992), 'Between a rock and a hard place: organizational change and performance under conditions of fundamental environmental transformation, *Administrative Science Quarterly*, **37**, 48–75.

Havemann, H. A. (1993a), 'Follow the leader: mimetic isomorphism and entry into new markets', *Administrative Science Quarterly*, **38**, 593–627.

Havemann, H. A. (1993b), 'Organizational size and change: diversification in the savings and loan industry after deregulation', *Administrative Science Quarterly*, **38**, 20–50.

Havemann, H. A. (1994), 'The ecological dynamics of organizational change: density and mass dependence in rates of entry into new markets, in J. A. C. Baum, and J. Singh (Eds.), *Evolutionary Dynamics of Organizations*, New York: Oxford University Press, 152–67.

Havemann, H. A. (1995), 'The demographic metabolism of organizations: Industry dynamics, turnover, and tenure distributions', *Administrative Science Quarterly*, **40**, 586–618.

Hawley, A. H. (1968), 'Human ecology', in D. L. Sills, (Ed.), *International Encyclopedia of the Social Sciences*, Vol. 4, Free Press, 328–37.

Hipp, C. (2000), *Innovationsprozesse im Dienstleistungssektor*, Heidelberg: Physica-Verlag.

Höft, U. (1992), *Lebenszykluskonzepte: Grundlage für das strategische Marketing- und Technologiemanagement*, Berlin: Erich Schmidt Verlag.

Jovanovic, B. and G. M. MacDonald (1994), 'The life cycle of a competitive industry', *Journal of Political Economy*, **102**, 322–47.

Kelly, D. and T. L. Amburgey (1991), 'Organizational inertia and momentum: a dynamic model of strategic change', *Academy of Management Journal*, **34**, 591–612.

Klepper, S. (1996), 'Entry, exit, growth and innovation over the product life cycle', *American Economic Review*, **86**, 562–83.

Klepper, S. (1997), 'Industry life cycles', *Industrial and Corporate Change*, **6**, 145–81.

Klepper, S. and E. Graddy (1990), 'The evolution of new industries and the determinants of market structure', *RAND Journal of Economics*, **21**, 27–44.

Klepper, S. and K. Simons (1997), 'Technological extinctions of industrial firms: an inquiry into their nature and causes', *Industrial and Corporate Change*, **6**, 379–460.

Koch, P. (1988), *Versicherungsgeschichte in Stichworten*, Verein zur Förderung der Versicherungswissenschaft e.V.

Koeniger, W. (2001), 'Labor and financial market interactions: the case of labor income risk and car insurance in the UK 1969–1995', Discussion Paper No. 240, European University Institute, Florence and IZA, Bonn.

Kubli, U. D. (1988), *Aufsicht und unternehmerisches Handeln*, St Gallen.

Maslow, A. H. (1977), *Motivation und Persönlichkeit* (First edition translated from the German under the title 'Motivation and Personality'), Olten: Walter-Verlag.

Messallam, A. A. (1998), 'The organizational ecology of investment firms in Egypt: organizational founding', *Organization Studies*, **19**, 23–46.

Mitchell, W. (1995), 'Medical diagnostic imaging manufacturers', in G. R. Carroll, and M. T. Hannan, (Eds.), *Organizations in Industry*, New York: Oxford University Press, 244–77.

Müller, W. (1981), 'Das Produkt der Versicherung', in M. Jung, R. R. Lucius and W. G. Seifert (Eds.), *Geld und Versicherung, Festgabe für Wilhelm Seuß*, Karlsruhe: Verlag Versicherungswirtschaft e.V., 155–71.

Muth, M. (1988), *Wer gewinnt den Wettlauf um den Privatkunden?*, *Versicherungswirtschaft*, 43, Karlsruhe: Verlag Versicherungswirtschaft e.V., 1586–88.

Pearson, R. (1997), 'Towards an historical model of services innovation: the case of the insurance industry 1700–1914', *Economic History Review*, **50**, 235–56.

Perez, C. and L. Soete (1988), 'Catching up in technologies: entry barriers and windows of opportunity', in G. Dosi, C. Freeman, R. R. Nelson, G. Silverberg and L. Soete (Eds.) *Technical Change and Economic theory*, London: Pinter Publishers, 458–79.

Pyka, A., B. Ebersberger and H. Hanusch (2004), 'A conceptual framework to model long-run qualitative change in the energy system', in J. S. Metcalfe and J. Foster (Eds), *Evolution and Economic Complexity*, Cheltenham, UK and Northampton, MA, USA: Edward Elgar.

Schieren, W. (1990), 'Festansprache zum 100. Geburtstag der Allianz AG', in Allianz Aktiengesellschaft Holding (Eds.), *100 Jahre Allianz AG – Festansprachen 9. März 1990*, München, 21–55.

Singh, J. V., D. J. Tucker and A. G. Meinhard (1991), 'Institutional change and ecological dynamics', in W. W. Powell and P. J. DiMaggio (Eds.), *The New Institutionalism in Organizational Dynamics*, Chicago, London, The University of Chicago Press, 390–463.

Staber, U. (1989a), 'Organizational foundings in the cooperative sector of Atlantic Canada: an ecological perspective', *Organization Studies*, **10**, 381–403.

Statistisches Bundesamt (Eds.) (2001), *Statistisches Jahrbuch 2001*, Stuttgart: Metzler-Poeschel.

Surminsky, A. (2000a), 'Das Jahrhundert der Assekuranz – 1. Begrüßung des 20. Jahrhunderts', *Zeitschrift für Versicherungswesen*, **51**, 111–15.

Surminsky, A. (2000e), 'Das Jahrhundert der Assekuranz – 5. Die Weltkriege', *Zeitschrift für Versicherungswesen*, **51**, 251–3.

Swaminathan, A. (1995), 'The proliferation of specialist organizations in the American wine industry 1941–1990', *Administrative Science Quarterly*, **40**, 653–80.

Tucker, D. J., J. V. Singh and A. G. Meinhard (1990), 'Organizational form, population dynamics, and institutional change: the founding patterns of voluntary organizations', *Academy of Management Journal*, **3**, 151–78.

Utterback, J. M. and W. J. Abernathy (1975), 'A dynamic model of process and product innovation', *Omega, The International Journal of Management Science*, **36**, 639–56.

Utterback, J. M. and F. F. Suárez (1993), 'Innovation, competition and industry structure', *Research Policy*, **22**, 1–21.

Vielreicher, P. (1995), *Produktinnovationsmanagement in Versicherungsunternehmen*, Wiesbaden, Gabler-Verlag.

Wade, J. (1996), 'A community-level analysis of sources and rates of technological variation in the microprocessor market', *Academy of Management Journal*, **39**, 1218–44.

Wagner, A. (1876), *Grundlegung der politischen Ökonomie, 3. Auflage, 1892*, Leipzig: C. F. Winter'sche Verlagshandlung.

Wandel, E. (1998), *Banken und Versicherungen im 19. und 20. Jahrhundert*, München: R. Oldenbourg Verlag.

Widmer, A. (1986), 'Innovationsmanagement in Banken', St Gallen, Dissertation.

Wiedenmayer, G. (1992), *Die Entwicklungsdynamik in der deutschen Brauindustrie: Eine empirische Überprüfung des organisationsökologischen Ansatzes, Beiträge zur Gesellschaftsforschung, Bd. 10*, Frankfurt am Main *et al.*: Peter Lang.

Wiedenmayer, G., H. E. Aldrich and U. Staber (1995), 'Von Gründungspersonen zu Gründungsraten: Organisationsgründungen aus populationsökologischer Sicht', *Die Betriebswirtschaft*, 221–36.

Windzio, M. (2001), 'Organisationsökologie und Arbeitsmarktmobilität im sozialen Wandel: Eine empirische Analyse am Beispiel Ostdeutschlands', *Zeitschrift für Soziologie*, **30**, 116–34.

Winkelmann, R. (1994), *Count Data Models (Econometric Theory and an Application to Labor Mobility)*, Berlin, Heidelberg: Springer Verlag.

PART III

The Geographical Dimension of Knowledge-based Economies

7. A process model of locational change in entrepreneurial firms: an evolutionary perspective

Erik Stam[1]

INTRODUCTION

Entrepreneurship is a highly localized process. Many studies have shown that almost all entrepreneurs start in their home region (Cooper, 1985; Allen and Hayward, 1990; Stam, 2003), or even within their home (Stam and Schutjens, 2000). Most of these firms do not survive the first ten years after start-up (Storey, 1997). It seems irrelevant to study the location of new firms, as new firm formation is almost per definition a local process, and most new firms fail. However, a small percentage of the firms in new cohorts is responsible for the majority of the net new job creation in the region where they are located (Birch, 1987; Kirchhoff, 1994; Storey, 1997). These fast-growing firms reveal very high locational dynamics, within as well as outside their region of origin (Stam, 2003). This special group of young fast-growing firms is highly relevant both in a societal perspective as job creators and in a scientific perspective as revealing very high locational dynamics. In contrast to the location of new firms in general (Cooper, 1998; Stuart and Sorenson, 2003) and the location of multinational enterprises (Dunning, 1998; Cantwell and Santangelo, 2002), we know almost nothing about the location of young fast-growing firms. This chapter aims to gain insight into the locational dynamics of these firms. Locational dynamics involves changes in the spatial organization, which is defined as the spatial configuration of physical resources of the firm. These changes necessarily involve (dis)investment decisions.

The research problem in this chapter is 'How do changes in the spatial organization of entrepreneurial firms come about?' and the main purpose of the chapter is to provide a conceptualization of the process of locational change. A process model of locational change is constructed on the basis of an empirical study of 109 locational events during the life course of 25 young firms in knowledge intensive sectors (knowledge services and biomedicals). This process model of locational change maps both internal and external variation and selection processes. This model contributes to the development of a causal process theory[2] of the spatial development of (new) firms.

The chapter is organized as follows. In the next section we will discuss the relevant concepts and theories on location and the firm. The following section describes the comparative longitudinal research design and methods. Subsequently, we present a process model of locational change that is based on the empirical study and the conceptual framework. The final section presents the conclusion.

THEORIZING LOCATIONAL CHANGE AND THE ENTREPRENEURIAL FIRM

In the 1990s a new genre of research in mainstream economics – the so-called 'new economic geography' (Krugman, 1991, 1998; Fujita et al., 1999) or 'geographical economics' approach (Brakman *et al.*, 2001) – has rediscovered location theory. In spite of the contribution of this new approach to the understanding of the location of production, there are at least three problems with using this approach for our study. First, this approach aims at explaining industry location, not location of individual firms (cf. Arthur, 1994; Boschma and Frenken, 2003). Second, this approach takes an atomistic view of firms and entrepreneurs, placing the whole explanatory burden on the (spatial) situation of the agent and a rationality imposed by the analyst (see for example Krugman, 1998; Fujita *et al.*, 1999). Third, this approach, like neoclassical economics in general (see Foss, 1994) does not offer an explanation of novelty (see Witt, 1992; Nooteboom, 2000), for example novel spatial structures. Locational change might involve new markets and new sources of supply for inputs, that is two types of Schumpeterian innovation (Schumpeter, 1934:66; see also Mucchielli and Saucier, 1997). The first and third problems concern the explanandum of this study: not the location of industries (like in most neoclassical economic location theory) but the location behaviour, the novel spatial organization of firms. This brings us to the second problem: the explanans are not only to be found in the spatial situation of the firm, but also in the characteristics of the firm and the entrepreneur.

In order to choose the most useful theories or concepts, one should first specify the research object and the explanandum. Our research object is the entrepreneurial firm. Entrepreneurial firms are independent young firms that are still owner-managed (most likely by the founder-entrepreneur), in contrast with managerial firms, in which ownership and management are separate (Hart 1983). These entrepreneurial firms can be 'life style' firms, that fail to grow after start-up (Hanks *et al.*, 1993), but in this study we focus on the new firms that have grown substantially after start-up; these entrepreneurial firms are neither small (anymore) nor (yet) large. The explanandum in this study is the spatial organization of entrepreneurial firms. Spatial organization is defined as the spatial configuration of physical resources,[3] resulting from a location decision-making process. Our definition of spatial organization is based on both behavioural economics, as it can be considered as the outcome of an (investment) decision-making process, and on the resource-competence based view of the firm, as it conceptualizes the firm as a collection of productive resources.

In order to solve our research problem – 'How do changes in the spatial organization of entrepreneurial firms come about?' – we will present a conceptual framework based on behavioural economics (March and Simon, 1958; Cyert and March, 1963; Simon, 1979); the resource-competence view of the firm (Penrose, 1959; Richardson, 1972; Teece *et al.*, 2000) and evolutionary economics (Foss, 1994; Boschma and Lambooy, 1999; Hodgson, 1999; Loasby, 2001) in the following sections.

Behavioural Economics

Four concepts of behavioural economics are especially helpful for our research problem: bounded rationality, satisficing, problemistic search, and organizational slack. According to behavioural economics, decision makers are intendedly rational, but are only limitedly so due to the informational and computational limits on the decision-making capacity of human beings (Simon, 1959; Conlisk, 1996). Next to this bounded rationality, decision makers do not have optimal beliefs and choices as assumed in rational-agent models: instead of utility maximization they reveal satisficing behaviour. Strategic decision making is based on comparison of actual performance with an aspiration level (March and Simon, 1958). As a result they are not constantly searching for the optimal location, but only considering a locational change if the organization functions below their aspiration level (when it fails to satisfice). When the firm performs poorly, decision makers engage in problemistic search. Cyert and March (1963:121) have defined problemistic search as 'search that is stimulated by a problem (usually a rather specific one) and is directed toward finding a solution to that problem'. Problemistic search is motivated by constraints or problems that cause an insufficient performance of the firm. These problems lead to a search for a quick solution in the immediate environment (of alternatives), rather than trying to develop the optimal solution with extensive search. This solution is often chosen to 'satisfice' (satisfy and suffice) the organizationally determined targets rather than to optimize. This problemistic search is driven by heuristic rules.

These location decisions are probably not wholly rational, but – at least to some extent – are intended to be so (Simon, 1957). The (spatial production and transportation-cum-transaction; see McCann, 1995) costs and benefits of a certain location are of course taken into account in arriving at a satisficing outcome. Next to this problemistic search, firms are also assumed to search when they have slack resources,[4] such as extra time and financial resources that can be used for investments (Cyert and March, 1963).

Summarizing, in behavioural economics the firm is conceptualized as a 'processor of information' (cf. Cohendet *et al.*, 1999; Pred, 1967) and performance and slack are the causal drivers of locational change.

Resource-competence View of the Firm

The resource-competence view of the firm offers several conceptual building blocks like resources, competences, interfirm cooperation, and productive opportunity. According to Penrose (1959) a firm is 'a collection of productive resources the disposal of which between different uses and over time is determined by administrative decision'. If we want to know how these resources affect the performance of the firm,[5] we have to know how they are organized, and for what purposes they are used. The concept of competences refers to the firm-specific way in which these resources are deployed and organized (Penrose, 1959). The general purpose of the firm is 'to organize the use of its "own" resources together with other resources acquired from outside the firm for production and sale of goods and services at a profit' (Penrose, 1959:31).

This resource acquisition often takes place between interrelated firms in a dense network of co-operation and affiliation (Richardson, 1972). The productive activities of a firm are governed by its 'productive opportunity' which comprises 'all of the productive possibilities that its "entrepreneurs" see and can take advantage of' (Penrose, 1959:31). Opportunities are objectively identifiable but their recognition is subjective and requires exploratory activity. To realize the opportunity it is necessary to organize business activity, which calls for some kind of productive base. As it grows, the firm's resources may come to support a variety of productive bases, but Penrose pointed out that: 'movement into a new base requires a firm to achieve competence in some significantly different area of technology' (1959:110). Obtaining or creating complementary resources are solutions that enlarge the firm's knowledge base, from which new opportunities can be pursued (Penrose, 1959: 54). With regard to these opportunities, Penrose

(1959:32–3) makes a distinction between entrepreneurial and managerial services. Entrepreneurial services are 'those contributions to the operations of a firm which relate to the introduction and acceptance on behalf of the firm of new ideas, particularly with respect to products, location, and significant changes in technology, to the acquisition of new managerial personnel, to fundamental changes in the administrative organization of the firm, to the raising of capital, and to the making of plans for expansion, including the choice of method of expansion' which are contrasted with managerial services, which relate to 'the execution of entrepreneurial ideas and proposals and to the supervision of existing operations' (Penrose, 1959: 32–3). This view on entrepreneurship resembles the Schumpeterian view (1934:66) to a large extent. Entrepreneurial services may involve a new locational strategy that is enabled by certain resources, competences and dynamic capabilities that belong to managerial services, and which leads to an increased performance of the firm.

The causal mechanism of the resource-competence view is situated within the conceptualization of the firm as a bundle of resources co-evolving internally and externally. A firm's resources and competences together with additional resources and competences outside the firm will directly affect its choice of strategy, and the options open to it. On the one hand these resources and competences may constrain locational changes of firms as they have co-evolved internally and externally with resources and competences that are to some extent place-bound (for example human resources) and hard to replace[6] (for example relations with specialized resource providers). Firms can and perhaps need to be located in certain spatial contexts as they have to be in spatial proximity of resource providers. On the other hand specific resources and competences may enable locational changes of firms, for example in becoming multilocational. To some extent firms create their own environments. Changes in the spatial organization may broaden the firm's 'productive opportunity': it may increase the entrepreneur's awareness of opportunities in the environment and it may enable the firm to take advantage of these opportunities.

Evolutionary Economics

Evolutionary economics offers valuable concepts for the analysis of locational change of entrepreneurial firms. We will discuss four concepts here: market selection, routines, chance, and novelty.

While behavioural economics and the resource-competence view mainly focus on the internal structures of the firm, evolutionary economics shifts the focus to the environment of the firm. The spatial pattern of firms – their location – is assumed to be an outcome of a market selection process.[7] Only firms that deliver value on a product-market and capture returns as the outcome of market competition, survive in the long run. The spatial environment affects this survival of firms as it determines the costs of production and transportation: this is comprised in the so-called 'spatial margins of profitability' (Smith, 1966; 1970; Taylor, 1970). Location is thus not only determined by a decision making process in the firm (ex-ante selection), but also by an ex-post selection process in the market, that is to some extent spatially differentiated (see Lambooy, 2002).

Next to the selection environment, evolutionary economics takes into account the internal characteristics of firms with the concept of 'routines'. Evolutionary economics also rejects the assumption of optimal decision making, insofar as this involves some connotations of deliberation: firm behaviour is maintained to be basically characterized by automaticity. More precisely, 'behavioral options are selected, but they are not deliberately chosen' (Nelson and Winter, 1982:94). Routine or rule-guided behaviour[8] may have a rational basis, as it once was initiated as a thoughtful way to cope with a certain problem. After this initiation it is not questioned anymore, and this is also quite efficient as we cannot continuously dispute our actions. The only thing that probably changes this routine behaviour is a certain trigger that makes us aware that the circumstances have changed so much that the routine behaviour is not efficient (enough) anymore ('problemistic search'), and then it is consciously debated again.

These changes in action type can be clarified by the distinction proposed by Polanyi (1962) into focal and subsidiary awareness. An example of subsidiary awareness is the build-up of routine perception, interpretation and behaviour in specific relations, by which conformity of behaviour is taken for granted, and awareness of for example opportunities for opportunism has become 'subsidiary' (Nooteboom, 2000:105–6). People will stick to their routines until certain tolerance levels are reached, by a triggering event. This trigger brings the action into focal awareness, by which people will consciously reconsider their behaviour (rational action). For locational change this means that after a certain location decision has been made after a triggering event, decision makers will not consider changing the spatial organization of the firm unless a new triggering event makes them aware of needed and possible changes. Location decisions – especially those involving locational changes outside the region of origin – appear to be more of a strategic non-programmed decision than a routine type of action to the majority of firms, due to their infrequent occurrence and high cost of implementation. So location decision making is not likely to become a routine.

Evolutionary economics also enables the analysis of the role of chance in the spatial organization of firms (see Boschma and Lambooy, 1999). Chance events may trigger locational changes: they are potential sources of spatial-organizational innovations. These chance events may relate to problems ('problemistic search') and to opportunities ('productive opportunity'). This latter type of trigger relates to the fourth concept: novelty. Novelty is of central concern to evolutionary economists (Witt, 1992; Foss, 1994; Nooteboom, 2000). Novelty refers to radically new things that are the outcome of human creativity. For our study this concerns novel spatial structures of the firm, or locational changes that enable the realization of innovations.

Summarizing, there are infinite numbers of potential triggers for locational change both within the firm as well as in its environment. These sources of variation have to be taken into account in order to analyse which variations were both realized by the firm and selected by the external selection environment. To assess the role of chance and routines in the (non-) emergence of novel spatial structures, we need both 'pre-revelation analysis' before locational changes are considered and realized, and 'post-revelation analysis' after locational changes are realized (see Witt, 1992). There are certain necessary conditions for locational changes: for example financial resources to invest and capabilities to realize a well functioning new spatial organization, and the viability of the new form of spatial organization in the market environment (market selection).

RESEARCH DESIGN AND METHOD

This study is based on empirical research on 109 realized locational changes (post-revelation analysis) and even more considerations to change the spatial organization (pre-revelation analysis), during the life course of 25 entrepreneurial firms (see Eisenhardt, 1989). We studied both successful and failed variations: on the micro level, considerations to change the spatial organization that were (not) realized; and on the macro level, closed locations. The focal actors in the empirical study are the entrepreneurial firms. The case studies involved the life histories of these firms as told by the founder-entrepreneurs, but also a survey on indicators about the size, nature, inter-organizational relations and spatial organization of the firm. Next to these data obtained in the interview, other data from company archives, the press and other media were collected. The explanandum in this study is locational change and has been operationalized in the empirical study as locational events. These locational events can be considered as the microadaptation events (Lewin and Volberda, 1999) that reflect the changes in spatial organization of the firms.

Sample

This research relies on theoretical sampling (that is, cases are chosen for theoretical, not statistical, reasons; Glaser and Strauss, 1967). This means that we have chosen polar types (Pettigrew, 1995) on critical dimensions. We have chosen entrepreneurial firms in contrasting knowledge intensive sectors, namely knowledge services and biomedicals, with contrasting spatial organizations (oversampling firms that realized an exit out of their region of origin), and we have also contrasted the fast-growing with micro entrepreneurial firms ('lifestyle firms') (see Table 7.1, Appendix).

The entrepreneurial firms have been operationally defined as firms that have survived the first four years of existence (which are generally characterized by the highest failure rates), but are not older than ten years (which means that they probably have not become mature and managerial firms, and that the founder-entrepreneur could probably be traced). The fast-growing firms had to have created at least 20 FTEs, which is a rough indicator for company success, and also means that the nature of these firms has changed. Finally, they had to be independent, which means owner-managed (with a majority stake in the firm). The micro firms had to satisfy the same criteria, with exception of the size: they had to have created at most five FTEs.

The sample consisted of 20 knowledge service firms in five regions and five biomedical firms in two regions in the Netherlands. Within these cases 109 locational events and even more locational initiatives are studied (see Table 7.1, Appendix). The dynamics in the spatial organization of the firms can be analysed with locational events. Locational events refer to the changes in the state of the spatial organization of firms. The possible states in the spatial organization are summarized and coded in Table 7.1 (Appendix).

A more extensive discussion of the research design and methods can be found in Stam (2003, Chapter 5).

PROCESS MODEL OF LOCATIONAL CHANGE

In order to examine the central research question a process model[9] is constructed based on findings in the empirical research. The basis of generalization in a process model is not from a sample to a population (statistical generalization) but from cases to a theory (analytical generalization; see Yin, 2003). In that we focus on an explanation of the temporal order and sequence of events that unfold in change processes (observed patterns in the events). This explanation is built on the generative mechanisms that cause events to happen and the particular circumstances or contingencies

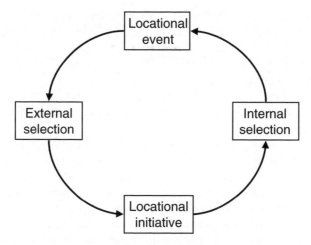

Figure 7.1   Process model of locational change

that exist when these mechanisms operate (see Sayer, 1992; Hedström and Swedberg, 1996). These mechanisms interact with contingent conditions (random, chance events for example)[10] in such a way that they cannot fully determine locational change of entrepreneurial firms.

The basic model explains locational events, with elements that have to be explained by necessary and contingent conditions. It may lead to a dynamic theory as the variables at a given time are a function (at least in part) of the same processes at an earlier time. The main thesis of the model is that locational initiatives have to be selected by the firm (internal selection) in order to become a locational event. The resulting new form of spatial organization has to be selected by an external environment (external selection) in order to be viable in the long run. Changes in the external environment may be followed by a new cycle starting with (a) new locational initiative(s). This process is depicted in Figure 7.1 with the four key elements.

Locational Initiative

The first element in the model is 'locational initiative'. By a locational initiative we mean a consideration to initiate a locational event. This locational initiative can be triggered by performance below aspiration levels (problemistic search) and by the recognition of opportunities. The performance below aspiration levels can be caused by constraints in the firm (for example lack of expansion space) and changes in the environment (for example a shrinking market or increased competition). The recognition of opportunities can also be caused by increased knowledge of the productive possibilities inherent in the firm's resources and by increased knowledge of the external world and the effect of changes in the external world (see Penrose, 1959:79). The actors involved in locational initiatives are those who suggest new ways of organizing the firm in space. The locational initiatives in the first development phases are mostly suggested by the entrepreneur(ial team), later on members of the management team or key employees, and members of the personal network of these decision makers may be important in this respect.

Almost all fast-growing firms in our research have considered starting a branch outside the home region, often triggered by an opportunity. Only six fast-growing firms never considered becoming multiregional, that is they have never been triggered by a problem or opportunity to initiate such a locational change. The micro firms in our research never considered becoming multilocational. The consideration to leave the original location is often triggered by a lack of expansion space that constrains the (future) performance of the firm (problemistic search). Only the considerations to move over a longer distance (out of the region), were more often triggered by an opportunity.

Internal Selection

Internal selection involves the ability and willingness to change the spatial organization. This explains whether or not the decision makers in the firm select a locational initiative. It involves the managerial activities through which resources and competences are internally redirected towards locational initiatives: a resource allocation process.

The ability of the firm to realize the proposed locational initiative depends on the resources, capabilities and organization structure of the firm and its dependence on or control over external organizations. There may be considerable locational inertia due to place bound human resources and sunk costs in physical assets (locational assets). Via the resource mobilization process, resources may be attracted from outside or created internally (for example through learning), which also enables a change.

The willingness to change depends on the intentions of the firm. However, as it is problematic to ascribe intentions to the firm, empirical research has to uncover who is defining these intentions. These intentions may be driven by personal factors, but are more often dominated by functional or strategic organizational factors. The strategic intent of the firm gives the evolutionary processes inside the firm something to 'aim' for (March, 1994). This strategic intent may even drive locational initiatives. However, for certain types of locational initiatives, especially relocations, strategic intent is often not involved at all. Sometimes the personal intent of the entrepreneur-founder might even overrule the strategic intent of the firm as a whole. Other people in the firm may be unwilling to change the spatial organization, due to vested interests, cultural factors, and fear of change. A few key actors often define the organizational success related to these intentions. A theory of social action is needed to make sense of how intentionality gives rise to outcomes in location decision-making processes.

Two types of agents may be involved in the internal selection: agents of selection and agents of retention. This selective retention shows who has control in location decision making, and by whom they are influenced ('stakeholders'). Agents of selection are those who decide which of the locational initiatives will be acted on, that is they are responsible for the level of additional variation in the spatial organization. Agents of retention are those who decide which of the existing parts of the spatial organization will be continued, and which will be discontinued (closing down of a branch, relocation). In other words, the agents of selection and the agents of retention are responsible for respectively the level of variation and the level of inertia in the spatial organization of the firm. Entrepreneurs themselves often make the relocation decisions, as it mostly affects their daily workplace. The decision to close down a certain branch is also made by the entrepreneur, as this often involves resistance of the employees involved. In most cases these agents of selection and agents of retention will be the same persons, that is the entrepreneur and the management team. In some cases these agents are different: the agents of retention are often still the entrepreneurs, but the agents of selection may also be 'empowered' employees taking up new initiatives, backed by the entrepreneurs. In firms that have developed decentralized control in decision making, employees have the freedom to start new locational initiatives that they regard as important, if they can find consensus among stakeholders of the firm and when it is regarded as good for the firm.

There might be an internal competition between alternative locational initiatives a firm may choose to invest their resources in pursuing. The processes of variation (which locational initiatives are considered) and selection (which are started) are guided by the expectations about how a locational initiative will perform. This also explains why not all locational initiatives survived the internal selection process to become a locational event. Many locational initiatives probably fall at the first hurdle (did not even go through the complete internal selection process) or did not leave the starting blocks (were only uttered, and have never been recognized as a 'serious' locational initiative). Our empirical study showed that many firms that have considered moving out of their region of origin, were not able or willing to realize this in the end. This is in contrast with the firms that considered starting a new branch in another region: those firms almost all realized such a locational change.

Locational Event

The outcome of the internal selection process is the preservation of the initial spatial organization (retention of the form of spatial organization) or a change of the spatial organization with a locational event, leading to a new form of spatial organization. This new form of spatial organization carries all the spatial structures of the past, unless a branch is closed down or a relocation has been realized.

External Selection

After a change in the form of spatial organization has been realized (as a locational event), the resulting form of spatial organization has to survive in an external selection environment. Fitness to the environment is the selection mechanism determining which forms of spatial organization survive. The introduction of a new form of spatial organization (variation) and its capacity for appropriating resources in the external environment (selective retention) define the evolutionary process. The external selection environment is normally taken to be a product market, but the labour market and the capital market may also be relevant. Competition takes place between firms that are active on the same or related markets. The outcome of this competition differs per market: profits in product markets, attraction and retention of human resources in labour markets, and attraction of different types of capital in capital markets.

The empirical study also showed that there are remarkable differences in the selection environment of knowledge services firms and biomedical firms. The knowledge service firms have to compete in a market on which there is demand from organizations for their services, while biomedical firms have to compete in the capital market to finance their research and development activities. In other words: knowledge service firms are already generating resources on their own, while biomedical firms are still mobilizing resources in order to reach a viable size and/or structure of operations. Both types of firms are affected by selection processes, but not by the same type of selection environment.

The spatial dimension of the selection environment is also highly industry-specific. The market environment for micro knowledge services firms can mainly be found at the regional and for fast-growing firms also at the national level. For biomedical firms the international level is most relevant.

Next to competition on goods and services, there are also other competitive processes that may be relevant as selection processes. Especially for biomedical firms the capital market is highly relevant. The spatial origin of capital providers and shareholders shift from national venture capitalists at the start to international shareholders after IPO. Finally, as we focus on knowledge intensive activities here, the knowledge inputs via the labour market are highly relevant for the survival and growth of fast-growing firms (not so much for micro firms as these have (almost) no employees). The spatial organization of these knowledge intensive fast-growing firms can in this respect be understood as a trade-off between two selection environments: the product and labour market for knowledge services and the capital and labour market for biomedical firms.

The spatial dimension of the labour market does not discriminate much between the two industries as all firms have 80–100 per cent of their employees within the region of the firm location(s). This does not necessarily mean that the personnel lives in the same region as the firm. It is more probably for biomedical activities as these are concentrated at the site of the firm. For the R&D activities co-location might even be necessary, enabling the transfer of tacit knowledge. This regional concentration is less probable for knowledge service activities as these can be executed at the location of the customers, at the homes of the employees, and of course also at the site of the firm. The offices of these knowledge service firms become more and more meeting points instead of working places.

The external selection environment of a firm is not given. The locational initiatives may include the choice to enter and exit certain selection environments (possibly incurring large entry and exit costs, see internal selection). Also without changing the spatial organization of the firm this environment may be changed when the firm chooses to serve other customers or attract other types of employees.

An evolutionary perspective requires a clear view on the unit of selection. What is the unit of selection for the external selection environment? Is it the new part of the spatial organization that is added in the form of a locational event, or the complete firm with its specific new organizational form in space? The unit of selection differs by the relative size of the firm. The vulnerability of smaller firms means that the entire organization constitutes a possible unit of selection. In contrast, larger firms with 'semi-independent' business units can add or lose spatial units without causing problems for the entire organization. New branches that cannot survive on their own in their specific environment may be retained because resources transferred from other parts of the firm support them. This latter situation is most probable for fast-growing firms that have accumulated organizational slack. Organizational slack and excess capacity may function as a buffer towards a strong selection environment; they have enough (financial) resources to 'subsidize' business units that are not yet viable in the market environment.

If the external selection environment operates very weakly and the regions in which the spatial units are located provide the necessary generic resources then human agency and chance involved in the locational initiatives and the factors related to the internal selection environment provide a more extensive explanation for the spatial organization than the external selection environment. The relative role of the internal and external selection environment cannot be predetermined.

A similar debate on the role of internal versus situational explanations can be found in psychology (Ross and Nisbett, 1991). Psychological research has shown that the influence of the person is stronger in explaining the decision to start a business and weaker in explaining the success of the business (Rauch and Frese, 2000). In evolutionary economics it has been stated that if the external selection environment operates very weakly[11] and the regions in which the spatial units are located provide the necessary generic resources,[12] then human agency and chance involved in locational changes and the factors related to the internal selection environment provide a more extensive explanation for the spatial organization than the external selection environment[13] (see Boschma and Lambooy, 1999).

IMPLICATIONS FOR THE ANALYSIS OF LOCATIONAL CHANGES DURING THE LIFE COURSE

We have defined and discussed the elements of the basic model of locational change. The basic model just represents one cycle, while a firm life course may consist of many cycles. For a complete understanding of the locational evolution of fast-growing firms during their life-course we have to formulate the initial conditions before the first cycle sets in, and we have to take into account the successive cycles after this first one, with changing conditions, internal as well as external. The spatial organization of a firm at time t constrains, informs, and affects probabilities of realizations of a certain new form of spatial organization at time $t + 1$ (see Murmann *et al.*, 2003:10). This involves different types of path dependence: for example cognitive path dependence[14] (prior knowledge), previous investments in the form of sunk costs, and structural lock-ins into webs of interdependent relationships.

Prior knowledge and experience of the founders to a large extent condition the location of the first activities of the new firm. However, a large 'amount' of experience of the entrepreneur-founders may also give them more possibilities for the location choices. This prior knowledge also explains to a large extent why some knowledge service firms started international activities and also opened branches in foreign countries. These firms were led by entrepreneurs with international experience or with international networks that originate from their former work environment. The biomedical firms in contrast are all active in international markets, both due to their former international experience and the nature of their 'products', but do not yet have international branches. During the life course certain firms develop capabilities to realize locational changes: for example to establish or take-over branches in a successful way.

The initial resource providers and customers of the firm may have long lasting effects on the development paths of fast-growing firms in space. Especially the small firms that are relatively dependent on large customers are bounded in their locational behaviour. The fast-growing firms become less dependent on specific customers and become multilocational in order to serve other customers.

The founding conditions also have some effects on the possibility of changing the spatial organization, depending on the amount of *sunk costs* involved in the initial location. For example one firm that relocated its headquarters outside the region of origin still had to be located at its initial site in order to keep important human resources and contacts with important knowledge providers (within the 'legal structure' of research contracts). These path dependences constrain and enable the range of possible options, mainly affecting the emergence of locational initiatives and the internal selection process.

The external selection environment may however also be changed by the firm during the life course, in two ways. First, the firm may seek other external selection environments by entering new product-market combinations in general. Second, the firm may affect its external selection environment by influencing important actors, for example in a process of co-evolution or political negotiations.

Our empirical study revealed that especially the fast-growing firms broaden their spatial selection environments. For example the biomedical firms initially acquire capital at a local or national scale, while in later phases they acquire this capital from venture capitalists and government agencies outside the national borders. The knowledge service firms also most often develop their markets from a regional scale to a national scale. When these firms also start with new products, or with existing products at new markets, they become involved in new selection environments. Exaptation[15] sometimes plays a role here as existing ideas or products are introduced in a new context. The knowledge service firms also affect their selection environment as they co-evolve with important clients. For these firms the competitive process of market selection is to some extent substituted by cooperation.

CONCLUSION

In this paper we have studied the locational changes of entrepreneurial firms. These changes have been analysed in two knowledge intensive industries: knowledge services and biomedicals. We have focused on location (initiatives and events), which directs attention to the relationship between the firm and its environment, instead of focusing only on the internal or external environments. We have made three major contributions to the literature on (new) firm location. The first contribution is the addition of 'opportunity-driven' location decision making next to the 'problem-driven' location decision making in the behavioural approach. These two types of decision making define the willingness to change the spatial organization of the firm. The second contribution is the identification of the contribution of willingness and ability (internal selection) aspects in the location decision-making process. The third contribution is the model of locational change that integrates two units of analysis and the two evolutionary processes involved. The model of locational change combines two basic process theories, teleological and evolutionary process theories, which are applied on the analysis of the spatial organization of entrepreneurial firms. The model conceptualizes a double two stage process of variation-selective retention. In a life course perspective this model offers a heuristic to study the successive cycles that make up the spatial development of firms. For the explanation of the changes in the spatial organization we focused on the developmental processes. The developmental processes refer to the accumulation of knowledge and resources (including sunk costs) that enable and constrain changes in the nature and spatial organization of the firms. Evolution becomes a three-stage scheme, not only involving variety and selection, but also including regeneration as firms face new opportunities or threats after they have changed their spatial organization (see Metcalfe *et al.*, 2000:15).

Future research may test the application of the model in other sectoral (mature industries like shipbuilding and transforming industries like graphics-media) and regional contexts. Further research may reveal the boundary conditions of the theory, as it has been developed in only one specific country (the Netherlands) and in two specific knowledge intensive industries. Finally, longitudinal research of a cohort of new firms could lead to statistical generalization in addition to the analytical generalization in this chapter.

NOTES

1. The author would like to thank Ron Boschma, Jan Lambooy and Jeroen van den Bergh for their comments. As usual, all errors are the responsibility of the author.

2. See Foss (1994) and Nooteboom (2000) for examples of causal process theories in evolutionary economics.
3. This also comprises the so-called 'locational assets' of firms (Teece *et al.*, 2000). Especially in the restaurant, retail, and hotel industries location can be a key asset, leading to competitive advantage (Aaker, 1989). A valuable location can act as an imperfectly imitable physical resource for the firm (Barney, 1991), or a tangible resource enabling a firm to exercise its capabilities, leading to a positional advantage (Day and Wensley, 1988). In this way, the spatial organization of the firm can be regarded as a portfolio of locational assets.
4. See Penrose's (1959) excess capacity of productive services that drives firm growth.
5. Location might play a role here as an asset that partly determines the market share and profitability of a firm (Teece *et al.*, 2000:345–6).
6. See Penrose (1959:25) and the more recent debate on sunk costs and corporate geography (Clark, 1994; Clark and Wrigley, 1997).
7. The initial evolutionary approach suggested by Alchian (1950) was proposed as a modification of economic analysis based on the assumptions of the *homo economicus*. Alchian argued that incomplete information and uncertain foresights made it impossible for business firms to maximize profits. And he thus dispensed the rational choice axiom of economic agents, operationalized as profit maximization. This led to the so-called Alchian-thesis, that is 'the view that competition represents a Darwinian selection mechanism that produces exactly the same outcome that would ensue from a world in which consumers maximized utility and businessmen maximized profits' (Blaug, 1992:249). This means that the bulk of traditional economics would be unaffected if we assumed that purposeful human behaviour does not matter in economic analysis (see Penrose (1952) for a critique on this kind of evolutionary economics).
8. See the similar concepts 'traditional action' (Weber, 1978) and 'habitual behavior' (Katona, 1951).
9. See Mohr (1982); Sayer (1992); Van de Ven (1992); Van de Ven and Poole (1995). Process theory is contrasted with variance theory, which aims to account for the input factors (independent variables) that statistically explain variations in some outcome criteria (dependent variables).
10. Chance is defined here in an Aristotelian sense as the intersection of two causally independent series of events (Van Woudenberg 2002: 21). The term should not be confused with contingent. Something is contingent if it is not necessary, which does not have to mean that it is improbable or unimportant (Van Woudenberg, 2002:23–4).
11. An economic boom period, similar to that during which most of the enterprises in this study were visited, may also reduce the external selection pressures.
12. The necessary inputs are not localized, but ubiquitous on higher spatial levels (Maskell and Malmberg, 1999; Weber, 1929). Maskell *et al.* (1998) see the process of 'ubiquitification' as an effect of globalization; many previously localized capabilities and production factors have become ubiquities.
13. This proposition relates to the discussion about the 'spatial margins of profitability' on pp. 147–9: firms are not constrained by location to make a profitable business in a relatively large spatial area.
14. The degree of choice – initiating, realizing, and retaining a change in the spatial organization – is constrained by internal and external selection, but also by limited information and the costs and limits to information processing (see Pred, 1967; Cohen and Levinthal, 1990). The latter constraint affects the range of locational initiatives that may emerge and the uncertainty surrounding internal selection related to the expectations on external selection.
15. The *Oxford Dictionary of Earth Sciences* defines exaptation as 'A characteristic that opens up a previously unavailable niche to its possessor.' 'Exaptation' differs from 'adaptation': adaptation means changing an entity towards a particular fit of its current context, while exaptation means that a certain entity is functional in a new context, while it was not initially selected in that selection environment; in other words its current primary function is the side effect of another (prior) adaptation in another context (see Gould and Vrba, 1982).

REFERENCES

Aaker, D. A. (1989), 'Managing assets and skills: the key to a sustainable competitive advantage', *California Management Review*, **31**(2), 91–106.

Alchian, A. A. (1950), 'Uncertainty, evolution, and economic theory', *Journal of Political Economy*, **58**(3), 211–21.

Allen, D. N. and D. J. Hayward (1990), 'The role of new venture formation/ entrepreneurship in regional economic development: a review', *Economic Development Quarterly* **4**, 55–64.

Arthur, W. B. (1994), *Increasing Returns and Path Dependence in the Economy*, Ann Arbor: University of Michigan Press.

Barney, J. (1991), 'Firm resources and sustained competitive advantage', *Journal of Management* **17**(1), 99–120.

Birch, D. (1987), *Job Creation in America*. New York: The Free Press.

Blaug, M. (1992), *The Methodology of Economics* (2nd edition), Cambridge: Cambridge University Press.

Boschma, R. A. and K. Frenken (2003), 'Evolutionary economics and industry location'. *Review for Regional Research*, **23**, 183–200.

Boschma, R. A. and J. G. Lambooy (1999), 'Evolutionary economics and economic geography', *Journal of Evolutionary Economics*, **9**, 411–29.

Brakman, S., H. Garretsen and Ch. van Marrewijk (2001), *An Introduction to Geographical Economics: Trade, Location, and Growth*, Cambridge: Cambridge University Press.

Cantwell, J. and G. D. Santangelo (2002), 'The new geography of corporate research in Information and Communications Technology (ICT)', *Journal of Evolutionary Economics* **12**(1–2): 163–97

Clark, G. L. (1994), 'Strategy and structure: corporate restructuring and the scope and characteristics of sunk costs', *Environment and Planning A*, **26**, 9–32.

Clark, G. L. and N. Wrigley (1997), 'Exit, the firm and sunk costs: reconceptualizing the corporate geography of disinvestment and plant closure', *Progress in Human Geography*, **21**(3), 338–58.

Cohen, W. M. and D. A. Levinthal (1990), 'Absorptive capacity: a new perspective on learning and innovation', *Administrative Science Quarterly*, **35**(1), 128–52.

Cohendet, P., F. Kern, B. Mehmanpazir and F. Munier (1999), 'Knowledge coordination, competence creation and integrated networks in globalised firms', *Cambridge Journal of Economics*, **23**, 225–41.

Conlisk, J. (1996), 'Why bounded rationality?', *Journal of Economic Literature*, **34**, 669–700.

Cooper, A. C. (1985), 'The role of the incubator organizations in the founding of growth-oriented firms'. *Journal of Business Venturing* **1**, 75–86.

Cooper, S. Y. (1998), 'Entrepreneurship and the location of high technology small firms: implications for regional development', in R. Oakey and W. During (eds), *New Technology-Based Firms in the 1990s*, London: Paul Chapman, pp. 247–67.

Cyert, R. M. and J. G. March (1963), *A Behavioral Theory of the Firm*, Englewood Cliffs, NJ: Prentice-Hall.

Day, G. S. and R. Wensley (1988), 'Assessing advantage: a framework for diagnosing competitive superiority', *Journal of Marketing* **52**(2), 1–20.

Dunning, J. H. (1998), 'Location and the multinational enterprise: a neglected factor?', *Journal of International Business Studies*, **29**(1), 45–66.

Eisenhardt, K. M. (1989), 'Building theories from case study research', *Academy of Management Review*, **14**(4), 532–50.

Foss, N. J. (1994), 'Realism and evolutionary economics', *Journal of Social and Evolutionary Systems*, **17**(1), 21–40.

Fujita, M., P. Krugman, and A. Venables (1999), *The Spatial Economy: Cities, Regions and International Trade*, Cambridge, MA: MIT Press.

Glaser, B. and A. Strauss (1967) *The Discovery of Grounded Theory*, Chicago: Aldine.

Gould, S. J. and E. Vrba (1982), 'Exaptation – a missing term in the science of form', *Paleobiology*, **8**, 4–15.

Hanks, S. H., C. J. Watson E. Jansen E., and G. N. Chandler (1993), 'Tightening the life-cycle construct: a taxonomic study of growth stage configurations in high-technology organizations', *Entrepreneurship: Theory and Practice*, **18**(2), 5–31.

Hart, O. (1983), 'The market mechanism as an incentive scheme'. *The Bell Journal of Economics*, **14**, 366–82.

Hedström, P. and R. Swedberg (1996), 'Social mechanisms', *Acta Sociologica*, **39**, 281–308.

Hodgson, G. M. (1999), *Evolution and Institutions: On Evolutionary Economics and the Evolution of Economics*, Cheltenham: Edward Elgar.

Katona, G. (1951), *Psychological Analysis of Economic Behavior*, New York: McGraw-Hill.

Kirchhoff, B. A. (1994), *Entrepreneurship and Dynamic Capitalism*. Westport, CT: Praeger.

Krugman, P. (1991), *Geography and Trade*, Cambridge, MA: MIT Press.

Krugman, P. (1998), 'What's new about the new economic geography?', *Oxford Review of Economic Policy*, **14**(2), 7–17.

Lambooy, J. G. (2002), 'Knowledge and urban economic development: an evolutionary perspective', *Urban Studies*, **39**(5–6), 1019–35.

Lewin, A. Y. and H. W. Volberda (1999), 'Prolegomena on coevolution: a framework for research on strategy and new organizational forms', *Organization Science* **10**(5), 519–34.

Loasby, B. J. (2001), 'The evolution of knowledge', paper presented at DRUID Summer Conference 2001, Aalborg.

March, J.G. (1994), 'The evolution of evolution', in J.A.C. Baum, and J. V. Singh (eds) *Evolutionary Dynamics of Organizations*, New York: Oxford University Press, pp. 39–49.

March, J. G. and H. Simon (1958), *Organizations*, New York: Wiley.

Maskell, P., E. Heikki, H. Ingjaldur, A. Malmberg and E. Vatne (1998), *Competitiveness, Localised Learning and Regional Development: Specialisation and Prosperity in Small Open Economies*, London: Routledge.

Maskell. P. and A. Malmberg (1999), 'Localised learning and industrial competitiveness', *Cambridge Journal of Economics*, **23**(2), 167–85.

McCann, P. (1995), 'Rethinking the economics of location and agglomeration', *Urban Studies*, **32**(3), 563–77.

Metcalfe, J. S., M. R. Fonseca, and R. Ramlogan (2000), *Innovation, Growth and Competition: Evolving Complexity or Complex Evolution*, Manchester: CRIC, University of Manchester.

Mohr, L. B. (1982), *Explaining Organizational Behavior. The Limits and Possibilities of Theory and Research*, San Francisco: Jossey-Bass.

Mucchielli, J.-L., and P. Saucier (1997), 'European industrial relocations in low-wage countries: policy and theory debates', in P. J. Buckley, and J.-L. Mucchielli (eds) *Multinational Firms and International Relocation*, Cheltenham: Edward Elgar.

Murmann, J. P., H. E. Aldrich, D. Levinthal and S. G. Winter (2003), 'Evolutionary thought in management and organization theory at the beginning of the new millennium – A symposium on the state of the art and opportunities for future research', *Journal of Management Inquiry*, **12**(1): 22–40.

Nelson, R. R. and S. G. Winter (1982), *An Evolutionary Theory of Economic Change*, Cambridge, MA: Belknap Press.

Nooteboom, B. (2000), *Learning and Innovation in Organizations and Economies*, Oxford: Oxford University Press.

Penrose, E. T. (1952), 'Biological analogies in the theory of the firm', *American Economic Review*, **42**(5), 804–19.

Penrose, E. T. (1959), *The Theory of the Growth of the Firm* (3rd edition 1995), Oxford: Oxford University Press.

Pettigrew, A. (1995), 'Longitudinal field research on change: theory and practice', in G. P. Huber, and A. H. Van de Ven (eds) *Longitudinal Field Research Methods*, Thousand Oaks: Sage, pp. 204–27.

Polanyi, M. (1962), *Personal Knowledge. Towards a Post-critical Epistemology* (1st edition 1958), London: Routledge & Kegan Paul.

Pred, A. R. (1967), *Behaviour and Location: Foundations for a Geographic and Dynamic Location Theory, Part I*, Lund: The Royal University of Lund.

Rauch, A. and M. Frese (2000), 'Psychological approaches to entrepreneurial success: a general model and an overview of findings', in C. L. Cooper, and I. T. Robertson (eds), *International Review of Industrial and Organizational Psychology*, New York: Wiley.

Richardson, G. B. (1972), 'The organization of industry', *Economic Journal*, **82**(327), 883–96.

Ross, L. and R. E. Nisbett (1991), *The Person and the Situation: Perspectives of Social Psychology*, Philadelphia: Temple University.

Sayer, A. (1992), *Method in Social Science*. London: Taylor & Francis.

Schumpeter, J. A. (1934), *The Theory of Economic Development. An Inquiry into Profits, Capital, Credit, Interest, and the Business Cycle* (first edition in German 1909), New York: Oxford University Press.

Simon, H. A. (1957), *Administrative Behavior* (2nd edition), New York: Macmillan.

Simon, H. A. (1959), 'Theories of decision making in economics and behavioral science', *American Economic Review*, **49**(3), 253–83.

Simon, H. A. (1979), 'Rational decision making in business organizations', *American Economic Review*, **69**(4), 493–513.

Smith, D. M. (1966), 'A theoretical framework for geographical studies of industrial location', *Economic Geography*, **42**(95), 95–113.

Smith, D. M. (1970), 'On throwing out Weber with the bathwater: a note on industrial location and linkage', *Area*, **2**(1), 15–18.

Stam, E. (2003), 'Why butterflies don't leave. Locational evolution of evolving enterprises', Ph.D. Dissertation, Utrecht: Utrecht University.

Stam, E. and V. Schutjens (2000), 'Locational behaviour of young firms: a life course perspective', Paper for the 40th European Congress of the Regional Science Association, Barcelona, Spain.

Storey, D. (1997), *Understanding the Small Business Sector*, London: International Thomson Business Press.

Stuart, T. and O. Sorenson (2003), 'The geography of opportunity: spatial hetero-geneity in founding rates and the performance of biotechnology firms', *Research Policy*, **32**(2): 229–53.

Taylor, M. J. (1970), 'Location decisions of small firms', *Area*, **3**, 51–4.

Teece, D. J., Pisano, G., and A. Shuen (2000), 'Dynamic capabilities and strategic management', in G. Dosi, R. Nelson, and S. G. Winter (eds), *The Nature and Dynamics of Organizational Capabilities*, New York: Oxford University Press.

Van de Ven, A. H. (1992), 'Suggestions for studying strategy process: a research note', *Strategic Management Journal*, **13**, 169–88.

Van de Ven, A. H. and M. S. Poole (1995), 'Explaining development and change in organizations', *Academy of Management Review*, **20**(3), 510–40.

Van Woudenberg, R. (2002), *Ontwerp en Toeval in de Wereld*, Amstelveen: De Zaak Haes.

Weber, A. (1929), *A Theory of the Location of Industries* (translated, original 1909), Chicago: Chicago University Press.

Weber, M. (1978), *Economy and Society* (translated, original 1922), Berkeley: University of California Press.

Witt, U. (1992), 'Evolutionary concepts in economics', *Eastern Economic Journal*, **18**(4), 405–19.

Yin, R. K. (2003), *Case Study Research: Design and Methods* (3rd edition). Thousand Oaks: Sage.

APPENDIX: LOCATIONAL EVENTS

In general the changing states in the spatial organization involve organic growth or decline of firms, but it is also possible that they involve external growth. Two modes of external growth are identified here: Merger or sale (code 'M') and Acquisition (code 'A'). When a change in state goes hand in hand with external growth this is shown with the addition of the relevant codes. For example, 'A5' means an acquisition of a firm outside the home region (acquired new branch). Some locational events occur simultaneously, for example '90' means exit from home-based to business premises outside the region of origin. Table 7.1 shows the sequences of locational events during the life courses of the firms studied.

Table 7.1   Sequences of locational events

	Cases	Sequence of locational events*
Fast-growing firms		
	A	01537851
	B	0155315355596
	C	0156
	D	01
	E	011111A511
	F	01
	G	9015
	H	0A39 A55A5A5A55#
	I	0515
	J	0
	K	90177
	L	901117
	M	0135535777788
	N	01175757
	O	011
	P	0111
	Q	0111
	R	01M95
	S	01
	T	01
Micro firms	a	0
	b	**
	c	0
	d	90
	e	01

Notes:
* codes: 0 = Initial location at (business) premises
        1 = In situ or intraregional expansion (relocation to larger premises)
        2 = In situ or intraregional contraction (relocation to smaller premises)
        3 = Set up of a branch within the home region
        4 = Close down of a branch within the home region
        5 = Set up of a branch outside the home region, within the home country
        6 = Close down of a branch outside the home region, within the home country
        7 = Set up of a branch outside the home country
        8 = Close down of a branch outside the home country
        9 = Relocation (headquarter) outside the home region.
** stays home-based.
# and at least ten more new and acquired branches.

8. The diffusion of the steam engine in eighteenth-century Britain

Alessandro Nuvolari, Bart Verspagen and Nick von Tunzelmann

INTRODUCTION

Whilst economic historians have long discussed the nature and the determinants of technical change in the early phases of industrialization (see Habakkuk, 1962; Landes, 1969; Mathias, 1983; just to mention a few classical contributions), comparatively less attention has been devoted to the diffusion of new technologies in this historical period. Reviewing the state of the art more than thirty years ago, Rosenberg noted:

> [I]f we focus upon the most critical events of the industrial revolution, such as the introduction of new techniques of power generation and the climactic events in metallurgy, our ignorance of the rate at which new techniques were adopted, and the factors accounting for these rates is, if not total, certainly no cause for professional self-congratulation. . . . Our knowledge of the sequence of events at the purely technical level remains far greater than our knowledge of the translation of technical events into events of economic significance. (Rosenberg, 1976: 189–90, note that the original paper was published in 1972)

At the time, Rosenberg was undoubtedly right in indicating the existence of a fundamental and largely unexplored research issue. Since then, some considerable progress has been made, so that today we have a number of studies which portray with some accuracy the patterns of diffusion for a number of key technologies of the industrial revolution. To name just a few major contributions, Hyde (1977) has analysed the diffusion of iron production techniques, David (1975, chs. 4, 5) has studied the diffusion of the reaper in the USA and in Britain, and von Tunzelmann (1978) and Kanefsky (1979) have examined the diffusion of power technologies. These studies have also ventured some way towards interpreting the factors driving the process of diffusion (sometimes igniting interesting controversies such as in the case of Alan Olmstead's (1975) critique of David's study of the reaping machine). Furthermore, in certain cases, the analysis of the diffusion process has also induced some overall reassessment of the role played by specific technologies in the process of economic growth.

This chapter serves a twofold purpose. The first is to provide a thorough reconstruction of the early diffusion of steam power technology (in the form of Watt and Newcomen engines) by providing new estimates for the timing, the pace and the geographical extent of steam engine usage during the eighteenth century. The second goal is to assess the factors influencing the adoption of steam engine technology in this period. In particular, the chapter will pay attention to the process of *spatial spread* of steam technology during the eighteenth century. The focus on the geographical aspects of the diffusion process is motivated by the fact that a growing number of contributions have argued (in our view rather compellingly) that a proper understanding of the processes of economic change taking place during the British industrial revolution needs to be based on a regional perspective (Pollard, 1981; Langton, 1984; Hudson, 1989; Berg and Hudson, 1992). In particular, these authors claim that industries exhibiting fast rates of output growth and extensive technical and organizational changes displayed a strong tendency towards regional concentrations. From these considerations, it is clear that, when accounting for the diffusion of new technologies in this period, due attention must be paid to spatial aspects.

The rest of the chapter is organized as follows. In the next section we present a brief overview of the development of steam power technology in the course of the eighteenth century. Clearly the aim of this section is to provide the necessary background (from the history of technology) to our diffusion study. In the third section, we provide a broad outline of the geographical diffusion patterns of Newcomen and Watt engines. In the fourth section, by estimating 'adoption equations' of various types of steam engines by county, we assess the relative role of a number of specific location factors. In the same section, we also attempt to interpret the results of our econometric analysis against the background of the existing historical accounts of the emergence of steam power technology. The final section draws conclusions.

THE DEVELOPMENT OF STEAM POWER TECHNOLOGY DURING THE EIGHTEENTH CENTURY

In the late seventeenth century mining activities began to be severely hampered by flooding problems. Following the scientific investigations of Torricelli and Pascal, there were several attempts to use atmospheric pressure to lift water out of mines. The Savery engine, clearly inspired by the

scientific investigations of the time, can be considered as the first successful effort in this direction. The engine was developed in the period
1695–1702. In the Savery engine, steam was first admitted and then condensed inside a 'receiving' vessel by pouring cold water over its outside.
Following steam condensation, atmospheric pressure drove the water to be
pumped up into the vessel. The engine suffered from two major shortcomings, which severely limited its practical utilization. The first defect was the
restricted height of operation: the suction lift could raise water only to a
height of 20 feet (about 6 metres). The second was the high fuel consumption due to the need to re-create steam inside the vessel at each stroke.
Undoubtedly, the historical importance of the Savery engine lies more in
its showing the general potentialities of the use of steam power rather than
in its practical applications, although a number of such engines continued
in practical use for many years.

The Newcomen engine, developed in 1712, resolved the problem of the
limited height of operation. The engine consisted of a piston-cylinder
arrangement connected to one arm of a working beam. The opposite end
of the working beam was connected to the mine pump-rod. Steam was
admitted from the boiler into the cylinder by means of a valve. Then a cold
jet of water was sprayed into the cylinder, condensing the steam. This
created a partial vacuum inside the cylinder, so that the piston was pushed
down by atmospheric pressure[1] (the top of the cylinder was open), lifting
the pump-rod at the other end of the beam. The use of the cylinder-piston
arrangement together with the beam made possible the use of the engine
for effective mine drainage, as pump-rods could easily be extended to reach
the necessary depth. Furthermore, the Newcomen engine was robust,
highly reliable and based on a fairly simple working principle.

Given these merits, it is not surprising that Newcomen engines soon
came into widespread use in mining activities. However, the Newcomen
engine had two main technical shortcomings. As with the Savery engine,
one deficiency was the high fuel consumption due to the need for cooling
and heating the cylinder at each stroke. The second limitation was the
irregularity of its movement, which prevented the use of this kind of engine
for directly delivering rotary motion.[2] Savery and Newcomen formed a
partnership to exploit the patent rights of their inventions (Savery had been
granted a patent for his invention in 1699). The patent expired in 1733.

The problem of the high fuel consumption of the Newcomen engine was
successfully tackled by James Watt in the late 1760s. In the Watt engine condensation was carried out in a separate vessel and not in the cylinder, so
there was no need to re-heat the cylinder at each stroke. The Watt engine,
like the Newcomen engine, consisted of a piston-cylinder arrangement connected with a working beam, but the piston was pushed down by the action

of steam and not by atmospheric pressure (the cylinder had a closed top). After having pushed down the piston, the steam was admitted by means of a system of valves into a separate vessel where it was condensed. This allowed for a much higher fuel economy compared with the Newcomen engine.

In the second half of the eighteenth century, there were also a number of attempts to introduce modifications to the Newcomen engine so that it could deliver a steady rotary motion. The most convenient solution was patented in 1780 by James Pickard. It involved the combined use of the crank and a flywheel (Hills, 1989: 60). At more or less the same time, Watt, at the insistence of his business partner Matthew Boulton, was also working on the transformation of reciprocating into rotary motion. Pre-empted by Pickard in the use of the crank, Watt was forced to contrive an alternative mechanical device, the 'sun and planet' gear. However, after the expiration of Pickard's patent, in 1794, Boulton and Watt resorted to the use of the simpler and more effective crank (von Tunzelmann, 1978: 20). The conversion of reciprocating into rotary motion was also facilitated by the development of the double-acting engine, another invention by Watt, which was patented in 1782. In the double-acting engine steam is alterna-tively admitted into the cylinder on both sides of the piston. This resulted in a more powerful action, but also in a much more uniform movement of the piston, making the Boulton and Watt double-acting design state-of-the-art for applications requiring rotary motion.

Finally, in the second half of the 1790s, Richard Trevithick developed the first high-pressure engine (Watt engines used steam at a little more than atmospheric pressure). This type of engine did not use the separate con-denser, but discharged exhaust steam directly into the atmosphere. For this reason, they were called 'puffers'. The main advantage of this type of engine was the compactness and the cheaper cost of installation due to elimination of the condenser, the air pump and the beam (von Tunzelmann, 1978: 23). The nineteenth-century development of steam power technology was to be increasingly characterized by the use of higher and higher steam pressures, though usually in combination with condensing.

DIFFUSION PATTERNS IN EARLY STEAM POWER TECHNOLOGY

Kanefsky and Robey (1980) compiled a survey of all the steam engines erected in Great Britain in the course of the eighteenth century.[3] For each (known) steam engine erected during the period 1700–1800, Kanefsky and Robey recorded the year of construction, the type or design of the engine (that is Newcomen, Watt, and so on), the county, and the sector of appli-cation.[4] It is worth remarking that this dataset intends to cover engine con-struction and not engine utilization. This means that besides the year of erection there is no other information on the time period over which the engine was actually used, and there is no information on the date at which the engine was scrapped or replaced.

As the authors would admit, the data collected by Kanefsky and Robey are probably affected by some biases in both upward and downward direc-tions. The principal source of overestimation is the double counting of engines that were moved from one place to another, whereas underestima-tion is mainly due to small engines that have left no trace in the records. Notwithstanding these problems (which might result in some revisions in the future), the survey constitutes the most accurate attempt to trace the growth of steam power in Britain over the eighteenth century. In this work, we employ an up-to-date version of this dataset compiled by Kanefsky.[5]

On the basis of the historical outline presented on pp. 167–9, the devel-opment of steam power technology in the eighteenth century can be divided rather naturally into three distinct 'epochs'. The first epoch (1700–33) goes from the invention of the Savery engine to the expiration of the Savery-Newcomen patent. This phase represents the early introduction of the new technology. The second epoch covers the period 1734–74. The final period goes from 1775 (the year of the first successful erection of a Watt engine) to 1800 (the year in which Watt's patent for the separate con-denser expired).

The maps presented in Figure 8.1 provide a preliminary 'impressionistic' view of the geographical (county) distribution of the engines erected in these three periods. Darker (lighter) areas indicate a higher (lower) number of engines. White areas indicate that no engines were erected in that par-ticular county. In addition, map 5 represents the geographical distribution of water-wheels (the 'predominant' power technology of the period) and map 6 illustrates the prevailing level of coal prices in the various counties in (*circa*) 1800 (again, darker areas indicate higher prices, lighter areas rep-resent lower prices, and in this case white areas correspond to missing values).[6]

The spread of steam power technology appears to have been, from the very outset, remarkably wide.[7] Available evidence indicates that it is highly likely that the first Newcomen engine was erected in Cornwall at the Wheal Vor tin mine in 1710. However, because of the high price of coal, Cornwall did not represent the most fertile soil for the diffusion of the new technol-ogy. The erection of the Wheal Vor engine remained a sporadic event and the introduction of Newcomen engines in Cornish mines actually took place only from the 1720s (Rolt and Allen, 1997: 45).

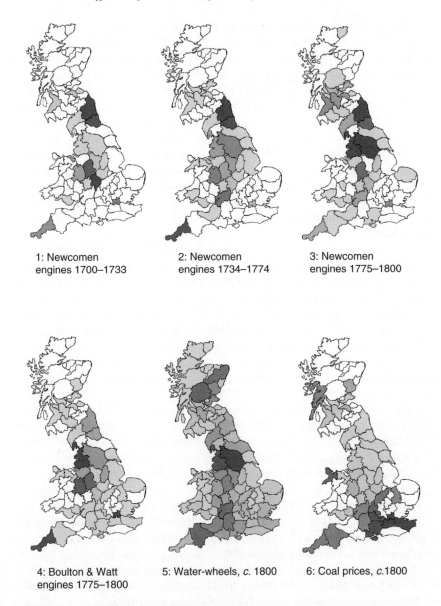

Figure 8.1   *Geographical diffusion of steam technology during the eighteenth century*

Coal mining represented of course a much more receptive environment for the new technology, since the coal would be relatively cheap. The Midlands coalfields (Stafford and Warwickshire) were the first location where Newcomen engines could take firm root. The commercialization of the engine was at first controlled by the Newcomen and Savery partnership. After Savery's death in 1715, a syndicate for the exploitation of the patent rights, the 'Committee of Proprietors of the Invention for Raising Water by Fire' was constituted. The Committee, under the direction of its secretary John Meres, promoted rather successfully the use of Newcomen engines for drainage in various mining areas by means of a network of agents and licensees.[8] Apart from the Midlands, as the map of Figure 8.1 indicates, by 1733, Newcomen engines had been adopted in some numbers in Cornwall and in the coalfields in the North East (Northumberland and Durham).

Overall, during the period of the monopoly of the 'Proprietors' about one hundred Newcomen engines were constructed. As Smith (1978: 12) has aptly remarked, for the time, this must be considered 'by any standards a colossal business achievement'. On the other hand, it should also be noted that historians (see for example, Flinn, 1984: 117) have generally contended that the high level of royalties claimed by the 'Proprietors' (up to £350 a year) hampered the diffusion process in this initial phase.[9] Be this as it may, one has to acknowledge that, under the 'Proprietors', a group of skilled engine-builders emerged, and although (as we have mentioned in the previous section) one of the main merits of Newcomen's invention was its relative easiness of construction and maintenance, in this initial phase, the engine still represented a rather sophisticated piece of equipment and its erection probably called for more than ordinary engineering skills. Thus, the formation and consolidation of this base of engine-building skills presumably represented a critical factor for the successful introduction of the engine in various locations. Among these engineers we may mention Henry Beighton, who worked for the Parrot-Sparrow partnership and compiled a table containing some rules of thumb for the proportions of the various components of the engine; Joseph Hornblower, who supervised the erection of various engines first in the Midlands and then in Cornwall;[10] Samuel Calley, the son of John Calley (the partner of Thomas Newcomen in the invention of the engine); and Marten Triewald, a Swedish engineer who installed various Newcomen engines in the North East and who would erect a (not very successful) Newcomen engine in Sweden at the Dannemora mine.

In the period 1734–74 Newcomen engines continued to be built in mining areas. However as we can we see from map 2, in this phase, steam power also penetrated new locations. This wider spread of the engine was mainly due to its adoption by the iron sector (Shropshire) where it was used to assist water-wheels in blowing coke blast furnaces during drought periods (Hyde, 1977: 69–75). Newcomen engines also began to be constructed in some numbers in Scotland in the counties of the Clyde Valley.[11]

In this second phase, the 'Proprietors' had completely ceased to control the installation of the engines and Newcomen engines were typically erected by local craftsmen, leaving the cylinder, the cylinder bottom and a small number of other critical components to be manufactured by 'specialist' firms and then shipped to the location of the engine. In this respect, it is worth noting that, up to the 1780s, in Britain there existed only four ironworks that could supply cast iron cylinders for steam engines, namely Coalbrookdale and New Willey (in Shropshire), Bersham (in Denbigh) and Carron (Stirling).

The period 1775–1800 is characterized by competition between Watt and Newcomen engines. In this phase, typically textile counties such as Lancashire and Renfrew (cotton) and West Riding (wool) began to resort to some use of steam to power machinery. The main difference in the spread of the two types of engines is that Watt engines appeared capable of achieving some penetration (although in low numbers) in the counties of the South East, an area which appears, by and large, to exclude Newcomen engines.

Table 8.1 reports Moran I statistics for the three periods we are considering. Moran I statistics assess whether a variable displays a tendency to be systematically clustered in space, or, on the contrary, it is randomly spread. Higher values of Moran I statistics indicate stronger degrees of (positive) spatial autocorrelation. In other words, higher values of the statistics mean that counties with relatively high numbers of engines tend to be neighbouring (see Cliff and Ord, 1981: 42–6 for more details on the calculation of the Moran I statistic). Here the statistic was computed using a spatial contiguity matrix indicating whether two counties have borders in common or not. Significance levels have been computed under two different hypotheses: the first one holds that the observations of our variable (number of engines

Table 8.1   Spatial autocorrelation between engines

Type of engine	Period	Number of engines	Moran I statistic	Significance (normal)	Significance (randomized)
Newcomen	1700–33	97	0.167	**	***
Newcomen	1734–74	442	0.124	*	**
Newcomen	1775–1800	616	0.192	***	***
Boulton & Watt	1775–1800	479	0.074		

Notes: *,**,*** indicate significance levels of 10 per cent, 5 per cent and 1 per cent respectively.

installed in each county) are normally distributed, whereas the second one assumes that the realizations of the variable were extracted from one of the possible $n!$ permutations of the n values of the variable over the n locations (counties).

Table 8.1 shows that the Moran I statistic is higher for Newcomen engines than for Watt engines. Notably, in the case of Newcomen engines the coffiecient appears to be significantly different from zero, both when the original variable is assumed to be characterized by a normal distribution and when it is supposed to be generated by an unspecified one (randomized).

On the contrary, the Moran I statistic for Boulton and Watt engines does not turn out to be significant. This seems to indicate that the adoption of Boulton and Watt engines was less susceptible of being conditioned by specific locational factors. This finding may be accounted for by two possible sets of factors acting respectively on the demand and the supply side. On the demand side, given its superior fuel efficiency, it is likely that the adoption of Watt engines was less conditioned by the proximity to cheap coal (this is indeed consistent with the penetration of the Watt engine in the South East of England). Concerning the possible existence of spatial constraints from the supply side, it is worth noting that, apart from the early period of the 'Proprietors', the installation of Newcomen engines was typically in the hands of local millwrights and for this reason, the geographical adoption of the engine could have been limited to areas endowed with the necessary amount of engineering skills. On the contrary, as we shall see, Boulton and Watt instead adopted immediately a much wider horizon in their marketing of steam engines, aiming to serve the entire national market for power.

To compare the speed of the diffusion between counties, we have fitted logistic curves to our data.[12] In particular, we have fixed the saturation level at 100 per cent (which amounts to assuming that all the potential adopters at the end of the diffusion process will have adopted the technology). This allows us to make use of the following log-linear transformation, which can then be easily estimated using ordinary least squares.

$$\log_e\left(\frac{P_t}{1 - P_t}\right) = a + b \cdot t \tag{1}$$

In Equation (1), P_t is equal to the percentage of adopters that, at time (year) t, have erected a steam engine, a is the intercept that defines the position of the logistic curve and the slope parameter b indicates the rate of diffusion (higher values of b indicate a faster diffusion process).

We have calculated the values for P_t from the last observation (cumulative number of engines erected) in our possession (1800), assuming that this final observation corresponds to levels of saturation going from 5 to 99 per cent, adopting steps of 1 per cent. Within this set of estimations we have chosen the one with the best fit (highest R^2). Tables 8.2 and 8.3 give the results, for Newcomen and Watt engines (note that we have performed this exercise only for counties with more than four engines). The table also reports the growth time (Δt) in terms of the time interval needed for moving from 10 per cent to 90 per cent of the final saturation level and the estimated midpoint of the logistic curve. Finally, we have also calculated average compound growth rates for the number of engines constructed in each county (which represents the 'limit' case of a growth rate invariant over time).

Table 8.2 reveals some interesting aspects of the spread of Newcomen engines. Looking at the midpoint values there appears to exist a relatively ordered sequence in the penetration of the engine in various locations. The technology is first adopted in the coal mining areas of the Midlands (Stafford and Warwick), of the North East (Northumberland, Durham) and in Cornwall (copper and tin mining). In a second phase, Newcomen engines are adopted in ironworks (Shropshire). Finally, we have the penetration in typically 'textile' counties, such as West Riding (wool) and Lancashire, where the adoption appears to be characterized by slower diffusion rates. It is interesting to note that Scottish counties (Lanark, Fife and Stirling) display the highest rates of diffusion. This is probably to be explained by the initially delayed penetration of the engine in these counties. Presumably, the establishment of the Carron ironworks (which made use of the cylinder boring machine designed by John Smeaton) in Stirling in 1760 spurred the rapid adoption of steam power in Scottish counties from the early 1760s, triggering a 'catching-up' type of process.[13] Figure 8.2 charts the estimated diffusion paths for a number counties which were particularly intensive users of Newcomen engines.

If we compare Table 8.2 with Table 8.3, the much higher values of the rates of diffusion for Boulton and Watt engines are immediately evident. The average rate of diffusion (b) for Newcomen engines is equal to 0.07, whereas for Watt engines it is equal to 0.26, indicating that the diffusion process of the latter was indeed much faster.[14]

Considering midpoint values, as in the case of Newcomen engines, the adoption of the Watt engine in various locations also seems to have been characterized by a sequential order. First we have Cornwall and Shropshire (where steam engines were mainly used in ironworks), followed by the textile districts of Nottingham and later on of Lancashire and the West Riding. The table also indicates a comparatively slow rate of diffusion of the Watt engine in Northumberland (coal mining), where the cheap price of coal presumably

Table 8.2 Rates of diffusion of atmospheric engines

County	Number of engines	First erected	Growth rate	Saturation point reached in 1800 (%)	R^2	Intercept (a)	Rate of adoption (b)	Growth time (Δt)	Midpoint
Cornwall	75	1710	0.048	91	0.968	−4.150 (0.1589)	0.0761 (0.0033)	57.7	1765
Cumberland	23	1717	0.038	5	0.965	−5.946 (0.1975)	0.0367 (0.0028)	119.8	1879
Derby	62	1717	0.050	68	0.989	−4.078 (0.1133)	0.0564 (0.0018)	78.0	1789
Durham	103	1717	0.056	88	0.953	−3.437 (0.1568)	0.0606 (0.0033)	72.5	1774
Gloucester	49	1735	0.060	96	0.977	−3.297 (0.1434)	0.1008 (0.0035)	43.6	1768
Lancashire	85	1719	0.055	5	0.993	−7.725 (0.0977)	0.0579 (0.0015)	76.0	1853
Leicester	10	1724	0.030	78	0.996	−2.601 (0.0917)	0.0510 (0.0015)	86.1	1775
Middlesex	44	1698	0.037	48	0.975	−3.936 (0.1178)	0.0373 (0.0015)	117.7	1803
Northumberland	163	1718	0.063	83	0.965	−3.745 (0.1240)	0.0605 (0.0027)	72.7	1780
Nottingham	16	1728	0.038	41	0.942	−3.262 (0.2261)	0.0390 (0.0041)	112.7	1812
Shropshire	74	1715	0.051	79	0.976	−3.963 (0.1068)	0.0563 (0.0018)	78.1	1785

Somerset	8	1745	0.037	70	0.983	−1.582 (0.0908)	0.0427 (0.0018)	102.8	1782
Stafford	59	1706	0.043	72	0.952	−3.615 (0.1648)	0.0452 (0.0023)	97.2	1786
Warwick	39	1714	0.043	96	0.834	−1.877 (0.3225)	0.0468 (0.0054)	93.9	1754
Worcester	13	1725	0.034	66	0.892	−2.338 (0.2310)	0.0340 (0.0048)	129.1	1794
West Riding	100	1715	0.054	26	0.986	−5.852 (0.0949)	0.0550 (0.0014)	80.0	1821
North Riding	4	1754	0.029	85	0.894	−1.034 (0.4393)	0.0846 (0.0198)	51.9	1766
Carmarthen	5	1750	0.031	5	0.931	−4.580 (0.0946)	0.0292 (0.0050)	150.7	1907
Flint	19	1715	0.034	96	0.916	−2.079 (0.2237)	0.0554 (0.0051)	79.4	1753
Glamorgan	13	1717	0.031	83	0.939	−2.961 (0.2020)	0.0575 (0.0034)	76.4	1769
Ayr	32	1720	0.043	5	0.937	−6.002 (0.2022)	0.0361 (0.0030)	121.8	1886
Clackmannan	5	1764	0.043	5	0.968	−4.573 (0.1154)	0.0416 (0.0039)	105.7	1874
Dumfries	6	1787	0.127	99	0.993	−1.811 (0.1672)	0.4645 (0.0237)	9.5	1791
East Lothian	6	1720	0.022	5	0.702	−4.845 (0.7303)	0.0171 (0.0105)	257.0	2003
Fife	21	1764	0.083	74	0.850	−2.616 (0.3205)	0.0959 (0.0146)	45.8	1791

Table 8.2 (continued)

County	Number of engines	First erected	Growth rate	Saturation point reached in 1800 (%)	R^2	Intercept (a)	Rate of adoption (b)	Growth time (Δt)	Midpoint
Lanark	26	1760	0.081	24	0.976	−4.467 (0.1438)	0.0883 (0.0048)	49.8	1811
Midlothian	26	1720	0.041	5	0.858	−6.004 (0.2566)	0.0329 (0.0039)	133.4	1902
Renfrew	8	1767	0.061	5	0.969	−5.179 (0.2966)	0.0669 (0.0107)	65.6	1844
Stirling	18	1760	0.071	78	0.926	−2.517 (0.2366)	0.0896 (0.0080)	49.1	1788
West Lothian	9	1764	0.060	7	0.949	−3.693 (0.0792)	0.0274 (0.0027)	160.5	1899

Notes: The growth rate is the average compound growth rate. The logistic trend is estimated using the formula $\log_e[P_t/(1 - P_t)] = a + b \cdot t$. Standard errors are reported in parentheses. Growth time ($\Delta t = \ln 81/b$) is the time interval (in years) for moving from 10 per cent to 90 per cent of the diffusion path. Midpoint $= -(a/b) +$ year in which the first engine was installed in the county.

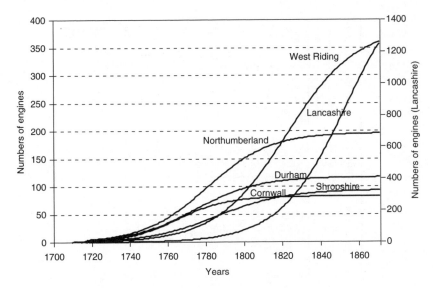

Figure 8.2   Estimated diffusion paths for Newcomen engines

gave some advantage to Newcomen engines with respect to Watt. The estimated diffusion curves for Watt engines in a number of steam-using counties are displayed in Figure 8.3.

The rank correlation coefficient between the total number of Newcomen and Watt engines erected in each county (Spearman's rho) is equal to 0.7, whereas that between the rates of diffusion is equal to 0.53. They are both significant at the 1 per cent level. This finding can be interpreted as indicating that the rates of diffusion and the extent of usage of the two types of engines were affected by a number of common factors.

Our inquiry on the patterns of diffusion reveals that steam engine technology was, from a very early stage, integrated rather successfully into several of the different 'regional production systems' which comprised the British economy during the eighteenth century (see Pollard (1981) for an overview of the distinguishing features of each regional economy). In other words, by the end of the eighteenth century steam technology had already become source of power capable of being used in a wide variety of production processes and in different local contexts.

As mentioned in the previous section, the distinctive feature of the Boulton and Watt engine was its superior fuel economy with respect to the Newcomen. Watt engines, however were normally more expensive, because of their additional components (separate condenser, air pump, and so on) and because their erection required higher engineering standards.

Table 8.3 Rates of diffusion of Boulton and Watt engines

County	Number of engines	First erected	Growth rate	Saturation point reached in 1800 (%)	R^2	Intercept (a)	Rate of adoption (b)	Growth time (Δt)	Midpoint
Cheshire	17	1778	0.125	49	0.983	−3.875 (0.1756)	0.1699 (0.0096)	25.9	1801
Cornwall	56	1777	0.175	99	0.907	−2.798 (0.3673)	0.2848 (0.0285)	15.4	1787
Cumberland	5	1789	0.132	81	0.985	−0.890 (0.1257)	0.2299 (0.0161)	19.1	1793
Durham	18	1791	0.301	91	0.959	−4.088 (0.6223)	0.6387 (0.0776)	6.9	1797
Gloucester	7	1787	0.139	87	0.972	−2.399 (0.1495)	0.3323 (0.0137)	13.2	1794
Lancashire	74	1777	0.188	5	0.984	−7.749 (0.1534)	0.1967 (0.0088)	22.3	1816
Middlesex	77	1776	0.182	85	0.975	−3.930 (0.1106)	0.2125 (0.0067)	20.7	1794
Northumberland	20	1778	0.133	5	0.950	−6.446 (0.3905)	0.1468 (0.0203)	29.9	1822
Nottingham	18	1786	0.198	99	0.940	−1.958 (0.3065)	0.4402 (0.0373)	10.0	1790

Shropshire	44	1776	0.157	99	0.966	-3.196 (0.2332)	0.2999 (0.0168)	14.7	1787
Stafford	38	1775	0.144	95	0.975	-3.123 (0.2104)	0.2146 (0.0116)	20.5	1790
Warwick	11	1777	0.101	8	0.965	-4.866 (0.1694)	0.1026 (0.0093)	42.8	1824
West Riding	22	1782	0.167	27	0.968	-4.283 (0.1929)	0.1851 (0.0141)	23.7	1805
East Riding	6	1779	0.081	81	0.957	-1.933 (0.1530)	0.1784 (0.0192)	24.6	1790

Notes: See Table 8.2.

181

On the basis of the available data on the fuel consumption of the two types of engines and of their capital costs, von Tunzelmann (1978, ch. 4) calculated the threshold levels of the price of coal at which it would have been convenient for a fully rational entrepreneur to adopt a Boulton and Watt engine. Figures 8.4 and 8.5 contain scatter diagrams showing the relation between price of coal and the share of Watt engines in the total number of engines erected in the county during the period 1775–1800. We have also plotted the threshold levels as calculated by von Tunzelmann (1978). Note that there are two threshold levels in each diagram: the first (and lower) one (I) indicates the threshold for a new engine, the second one (II), the threshold for the replacement of an existing Newcomen engine with a new Boulton and Watt one.[15] Figure 8.4 considers the case of reciprocating engines (where the gap in fuel efficiency between the Newcomen and Watt engines was larger), whereas Figure 8.5 displays the scatter diagram for rotary engines. It is important to remark that these threshold levels are computed for best-practice techniques.

Figures 8.4 and 8.5 suggest that the price of coal was indeed one of the major determinants (acting on the demand side) dictating the adoption of a Watt *vis-à-vis* a Newcomen engine. In other words, an interpretation of the patterns of adoption of steam engine in terms of the threshold model is surely consistent with some broad features of the diffusion process. However, considering that most counties are situated in what seems to be

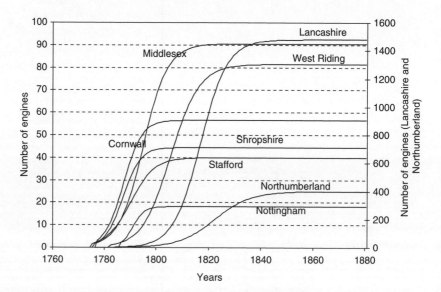

Figure 8.3   Estimated diffusion paths for Watt engines

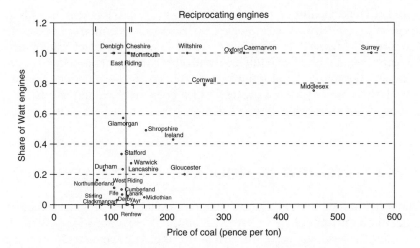

Figure 8.4   Price of coal and share of Watt reciprocating engines

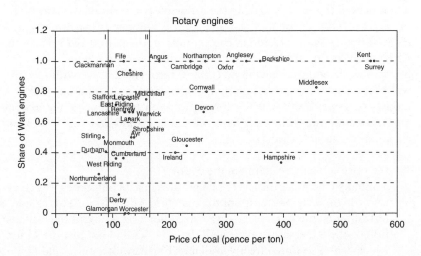

Figure 8.5   Price of coal and share of Watt rotary engines

a 'transitional' state, it is clear that non-economic factors, possibly in combination with information delays and 'entrepreneurial failures', also affected
the geographical spread of steam power technology.[16] In this respect, it must
be recognized that the adoption of a new technology involves much more
than the assessment of the direct costs and benefits between different pieces
of equipment as is assumed in threshold view of the diffusion process, but is

likely to reflect a host of other factors, such as the development of skills in operating the various technologies, the expectations concerning possible future technological developments and the fit of the new technology with complementary pieces of equipment and other contingent production activities. All this makes the adoption of new technologies the outcome of a particularly complex decision process, which goes well beyond the relatively straightforward profitability calculation based on current factor prices (Gold, 1980).

AN ECONOMETRIC MODEL OF ENGINE ADOPTION

In order to shed some additional light on the factors driving the spread of steam power technology we estimate 'adoption' equations for eighteenth century steam engines. We focus on the late eighteenth century (1775–1800) and estimate two distinct models for Newcomen and Watt engines. Clearly, the aim is to check whether there were noteworthy differences in the factors driving the diffusion processes of the two types of engines. Our dependent variable is the number of steam engines (Newcomen or Watt) erected in each county in the period 1775–1800. In both cases, the distribution of the variables is skewed, with a non-negligible number of counties having no (that is, zero) engines. Accordingly, we will make use of negative binomial regressions for estimating the two models (Greene, 2000: 880–93; for a thorough treatment of regression analysis techniques with count data, see Cameron and Trivedi, 1998). Our explanatory variables are:

1. the price of coal prevailing in the county;
2. a dummy indicating the level of coal prices in a dichotomous way (that is low/high, with low being approximately less than 14 s.). This characterization of the price of coal variable allows us to use in the estimation of the regression equation all the counties and not just the 41 for which coal prices are directly available. Furthermore, one could argue that the dummy specification is a more appropriate representation of 'threshold' behaviour. The dummy variable has been constructed considering the studies of the coal mining industry of Flinn (1984), von Tunzelmann (1986) and Turnbull (1987);
3. the number of water-wheels, which can be considered as a proxy for the demand for power (note that in some applications such as ironworks and textiles, steam engines were initially used to assist the operation of water-wheels during drought periods);
4. the number of steam engines erected in the previous period (that is

1734–74) which captures, admittedly in a rough way, both the familiarity of potential users with steam technology and the (possibly related) level of 'mechanical skills' in the county in question;
5. the number of blast furnaces in operation existing in the county *c*. 1800;
6. the number of cotton mills existing in the county *c*. 1800;
7. the number of woollen mills existing in the county *c*. 1800.

The last three variables are included in order to assess the influence of industries (ironworks and textiles) that were among the most intensive users of steam power. A complete description of the sources and the construction of the variables used is given in the Appendix.

Admittedly, our set of explanatory variables is far from covering all the potential factors affecting the diffusion of steam technology in the period in question. In particular, our variables consider mainly factors acting on the demand side. Coal prices reflect the cost of a unit of power for the adopter of a steam engine. However this coefficient can also reflect the use of the steam engine in coal mines (as in coal mining areas coal was cheap). Similarly, the number of water-wheels is a proxy for the overall demand of power existing in the county, but, at the same time, the variable can also capture some 'substitution' or 'complementarity' effects between steam and water power. The sectoral variables (number of blast furnaces, number of cotton mills, number of woollen mills), indicating the size of different branches of economic activities in various counties, are obviously aimed at accounting for the different (steam) power requirements of a number of application sectors. Note that our coverage of application sectors cannot by any means considered as exhaustive. Lack of suitable data has prevented us from estimating for a sufficient number of counties the size of a number of sectors which were very intensive users of steam power, such as mining, food and drink (breweries) and waterworks and canals. As already mentioned, the variable 'engines erected in the previous period (1734–74)' aims at capturing the degree of familiarity (of both adopters and suppliers) with steam technology extant in each county. In this sense the variable controls for a mix of effects operating both on the supply and on the demand side.

It is fair to say that our model neglects the possible 'proactive' role played by the suppliers of the technology in the diffusion process. As we have already mentioned, the high rates of diffusion for Watt engines estimated in Table 8.3 were plausibly not only determined by the superior fuel efficiency of the Watt engines, but also by the effectiveness of Boulton and Watt's organization of steam engine production and marketing techniques. From the very outset, Boulton and Watt wanted to establish themselves as a leading 'national' producer of steam engines.[17] Instead, the construction of Newcomen engines was mainly undertaken by local manufactures with narrower and less ambitious business horizons.[18]

In this respect, Roll (1930) and Dickinson (1936) stressed the critical role played by Boulton's entrepreneurial and marketing abilities for the success of the partnership.[19] Boulton's efforts ensured that Watt engines were quickly adopted in a wide range of industrial applications, which before had not made much use of steam power (breweries, textiles, and so on). For example, the erection of the famous Albion Mills in London is frequently pointed out as an example of a successful marketing strategy which succeeded in triggering the interest in steam power of many industrialists (in particular, breweries) in the London area.[20] Another initiative aimed at broadening the use of steam technology was the publication by Boulton and Watt of small technical booklets (of course only reserved for their customers) providing detailed descriptions of the procedures for erecting and operating their engines. In this way, 'distant' customers could hopefully be able to cope with minor technical difficulties without the assistance of Boulton and Watt's men.

Furthermore, Boulton and Watt successfully established standard units of measure for both the fuel efficiency (duty) and the power (horsepower) of steam engines. Note that the establishment of a standardized unit of power was an event not only of technically, but especially of economic significance (perhaps one of the main determinants of the successful adoption of the engine in various manufacturing applications). The horsepower unit permitted industrialists to have a rather reliable assessment of their power requirements and it also permitted a rough, but rather effective, cost-benefit analysis of the adoption of various power sources. Rules of thumb soon came into common usage for expressing the power requirements of a number of industrial processes (for example in cotton spinning 1 horsepower was typically supposed to drive 100 spindles).

From these considerations it is clear that our econometric exercise can hope to provide just a partial appraisal of the determinants of the usage of steam technology in the late eighteenth century. Hence, the results ought to be regarded with care, taking into account the possible influence of factors not included in our set of explanatory variables.

Tables 8.4 and 8.5 give the results of the estimates for Newcomen engines. Table 8.4 includes all the specifications with the coal dummy variable (these regressions include all observations in our sample), whereas Table 8.5 covers the specifications employing the price of coal variable (these regressions refers to a more restricted sample of 41 counties). We have estimated the coefficients considering two different forms of the negative binomial density function. In the first case we have assumed that the negative binomial density function has mean equal to μ and variance

Table 8.4 'Adoption' equations for Newcomen engines, 1775–1800

Model	(I)		(II)		(III)		(IV)	
Type	NB 2	NB 1	NB 2	NB 1	NB 2	NB 1	NB 2	NB 1
Number of counties	84	84	84	84	84	84	84	84
Constant	1.122***	1.328***	0.270	0.633**	1.497***	1.855***	1.390**	1.647***
	(0.334)	(0.261)	(0.363)	(0.273)	(0.463)	(0.273)	(0.285)	(0.218)
Dummy coal	−1.919***	−1.740***			−2.021***	−1.901***	−1.900***	−1.613***
	(0.359)	(0.333)			(0.436)	(0.346)	(0.369)	(0.335)
Water-wheels	0.003	0.004**	0.003	0.002	0.008**	0.004**		
	(0.002)	(0.002)	(0.003)	(0.002)	(0.003)	(0.002)		
Engines	0.079***	0.035***	0.078***	0.046***			0.087***	0.037***
	(0.021)	(0.004)	(0.028)	(0.005)			(0.022)	(0.004)
Blast furnaces	−0.005	0.032*	0.063	0.068***	0.008	0.035	0.011	0.045***
	(0.043)	(0.016)	(0.059)	(0.017)	(0.046)	(0.023)	(0.045)	(0.015)
Cotton mills	0.003	0.004*	0.015	0.010***	−0.002	0.005	0.008	0.009***
	(0.008)	(0.003)	(0.014)	(0.003)	(0.010)	(0.003)	(0.008)	(0.002)
Wool mills	−0.008	−0.015*	−0.014	−0.008	−0.018	−0.011	−0.001	0.002
	(0.012)	(0.009)	(0.013)	(0.009)	(0.015)	(0.009)	(0.011)	(0.004)
α	1.474***		2.586***		2.795***		1.572***	
	(0.391)		(0.603)		(0.630)		(0.403)	
δ		6.268***		9.828***		13.744***		7.331***
		(1.8)		(2.748)		(3.946)		(2.051)
Log likelihood	−172.122	−159.629	−184.825	−173.546	−186.199	−173.969	−173.160	−162.241
Pseudo R^2	0.154	0.215	0.091	0.147	0.084	0.144	0.148	0.202

Notes: Negative binomial estimations. Standard errors in brackets. *, **, *** indicate significance levels of 10, 5 and 1 per cent. The α and δ statistic verify the existence of 'overdispersion' (χ^2 test).

Table 8.5 'Adoption' equations for Newcomen engines, 1775–1800

Model	(I)		(II)		(III)	
Type	NB 2	NB 1	NB 2	NB 1	NB 2	NB 1
Number of counties	41	41	41	41	41	41
Constant	1.817***	2.442***	1.962***	2.509***	2.933***	3.423
	(0.463)	(0.427)	(0.405)	(0.422)	(0.455)	(0.464)
Coal price	−0.003**	−0.007***	−0.003**	−0.006***	−0.004**	−0.008***
	(0.002)	(0.002)	(0.002)	(0.002)	(0.002)	(0.003)
Water-wheels	0.002	0.003*				
	(0.003)	(0.002)				
Engines	0.047***	0.028***	0.049***	0.031***		
	(0.016)	(0.005)	(0.016)	(0.005)		
Blast furnaces	0.047	0.039**	0.059	0.050***	0.065	0.049**
	(0.042)	(0.017)	(0.040)	(0.015)	(0.048)	(0.020)
Cotton mills	0.010	0.006**	0.012*	0.010***	0.011	0.010**
	(0.008)	(0.003)	(0.007)	(0.002)	(0.008)	(0.002)
Wool mills	−0.015	−0.013	−0.011	−0.001	−0.009	−0.001
	(0.011)	(0.008)	(0.009)	(0.004)	(0.013)	(0.006)
Log likelihood	−126.331	−113.44	−126.515	−115.116	−134.141	−125.594
α	1.190***		1.214***		2.019***	
	(0.359)		(0.362)		(0.520)	
δ		6.970***		8.124***		17.812***
		(2.301)		(2.626)		(5.853)
Pseudo R^2	0.096	0.188	0.095	0.176	0.040	0.101

Notes: See Table 8.4.

equal to $\mu(1 + \alpha\mu)$. Cameron and Trivedi (1998: 62) refer to this model as 'NB 2'. In the second case we have assumed a density function with mean equal to μ and variance equal to $\mu(1 + \delta)$. This case is termed 'NB 1' by Cameron and Trivedi (1998: 62). It is possible to test for the actual existence of 'overdispersion' (that is, that the variance is larger than the mean) by verifying that α or δ are different from zero. In our case this was done by means of a likelihood ratio test (Cameron and Trivedi, 1998: 77–8).

In all specifications, α and δ are significantly different from zero, confirming the existence of overdispersion and supporting our choice of negative binomial estimations. In this respect, one can note that the existence of overdispersion points to the fact that the data exhibit a higher degree of cross-sectional heterogeneity (that is clustering in counties with 'high' or 'low' number of engines), than in the case of a spatially homogeneous Poisson process.[21] In other words, the existence of overdispersion points to a pattern of spatial clustering among counties in terms of their extent of steam usage that goes beyond what can be accounted for by our set of explanatory variables. Furthermore, one could actually suggest that this cross-sectional heterogeneity reveals the existence of county-specific 'absorptive capabilities' affecting the spread of steam technology.

The coefficient for the coal dummy variable is significant with a negative sign in all the specifications in which it is included. Similarly, the price of coal (whose inclusion restricts the sample to 41 counties) is also negative and significant. These results confirm rather clearly that high coal prices deterred the adoption of Newcomen engines.

The coefficient for the variable 'engines erected in the previous period' is positive and significant in all specifications, showing the positive influence of a certain degree of 'previous' familiarity with steam technology.

The coefficient for water-wheels is significant (with a positive sign), only in the NB1 type of model. Similarly, also the sectoral variables turn out to be significant only in NB1 type of models. In this respect, one may note that NB1 models seems to display consistently a better 'fit' to the data, at least, so far as this is reflected in the 'pseudo R^2'.

The coefficient for the blast furnaces appears to be higher than the one for cotton mills, indicating a stronger relationship between iron manufacturing and the adoption of Newcomen engines. Unfortunately, lack of suitable data has prevented us from assessing the impact of the main sector of application of the Newcomen engine, coal mining.

This result probably reflects the different degree of familiarity that these user sectors had with the Newcomen engine. Newcomen engines were successfully adopted in ironworks from the early 1740s. Instead they had begun to be used to drive cotton machinery only from the 1780s. In general, the motion they delivered was rather unsteady and it was not particularly suited for powering textile machinery (Hills, 1970: 141–3). Some ingenious technical solutions that could mitigate this problem were introduced in the early 1790s by Francis Thompson and Bateman and Sherrat for the Newcomen engines installed in cotton mills in Lancashire and Nottinghamshire (Hills, 1970: 147–8; see also Frenken and Nuvolari, 2004). Finally, it is worth noting that the adoption of Newcomen engines in ironworks and in cotton mills in the period we are considering was limited by the competition of Watt engines.

The coefficient of the wool mills variable is not significant (with the only exception of regression I (NB1) in Table 8.4 where it has a negative sign). This can be accounted for by the fact that the transition to steam power mechanization in the wool textile industry (which was concentrated in Yorkshire (West Riding) and in the West of England) was much slower than in cotton. Furthermore, in this industry, the diffusion of steam technology proceeded at two very different paces in the two areas. In the West Riding, atmospheric returning engines were rapidly and rather successfully adopted for power carding and spinning machines (jennies). Table 8.2 indicates that about 100 engines were installed in the West Riding by 1800. Instead in the other wool regions of the West of England (Gloucester, Wiltshire) and of Scotland, steam power technology was introduced very slowly (Jenkins and Ponting, 1982: 50–6). The combined effect of these two contrasting patterns of adoption can help explain why the coefficient for wool mills is not significant in the majority of the specifications.

Tables 8.6 and 8.7 contain the results of the set of regressions having the number of Watt engines as dependent variable. As in the case of Newcomen engines, the tests on α and δ confirm the presence of overdispersion, upholding our choice of negative binomial estimations.

The coal dummy is significant with a negative sign in three specifications (Model I (NB 2), Model III (NB 1) and Model IV (NB 2)). It is worth noting that the (negative) coefficient is lower than in the Newcomen case. In our interpretation, rather than reflecting a direct impact of coal price on the adoption of Watt engines, this result is due to the fact that a number of counties with high levels of coal prices were also 'peripheral' or 'rural' counties with low demand for steam power. In particular, this is true for the 'northern' Scottish counties. In fact, when the model is specified in terms of coal prices (as we have said, this reduces the sample to 41 counties, centred essentially on 'industrial' counties (North of England, Wales, South of Scotland), see Appendix), the coal price coefficient appears to be generally positive and significant, providing support for the idea that high coal prices tend to enhance the adoption of Boulton and Watt engine, on account of their superior fuel efficiency.

Table 8.6 *'Adoption' equations for Watt engines, 1775–1800*

Model	(I)		(II)		(III)		(IV)	
Type	NB 2	NB 1	NB 2	NB 1	NB 2	NB 1	NB 2	NB 1
Number of counties	84	84	84	84	84	84	84	84
Constant	0.524	0.970***	0.036	0.616**	1.082*	1.420***	0.608	1.162***
	(0.469)	(0.366)	(0.399)	(0.296)	(0.628)	(0.337)	(0.388)	(0.318)
Dummy coal	−0.831*	−0.555			−0.341	−0.934***	−0.821*	−0.541
	(0.466)	(0.355)			(0.555)	(0.328)	(0.463)	(0.357)
Water-wheels	0.001	0.002	0.001	0.002	0.004	0.003		
	(0.003)	(0.002)	(0.003)	(0.002)	(0.004)	(0.002)		
Engines	0.113***	0.033***	0.101***	0.038***			0.113***	0.034***
	(0.028)	(0.007)	(0.027)	(0.005)			(0.028)	(0.006)
Blast furnaces	0.0002	0.061***	0.044	0.076***	0.054	0.060**	0.006	0.066***
	(0.055)	(0.022)	(0.052)	(0.019)	(0.057)	(0.026)	(0.052)	(0.021)
Cotton mills	0.008	0.011***	0.015	0.013***	0.008	0.010***	0.009	0.013***
	(0.010)	(0.003)	(0.011)	(0.003)	(0.012)	(0.004)	(0.009)	(0.002)
Wool mills	0.002	−0.016	0.009	−0.016	−0.011	−0.014	0.003	−0.006
	(0.014)	(0.011)	(0.014)	(0.011)	(0.016)	(0.011)	(0.014)	(0.006)
α	2.351***		2.452***		4.165***		2.346***	
	(0.516)		(0.542)		(0.821)		(0.515)	
δ		10.805***		10.457***		14.941***		10.916***
		(3.076)		(2.956)		(4.350)		(3.095)
Log likelihood	−166.275	−164.164	−167.919	−165.364	−181.911	−170.660	−166.329	−164.754
Pseudo R^2	0.114	0.125	0.105	0.119	0.031	0.090	0.114	0.122

Notes: See Table 8.4.

Table 8.7 'Adoption' equation for Boulton and Watt engines, 1775–1800

Model	(I)		(II)		(III)	
Type	NB 2	NB 1	NB 2	NB 1	NB 2	NB 1
Number of counties	41	41	41	41	41	41
Constant	0.794*	1.111***	0.554	1.053**	1.502***	1.918***
	(0.426)	(0.426)	(0.391)	(0.415)	(0.436)	(0.378)
Coal price	0.003**	0.002*	0.003**	0.002*	0.002	0.0004
	(0.001)	(0.001)	(0.001)	(0.001)	(0.002)	(0.001)
Water-wheels	−0.003	−0.001				
	(0.002)	(0.002)				
Engines	0.046***	0.033***	0.044***	0.032***		
	(0.011)	(0.006)	(0.011)	(0.006)		
Blast furnaces	0.076**	0.060***	0.058**	0.058***	0.064*	0.057**
	(0.034)	(0.018)	(0.030)	(0.018)	(0.034)	(0.022)
Cotton mills	0.017***	0.014***	0.014***	0.013***	0.013**	0.012***
	(0.006)	(0.003)	(0.005)	(0.002)	(0.006)	(0.003)
Wool mills	0.005	−0.003	0.0004	−0.007	−0.006	−0.004
	(0.010)	(0.009)	(0.009)	(0.006)	(0.010)	(0.006)
α	0.854***		0.891***		1.479***	
	(0.221)		(0.227)		(0.329)	
δ		7.847***		7.948***		13.339***
		(2.338)		(2.363)		(3.937)
Log likelihood	−121.9162	−123.5604	−122.6542	−123.6762	−132.7414	−131.1648
Pseudo R^2	0.1154	0.1035	0.1101	0.1027	0.0369	0.0483

Notes: See Table 8.4.

The coefficient for the variable 'engines erected during the previous period' is positive and significant in all specifications (as it was for Newcomen engines). The coefficient for the number of water-wheels, instead, is never significant.

Turning our attention to the role of application sectors, Tables 8.6 and 8.7, in a number of specifications, report a positive and significant sign for the number of cotton mills and the number of blast furnaces. (In Table 8.6 the sectoral variables are significant only in NB1 regressions, as in the case of Newcomen engines, the NB1 model is characterized by a better fit as measured by the 'pseudo R^2'). Notably, the size of these coefficients is similar to the ones reported for Newcomen engines. This finding is indeed fully in line with historical accounts which pointed out that ironworks and cotton mills were among the first intensive users of the Watt engines. However, it should be noted that in the case of Watt engines as well, our adoption equations do not include a number of application sectors which were intensive users of these engines such as (non-coal) mining ventures, breweries, and so on, and that, for this reason, the estimates of the impact of application sectors should be considered with care. Finally, as in the case of the Newcomen engines, the coefficient for wool mills is not significant.

CONCLUDING REMARKS

In this chapter we have provided a reconstruction of the patterns of diffusion and adoption of steam engine technology during the eighteenth century. Our findings indicate that the level of coal prices was indeed one of the major determinants of the distinctive patterns of adoption of Newcomen and Watt engines, giving further support to the previous studies of von Tunzelmann (1978) and Kanefsky (1979). However, it is also clear that, together with the level of coal prices, a number of other factors were also at work. In this respect, it must be also acknowledged that the design of the engine did not only determine its fuel efficiency, but also the quality of the power delivered (smoothness and regularity of motion, susceptibility to breakages, and so on). Hence, particular types of engines turned out to better suited for particular applications (in some cases, despite their level of fuel efficiency). This issue is examined more in detail in Frenken and Nuvolari (2004).

Our diffusion study has also revealed that steam engine technology was, from a very early stage, integrated rather successfully into different regional production systems of the eighteenth-century British economy. However, our econometric analysis has also indicated that the regional patterns of adoption displayed considerable diversity reflecting the influence of location factors such as the price of coal and the productive structure of the various counties, but, also of more complex and idiosyncratic factors impinging on the absorptive capabilities of individual counties. In a more general perspective, this finding confirms the need of taking regional differences properly into account when examining the diffusion of new technologies during the British industrial revolution (Hudson, 1989).

These considerations also provide some indications for further research. As noted by Dosi:

> [T]he 'logistic curves' approaches to technological diffusion . . . show the same descriptive usefulness as well the same limitations of the epidemic curves (or, for that matter, probability models) to which they are formally similar: they show the pattern of diffusion of, say cholera, and they can also relate it to some broad environmental factors, such as the conditions of hygiene of a town, the reproduction time of bacteria, etc. but they cannot explain *why* some people get it and other do not, which relates to the immunological mechanisms of human bodies, the precise ways bacteria are transmitted, and so on. (Dosi, 1984: 286, italics in the text)

Thus, the reconstruction of the patterns of technological diffusion needs to be supplemented by further research on the 'microbiology' of the adoption process. In this respect, it would be wrong to assume that the diffusion of Newcomen and Watt engines proceeded neatly along 'equilibrium' paths. The available evidence on individual adoption decisions reveals that at the county level, the process of diffusion was driven by an 'epidemic' information spread. For example, Boulton and Watt frequently asked their 'first' customers in different counties to let potential buyers inspect the engines they had just installed (Hills, 1970: 156 and 158). Furthermore, one should also consider the 'proactive' role played by the suppliers of the new technology. As a consequence, the high rates of diffusion of Watt engines estimated in Table 8.3 are not simply determined by the superior fuel efficiency of the Watt engine, but they also reflect the effectiveness of Boulton and Watt's organization of steam engine production and marketing techniques. Boulton and Watt aimed immediately at establishing themselves as a 'national' producer of steam engines. Instead, in the period 1775–1800, the construction of atmospheric engines was mainly in the hands of local manufacturers with 'narrower' horizons. The wider spread of Watt engines should be also considered in this light. In this respect, Dickinson (1936) and Roll (1930) emphasized Boulton's entrepreneurial and marketing abilities, which ensured that steam power, in the form of the Watt engine, was quickly adopted in a wide range of industrial applications (for example the food industry especially breweries, textiles, and so on). Overall, the early diffusion process of steam technology in each county appears to have been driven by a complex interplay of factors (resource prices and availability, information delays, entrepreneurial failures) acting contextually both on the user's and the supplier's side. On theoretical grounds, one could consider this proposed interpretation (which, of course, needs to be corroborated by further research) as broadly consistent with 'evolutionary' types of diffusion models, where patterns of technological diffusion are seen as the emerging outcome of micro-processes of technological learning and market selection among boundedly rational agents (Silverberg *et al.*, 1988).

APPENDIX: SOURCES AND CONSTRUCTION OF THE DATA

Number of Steam Engines (Newcomen ('atmospheric') and Boulton & Watt) Installed During the Period 1775–1800 and Number of Engines Installed in the Period 1734–74

Data taken from the updated version of the Kanefsky and Robey (1980) list.

Price of Coal, *c.* 1800

Data taken from von Tunzelmann (1978: 148). The 41 counties for which coal prices were available are:

Cornwall, Devon, Wiltshire, Hampshire, Berkshire, Surrey, Middlesex (London), Kent, Cambridge, Northampton, Oxford, Leicester, Warwick, Worcester, Gloucester, Monmouth, Glamorgan, Shropshire, Stafford, Anglesey, Caernarvon, Denbigh, Cheshire, Derby, Nottingham, Lancashire, East Riding, West Riding, North Riding, Durham, Northumberland, Cumberland, Ayr, Renfrew, Lanark, Stirling, Argyll, Clackmannan, Midlothian, Fife, Angus.

Coal Dummy, *c.* 1800

The variable distinguishes between 'cheap' and 'dear' coal counties. Counties with coal prices higher than 14 s. per ton are considered as having a 'high' price of coal. The counties have assigned on the basis of the price list in von Tunzelmann (1978: 148) and of the maps and discussion of Flinn (1984), von Tunzelmann (1986) and Turnbull (1987).

Low coal price counties
Cheshire, Cumberland, Derby, Durham, Lancashire, Leicester, Monmouth, Northumberland, Nottingham, Shropshire, Stafford, Warwick, Worcester,

West Riding, East Riding, Carmarthen, Denbigh, Flint, Glamorgan, Pembroke, Angus, Ayr, Berwick. Clackmannan, Dunbarton, East Lothian, Fife, Kinross, Lanark, Midlothian, Renfrew, Stirling, West Lothian.

High coal price counties
Bedford, Berkshire, Buckingham, Cambridge, Cornwall, Devon, Dorset, Essex, Gloucester, Hampshire, Hereford, Hertford, Huntingdon, Kent, Lincoln, Middlesex (London), Norfolk, Northampton, Oxford, Rutland, Somerset, Suffolk, Surrey, Sussex, Westmorland, Wiltshire, North Riding, Anglesey, Brecknock, Caernarvon, Cardigan, Merioneth, Montgomery, Radnor, Aberdeen, Argyll, Banff, Caithness, Dumfries, Inverness, Kincardine, Kirkcudbright, Moray, Nairn, Peebles, Perth, Ross and Cromarty, Roxburgh, Selkirk, Sutherland, Wigtown.

Water-wheels, *c.*1800

Data taken from Kanefsky (1979: 215–16). The data have been constructed on the basis of contemporary maps (that is they are presumably likely to underestimate the actual figures). For more details, see Kanefsky (1979).

Blast Furnaces, *c.*1800

Data taken from Scrivenor (1854). The original source is government survey after the proposal of a tax on coal. The data refer to the year 1796.

Cotton Mills, *c.* 1800

Data taken from Chapman (1970: 257–66). Chapman's figures are based on insurance records and they mostly refer to the year 1795. For Lancashire we have estimated a figure of 204 mills, which is based on the assumption that the county had 50 per cent of large mills (types B and C) and 50 per cent of type A (that is small) mills. This is in line with the considerations contained in Chapman's paper.

Wool Mills, *c.* 1800

Data taken from Jenkins and Ponting (1982, pp. 34–38). The data refer to the year 1800. When more detailed information was lacking, an equal share of wool mills was assigned to the counties in the wool regions for which Jenkins and Ponting provide figures for the number of wool mills.

ACKNOWLEDGEMENTS

We would like to thank John W. Kanefsky for providing us with the updated version of his dataset of British steam engines. We are also grateful to Carolina Castaldi, Nicoletta Corrocher, Roberto Fontana, Koen Frenken, Francesco Lissoni and Laura Magazzini for helpful discussions. The usual disclaimers apply.

NOTES

1. For this reason, Newcomen and Savery engines were also commonly termed 'atmospheric' engines.
2. A number of Newcomen engines were successfully used to raise water over a water-wheel which, in turn, delivered rotary motion for factory machinery. This type of engine was usually called a 'returning engine'. One major limitation of this engine was that the inefficiency of the water-wheel was combined with the inefficiency of the engine. See Hills (1989: 49).
3. See Kanefsky (1979) for a detailed account of the construction of the database.
4. Other information available for some of the engines are the maker, the cylinder size and the horsepower.
5. The list originally compiled by Kanefsky and Robey contained a total of 2191 steam engines, the new updated dataset contains 2279 engines. The updated version of the list has been kindly provided to us by John Kanefsky. Concerning Watt engines, the updated list by Kanefsky contains 479 engines. Tann (1988) on the basis of a careful examination of the Boulton and Watt papers considers this total too high. Her estimation of the engines constructed by Boulton and Watt by 1800 is 449. In this work, mainly for sake of convenience, we have utilized Kanefsky's list without attempting corrections.
6. The source for the number of water-wheels is Kanefsky (1979: 215–16) and for coal prices von Tunzelmann (1978: 148). For more details on the sources of the data used in this chapter, see Appendix.
7. Note that maps 1, 2 and 3 show the distribution of Newcomen and Savery engines considered together. As a consequence, a more precise definition would be 'atmospheric engines'. Given the relatively small number of Savery engines installed, the results of our study are not affected by ignoring this distinction.
8. The most active licensee of the 'Proprietors' was the partnership formed by Stonier Parrot and George Sparrow who were engaged in the erection of more than 15 Newcomen engines. According to Flinn (1984: 120), the high number of engines erected in Warwick and Stafford (far in excess of the two counties' share in British coal production) is to be accounted for by the fact this was the 'home stronghold' of the Parrot–Sparrow partnership. For an account of the activities of Stonier Parrot, see Rowlands (1969).
9. Kanefsky's data provide some quantitative support for this view. From 1710 to 1733, 95 Savery-Newcomen engines were constructed. This is approximately equal to four engines erected per year. In the period 1734–1774, instead, 442 engines were built, corresponding to 11 engines per year.
10. Joseph Hornblower would decide to settle definitely in Cornwall. He was the grandfather of Jonathan, the inventor of the compound engine.
11. For an account of these cases of early installation of Newcomen engines in Scotland, see Hills (2002: 297).
12. Note that here we are not interested primarily in the relative virtues of various types of S curves for the estimation of diffusion process (as one would be when engaged in a forecasting type of exercise). Following Griliches (1957), we estimate logistic trends as

'summary devices' for comparing the rate of diffusion across counties. In other words, we are more willing to accept some loss of fit in order to get results that are easily comparable.

13. In the late 1760s and 1770s, Watt himself was involved in the installation of several Newcomen engines in Scotland. The erection of these engines provided Watt, who was until then acquainted only with experimental models, with a good deal of practical experience with the problems related with the installation and operation of full scale engines (Hills, 2002: 358).

14. As a term of comparison the rate of diffusion of the high pressure expansive engine in Cornwall estimated by von Tunzelmann (1978: 258) in the early nineteenth century is equal to 0.25. Von Tunzelmann considers this as a case of a relatively fast diffusion process.

15. The threshold prices calculated by von Tunzelmann are, in case of rotary engines, 7s. 10d. for installation of a new engine and 14s. for replacement, in case of reciprocating engines 5s. 10d. for installation and 11s. 3d. for replacement, see von Tunzelmann (1978: 76–7).

16. This was also the speculative conclusion reached by von Tunzelmann (1978, ch. 4).

17. In a famous letter to Watt (7 February 1769), Boulton, declining the offer of Watt and Roebuck (the first partner of Watt) of becoming the licensee of the Watt engine in three counties, wrote: '. . . I was excited by two motives to offer you my assistance which were love of you and love of a money-getting ingenious project. I presumed that your engine would require money, very accurate workmanship and extensive correspondence to make it turn to best advantage, and that the best means of keeping up the reputation and doing the invention justice would be to keep the executive part out of the hands of the multitude of empirical engineers, who from ignorance, want of experience and want of necessary convenience would be very liable to produce bad and inaccurate workmanship; all of which deficiencies would affect the reputation of the invention. To remedy which and produce the most profit, my idea was to settle a manufactory near to my own by the side of our canal where I would erect all the conveniences necessary for the completion of engines and from which manufactory we would serve all the world with engines of all sizes. By these means and your assistance we could engage and instruct some excellent workmen (with more excellent tools that would be worth any man's while to procure for one single engine) could execute the invention 20 per cent cheaper than it would be otherwise executed, and with a great difference of accuracy as there is between the blacksmith and the mathematical instrument maker. *It would not be worth my while to make for three counties only, but I find it very well worth my while to make for all the world'* (quoted in Dickinson and Jenkins, 1927: 30–1, italics added).

18. For an account of the activities of local producers of atmospheric engines in Lancashire in the second half of the eighteenth century, see Musson and Robinson (1969: 393–426).

19. In his *Memoir* of Matthew Boulton written in 1809, Watt stressed the role played by Boulton's entrepreneurial abilities (and by his extensive network of acquaintances) for the successful development of the engine partnership: 'Boulton . . . possessed in a high degree the faculty of rendering any new invention of his own or others useful to the publick, by organizing and arranging the processes by which it could be carried on, as well as promoting the sale by his own exertions and by his numerous friends and correspondents' (cited in Dickinson, 1936: 195–6).

20. The engines constructed for the Albion Mills were among the first rotary double acting engines constructed by Boulton and Watt. The choice of a plant of the almost unprecedented size of the Albion Mills was meant to attract the maximum of attention towards the new engine. From a strictly economic point of view the undertaking was not successful, however, according to many contemporaries, following the 'mechanical' success of the mill, double-acting rotary engines were adopted in a variety of industrial mills where direct rotary motion was needed (Westworth, 1933). The engine erected at the Albion Mill also convinced some textile manufacturers in the North to install Boulton and Watt engines for powering their mills, see Hills (1970: 156).

21. Silverberg and Verspagen (2003) have originally proposed this intuitive interpretation of the overdispersion test in the context of the temporal clustering of basic innovations.

REFERENCES

Berg, M. and P. Hudson (1992), 'Rehabilitating the industrial revolution', *Economic History Review*, **45**, 24–50.

Cameron, A. C. and P. K. Trivedi (1998), *Regression Analysis of Count Data*, Cambridge: Cambridge University Press.

Chapman, S. D. (1970), 'Fixed capital formation in the British cotton industry, 1770–1815', *Economic History Review*, **23**, 235–66.

Cliff, A. D. and J. K. Ord (1981), *Spatial Processes: Models and Applications*, London: Pion.

David, P. A. (1975), *Technical Choice, Innovation and Economic Growth*, Cambridge: Cambridge University Press.

Dosi, G. (1984), *Technical Change and Industrial Transformation. The Theory and an Application to the Semiconductor Industry*, London: Macmillan.

Dickinson, H. W. (1936), *Matthew Boulton*, Cambridge: Cambridge University Press.

Dickinson, H. W. and R. Jenkins (1927), *James Watt and the Steam Engine*, Oxford: Clarendon.

Flinn, M. W. (1984), *The History of the British Coal Industry, 1700–1830.* (Volume II), Oxford: Clarendon Press.

Frenken, K. and A. Nuvolari (2003), 'The early development of the steam engine: an evolutionary interpretation using complexity theory', *Industrial and Corporate Change*, **13**, 419–50.

Gold, B. (1980), 'On the adoption of technological innovations in industry: superficial models and Complex Decision Processes', *Omega*, **8**, 505–16.

Greene, W. H. (2000), *Econometric Analysis*, (4th edn), Upper Saddle River: Prentice-Hall.

Griliches, Z. (1957), 'Hybrid Corn: an Exploration in the Economics of Technological Change', *Econometrica*, **25**, 501–22.

Habakkuk, H. J. (1962), *American and British Technology in the Nineteenth Century. The Search for Labour-Saving Inventions*, Cambridge: Cambridge University Press.

Hills, R. L. (1970), *Power in the Industrial Revolution*, Manchester: Manchester University Press.

Hills, R. L. (1989), *Power from Steam. A History of the Stationary Steam Engine*, Cambridge: Cambridge University Press.

Hills, R. L. (2002), *James Watt: His Time in Scotland, 1736–1774*, Ashbourne: Landmark.

Hudson, P. (1989), 'The Regional Perspective', in P. Hudson (ed.), *Regions and Industries: A Perspective on the Industrial Revolution in Britain*, Cambridge: Cambridge University Press.

Hyde, C. K. (1977), *Technological and the British Iron Industry, 1700–1870*, Princeton: Princeton University Press.

Jenkins, D. T. and K. G. Ponting (1982), *The British Wool Textile Industry, 1770–1850*, London: Heinemann.

Kanefsky, J. W. (1979), 'The diffusion of power technology in British industry', 1760–1870, University of Exeter, PhD Thesis.

Kanefsky, J. W. and J. Robey (1980), 'Steam engines in 18th century Britain: a quantitative assessment, *Technology and Culture*, **21**, 161–86.

Landes, D. S. (1969), *The Unbound Prometheus. Technological Change and Industrial Development in Western Europe from 1750 to the Present*, Cambridge: Cambridge University Press.

Langton, J. (1984), 'The industrial revolution and the regional geography of England', *Transactions of the Institute of British Geographers*, **9**, 145–67.

Mathias, P. (1983), *The First Industrial Nation*, (2nd edn), London: Methuen.

Musson, A. E. and E. H. Robinson (1969), *Science and Technology in the Industrial Revolution*, Manchester: Manchester University Press.

Olmstead, A. L. (1975), 'The mechanization of reaping and mowing in American agriculture, 1833–1870', *Journal of Economic History*, **35**, 327–52.

Pollard, S. (1981), *Peaceful Conquest. The Industrialization of Europe 1760–1970*, Oxford: Oxford University Press.

Roll, E. (1930), *An Early Experiment in Industrial Organisation. Being a History of the Firm of Boulton & Watt, 1775–1805*, London: Longman.

Rolt, L. T. C., and J. S. Allen (1997), *The Steam Engine of Thomas Newcomen*, Ashbourne: Landmark, (1st edn., 1977).

Rosenberg, N. (1976), *Perspectives on Technology*, Cambridge: Cambridge University Press.

Rowlands, M. B. (1969), 'Stonier Parrot and the Newcomen engine', *Transactions of the Newcomen Society*, **41** (1968–9), 49–67.

Scrivenor, H. (1854), *History of the Iron Trade: From the Earliest Records to the Present*, London: Longman, Brown, Green and Longmans.

Silverberg, G., G. Dosi, and L. Orsenigo (1988), 'Innovation, diversity and diffusion: a self-organisation model', *Economic Journal*, **98**, 1032–54.

Silverberg, G. and B. Verspagen (2003), 'Breaking the waves: a Poisson regression approach to Schumpeterian clustering of basic innovations', *Cambridge Journal of Economics*, **27**, 671–93.

Smith, A. (1978), 'Steam and the city: the Committee of Proprietors of the invention for raising water by fire, 1715–1735', *Transactions of the Newcomen Society*, **49** (1977–8), 5–20.

Tann, J. (1988), 'Fixed capital formation in steam power, 1775–1825. A case study of the Boulton and Watt engine' in C. H. Feinstein and S. Pollard (eds.), *Studies in Capital Formation in the United Kingdom, 1750–1920*, Oxford: Clarendon Press.

Turnbull, G. (1987), 'Canals, coal and regional growth during the industrial revolution', *Economic History Review*, **40**, 537–60.

von Tunzelmann, G. N. (1978), *Steam Power and British Industrialization to 1860*, Oxford: Clarendon.

von Tunzelmann, G. N. (1986), 'Coal and steam power', in J. Langton and R. J. Morris (eds.), *Atlas of Industrializing Britain*, London: Methuen.

Westworth, O. E. (1933), 'The Albion steam flour mill', *Economic History*, **2**, 380–95.

9. Knowledge diffusion with complex cognition

Piergiuseppe Morone and Richard Taylor

BACKGROUND

Modern economy has been described as knowledge-based, or a learning economy, due to the central role that knowledge and learning play for economic development (OECD, 1996). None the less, the processes of learning and knowledge diffusion are still largely undiscovered and require substantial theoretical and empirical efforts to be properly understood.

From the premise that learning is a complex and interactive process which can take place at all times (we learn at school, we learn at work, we learn reading a book, we learn watching TV, we learn talking with people, we learn while using ICT), we operate a logical simplification to understand this phenomenon. Following the theoretical structure defined in previous work (Morone, 2001; Morone and Taylor, 2001), we divide learning into two categories: *formal learning* and *informal learning*. We define *formal learning* as the kind of learning that occurs in certain environments which are meant for learning such as schools, workplaces, and training groups. On the other hand we call *informal* those learning processes that occur 'spontaneously', simply by interacting with peers. Following the more traditional approach, we could define the knowledge acquired by formal learning as a standard economic good (for which I'm paying a price; that is tuition fees, forgone earnings); and the knowledge acquired by informal learning as an unconventional public good. Some authors have defined the latter kind of knowledge as a *club* good (Cornes and Sandler, 1996; Breschi and Lissoni, 2003) which is non rival and non excludible only for restricted groups of people (that is the *members of the club*).

Formal learning has been extensively investigated both theoretically and empirically (Becker, 1964; Mincer, 1974; Psacharopoulos, 1994), whereas the second learning process has only recently captured the attention of scholars. Mechanisms of innovation diffusion (Clark, 1984; Rogers, 1995) are often viewed as good examples of informal learning processes because they tend to occur through interaction within geographical and other informal networks, involving social externalities. Several researchers have investigated the patterns through which different agents adopt new technologies by means of theoretical as well as simulation models (Ellison and Fudenberg, 1993, 1995; Bala and Goyal, 1995, 1998). Another common way of modelling the mechanisms of social learning and technology diffusion makes use of evolutionary game theory (Chwe, 2000; Ellison, 1993, 2000; Anderlini and Ianni 1996; Berningaus and Schwalbe, 1996; Goyal, 1996; Akerlof, 1997; Watts, 2001).

Along with the speed of new technologies diffusion, several researchers have focused on the impact of peers' behaviour upon individual decisions in areas such as propensity to crime, use of drugs, school dropout and school attainments (Brock and Durlauf, 1995; Bénabou, 1993; Durlauf, 1996; Glaeser *et al.*, 1996).[1] What all the studies considered so far have in common is their reliance on the idea that learning from neighbours occurs and that under certain conditions it leads to the desirable stable equilibrium. However, none of these studies go beyond a binary definition of learning.

Jovanovic and Rob (1989) proposed for the first time a model in which incremental improvements in knowledge were defined as a complex process of assembling different ideas by means of information exchange among heterogeneous agents. The new insight brought by the authors is that knowledge was defined as something more complex than a binary variable and that, therefore, growth of knowledge could be defined as an interactive process tightly linked to its diffusion.

Cowan and Jonard (1999) made a subsequent attempt to study the effects of incremental innovations and their diffusion within a network of heterogeneous agents. Knowledge in their model is considered as a vector of values and is exchanged via a simple process of barter exchange. Depending on the network structure, the authors found that there is a trade-off between the speed of knowledge diffusion and the variance of knowledge. In other words, there is a spectrum of states of the world, varying from a situation of high knowledge inequality and fast knowledge diffusion (that is small-world), to the opposed situation, more equal in terms of knowledge variance but less efficient in terms of knowledge diffusion.

Along the lines of these works, Morone and Taylor (2001) defined a model in which agents exchanged knowledge exclusively by means of face-to-face interactions. The network structure was endogenous to the model and could vary over time. The authors showed how small-world networks emerged and coexisted with both a very unequal and a very equal diffusion of knowledge, different outcomes depending upon the initial conditions.

The objective of this chapter is to shed some light on informal learning by means of an agent-based simulation model in which we investigate the knowledge diffusion dynamics amongst agents interacting through a process of face-to-face knowledge exchange. Departing from previous works on knowledge diffusion, we aim to develop a model which takes into consideration the complexity of the process of knowledge acquisition. In doing so we define a complex cognitive structure for each agent (cognitive map) which regulates the processes through which knowledge diffuses. The paper is organised as follows: the following section presents our model of knowledge diffusion; the third section discusses how learning is defined in a framework of complex cognition; the fourth section explains how network properties of the model are calculated; the fifth section presents the results of a simulation exercise based on the model; the sixth section reviews the findings of an investigation applying this model to a case study based upon the data and geography of the Greater Santiago region in Chile; and finally, the seventh section concludes the chapter.

THE MODEL SPECIFICATIONS

We assume a population of N agents and a global environment consisting of a grid of cells. Each agent is initially assigned a random position in the grid, and interacts with her/his closest neighbours. Not all the cells of the grid are occupied by agents, and those occupied contain only one agent. We specify a wrapped grid (that is a torus) so that there are no edge effects – where we might have different behaviours due to the boundaries of the grid (peripheral agents have smaller neighbourhoods: hence fewer neighbours and fewer opportunities to interact).

The local environment of the agent is called the local-network and it is defined as the region on the grid that includes those cells adjacent in the four cardinal directions and within the agent's visible range (that is von Neumann neighbourhood structure). We also define a cyber-network as the ideal network connecting all those agents who have access to ICT. The cyber-network generates a second system which has no geographical dimension but connects all agents who have access to it. The two networks have different configurations: the local-network is defined as a regular system in which each agent represents a node and each connection represents an edge, while the cyber-network is structured with a central agent (star agent), external to the simulation, who works as a server and connects all other agents to one another. Each agent has an initial list of acquaintances including members of the local-network and (if the agent has access to ICT) the cyber-network.

Each connection has an associated strength, $\tau \in (0.05,1)$, which is a measure of the strength of the relationship from the agent to her/his acquaintance. Note that this model is not constrained to have symmetry of relationships between agents: in general, more prestigious agents (with higher levels of knowledge) will be the object of strong relationships from more peripheral agents (with lower levels of knowledge), which may be unreciprocated or reciprocated only weakly. At the beginning of the simulation, all strength values are set equal to one.

The unit of time we define in our model is called a cycle. In each cycle, all individuals are sorted into a random order, and then each is permitted to interact with one acquaintance. Each interaction is aimed at diffusing knowledge. Each agent is endowed with a cognitive map (CM), which contains information on the level and the kind of knowledge possessed by her/him. The structure of the CM is that of a tree, where each node corresponds to a bit of potential knowledge and each edge corresponds to an acquired knowledge. We will return to the CM in the next section.

In our simulation vertices correspond to agents and edges represent agents' connections. Formally, we have G (I, Γ), where $I = \{1, \ldots, N\}$ is the set of agents, and $\Gamma = \{\Gamma(i), i \in I\}$ gives the list of agents to whom each agent is connected. This can also be written $\Gamma(x) = \{(y \in I \mid \{x\} \mid d(x, y) \leq v) \cup (y \in \omega)\}$, where $d(x, y)$ is the length of the shortest path from agent x to agent v (that is the path which requires the shortest number of intermediate links to connect agent x to agent y), v (visibility) as already mentioned, is the number of cells in each direction which are considered to be within the agent's spectrum, and ω defines the cyber-network, which by definition encompasses all those agents endowed with ICT facilities. Intuitively, Γ_x (we will use this notation rather than $\Gamma(x)$ from now on) defines the neighbourhood of the agent (vertex) x.

Initial acquaintances in the local-network are the immediate neighbours (that is those within the visible spectrum). Subsequently, an agent can learn of the existence of other agents through interactions with her/his acquaintances (that is she/he can be introduced to the acquaintances of her/his acquaintances). If the acquaintance selected for interaction is connected to other individuals of whom the agent is not aware, then a new connection is made from the agent to the acquaintance of her/his acquaintance. If there is more than one unknown acquaintance, then the contacting agent will choose the one with the highest strength value (this would tend to avoid a situation where the agent is introduced to an acquaintance that is not considered to be a good choice). The new acquaintance will be added to the acquaintances list of the agent who initiated the interaction and the strength value will be equal to the one the new acquaintance had with the original acquaintance. Moreover, agents can stop interacting with some of their acquaintances if the connection does not tend to result in gain interactions and is therefore considered no longer useful. Hence the number of acquaintances changes over time, but does not necessarily increase over time. In this way we introduce a dynamic element into the network structure.

Having defined Γ_x as the set of initial acquaintances of agent x (or first generation connections), we define $\varphi_{x,t}$ as the set of acquaintances of the acquaintances at time t (or next generation connections), and the individual $m_t \in \varphi_{x,t}$ who is added at each t. We also define $\vartheta_{x,t}$ as the set of acquaintances dropped at time t and the individual $n_t \in \vartheta_{x,t}$ who is dropped at each t. Now we can define the total set of acquaintances for individual x at time $t = T$ as:

$$\Phi_{x,T} = (\Gamma_x \cup \varphi_{x,T}) \backslash \vartheta_{x,T} \tag{1}$$

We also define a rule governing how an agent chooses an acquaintance to interact with. In doing so, we make the assumption that an agent prefers interacting with acquaintances with whom she/he has strong relations. Agent y will be selected for interaction with agent x with probability given by:[2]

$$p^x(y) = \frac{\tau_y^x}{\sum_{j \in \Phi} \tau_i^x}, \tag{2}$$

In other words, the probability that x selects y for interaction can be understood as the relative strength of all the potential interactions. The selection mechanism is not based on the assumption that each agent has, at any moment of time, full information about other agents' knowledge levels. Rather, we introduce a mechanism whereby an agent adapts strength of relations depending upon previous experience of interaction.

Each cycle, the strength of the relationship between each agent and her/his acquaintances τ_i (where $i = \{1, \ldots, \Phi\}$), is adjusted (we drop for simplicity the index of the agent and use it only when strictly necessary) as follows:

$$\tau_{i,t} = \varepsilon \tau_{i,t-1} - \beta \tag{3}$$

where $\begin{cases} \varepsilon = 1.5 & \text{and } \beta = 0 \quad \text{if learning takes place;} \\ \varepsilon = 0.6 & \text{and } \beta = 0 \quad \text{if learning does not takes place;} \\ \varepsilon = 1 & \text{and } \beta = 0.05 \text{ if an agent is not selected for interaction.} \end{cases}$

As already mentioned, τ_i is bounded between 0.05 and 1. Whenever the τ_i attached to any acquaintance reaches the lowest threshold of 0.05, the acquaintance is dropped from the acquaintances list. However, acquaintances that are members of the local-network are never dropped due to the fact that they are geographical neighbours with whom we keep meeting unless we move to different neighbourhood (an option which is not considered in our simulation model).

In this way the agent will develop preferences to select an interaction with acquaintances with whom he/she has previously experienced positive learning interactions. In other words, the agent builds internal models of preference represented by the strength values τ_i. The strengthening of relationships increases the probability of interaction in subsequent periods.

COGNITIVE MAPS AND COMPLEX COGNITION

We will now discuss how learning takes place. One of the main limitations of simulation models that aim to formalise our understandings of knowledge diffusion processes (Cowan and Jonard, 1999; Morone and Taylor, 2001) is the oversimplifying assumption that knowledge is accumulated as a stockpile (that is a vector of cardinal numbers indicating the level of knowledge). The roots of this problem are to be found in the distinction between economics of information and economics of knowledge. As pointed out by Ancori *et al.* (2000), the economics of knowledge differs from the economics of information in the sense that knowledge is no longer assimilated to the accumulation of information as a stockpile. The distinction between these two concepts has been repeatedly ignored by a certain branch of the economic literature (economics of information), which does not consider the cognitive structure that agents use to elaborate knowledge.

Following this distinction, Ancori *et al.* (2000) develop an appreciative model in which the process of knowledge accumulation is disentangled into four major stages: identification of crude knowledge, learning how to use knowledge, learning how to transmit knowledge, and learning how to manage knowledge. The theoretical background of this model is the debate over the difference between tacit and codified knowledge. Three general observations are at the basis of the model: first, knowledge is closely dependent on the cognitive abilities of actors who hold it; second, knowledge cannot be considered separately from the communication process through which it is exchanged; and finally, knowledge demands knowledge in order to be acquired and exchanged.

For our purposes it is of a great interest to understand how people can exchange knowledge and how it is acquired once we dismiss the stockpile hypothesis. According to Ancori *et al.*, new knowledge is acquired 'by a backward process through which the new knowledge is confronted and articulated with previous experience [. . .] the appropriation of crude knowledge – that is its integration in one's cognitive context – is not the result of a transmission, but rather the result of a re-engineering process' (Ancori *et al.*, 2000: 267). What the recipient agent is basically doing is de-codifying the knowledge received in order to be able to position it in her/his own cognitive map.

Particularly useful is the following example: 'when the receiver knowing "blue" and "green" received the message "red", the result in his/her cognitive context is not to replace "blue", "green" by "blue", "green", "red", but to replace "blue", "green", "blue and green" by "blue", "green", "red", "blue and green", "blue and red", "green and red", and "blue, green and red"' (Ancori *et al.*, 2000: 267). This example leads to the idea that cognition follows combinatory rules rather than additive rules.

The theoretical framework created by Ancori *et al.*, in spite of its strictly appreciative nature, is of a great interest for the development of our model, establishing the theoretical guidelines required to characterise and construct the cognitive map that we will use in our simulation. We can think of the cognitive map as a tree in which each vertex (node) represents a piece of crude knowledge and each edge (link) represents knowledge that we have already mastered and learned how to use.

In the graphical representation below we present a possible cognitive map which shows only mastered knowledge (see Figure 9.1), while all the other possible nodes which would complete the tree represent knowledge that at present is not in the cognitive map but could be activated through individual as well as interactive learning.

As assumed by Ancori *et al.*, knowledge demands knowledge in order to be acquired; hence, in order to be activated, a new node would have to be

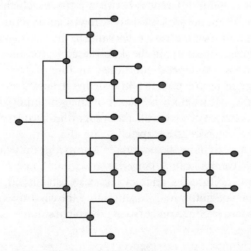

Figure 9.1   Cognitive map

directly connected to active (coloured) nodes. Moving from left to right in the cognitive map, we advance from less to more specialised knowledge, where each subsequent column corresponds to a higher level of knowledge. This observation justifies the assumption that new nodes can be activated (that is new knowledge can be acquired) only if they are directly connected to active nodes.

Each agent is initially endowed with a cognitive map determined by a random process. The number drawn at random from the uniform distribution corresponds to the 'column depth' up to which nodes are activated in the initial CM of that agent. Up to and including the first four columns, all nodes are fully activated. However, if the initial endowment exceeds the first four columns, then subsequent columns will not be fully activated, but will be activated according to the rule for endowment of specialised knowledge. We define specialisation as knowledge accumulation only in certain areas of the cognitive map. Agents will be specialised in one of two areas: the scientific area and the technical area.

The agent's interaction/exchange of knowledge can now be formalised as follows: each time an agent receives a message she/he will activate a new node, but only if this new knowledge can be pegged to pre-existing knowledge. From this analysis it follows that agents with a similar kind of knowledge (that is agents with similar patterns in the cognitive map) are more likely to have fruitful interactions. This fact is theoretically supported by the literature on 'epistemic communities' or 'communities of practice'.[3] Using this new approach will improve the simulation model, overcoming some of the limits of previous models.

To sum up, the main differences between a model which uses a 'knowledge vector' and a model which uses a 'knowledge structure' is that in the former cognition follows additive rules while in the latter cognition follows combinatory rules. Moreover, in the 'knowledge vector' model, knowledge accumulation does not depend upon the structure of previously accumulated knowledge, as it does with the 'knowledge structure' model. Formally, we have: $CM \ (X, N)$ where w is the set of the whole possible knowledge available (that is the set of vertices), and N identifies the piece of knowledge activated (that is edges of the graph).

We will now explain how the process of knowledge diffusion takes place. An agent, whom we shall call A, contacts an acquaintance, B, in accordance with Equation (2). Once the contact has been established, the algorithm compares the two cognitive maps, subtracting the cognitive map of A from that of B. This can produce one of two possible results:[4]

$$CM_A (X, N) \backslash CM_B (X, N) \begin{cases} = \varnothing \\ \neq \varnothing \end{cases} \qquad (4)$$

If the difference between the two sets is a non-empty set, there is possibility for interaction; if not, agent A will have no interest in interacting with agent B as there is no possible gain.

We present an example that will clarify the issue. Figures 9.2 and 9.3 represent the cognitive maps of agent A and an acquaintance, agent B. Now, let us assume that agent A contacts agent B. If we calculate the distance between the two maps, we get $CM_A(X, N) \backslash CM_B(X, N) \neq \emptyset$ (this can be clearly observed in Figure 9.3 below).

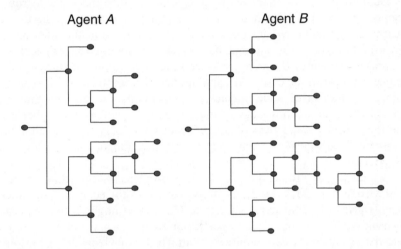

Figure 9.2   Comparing two cognitive maps

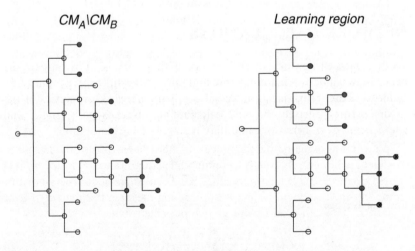

Figure 9.3   Knowledge interaction and the occurrence of learning

The left-hand picture of Figure 9.3 illustrates the difference between the two CMs. Once we have identified this difference, we need to identify the possible learning region where knowledge can be gained (that is additional nodes can be activated). To do so we recall the condition that new knowledge has to be pegged to already existing knowledge, and thus we can cross out several of the coloured nodes in the first diagram. We conclude that the only knowledge that agent A can learn from agent B is that which is connected to activated nodes.

Defining the nodes of the learning region as Ω, then the actual learning can be expressed as $p\Omega$, where p represents the percentage of nodes of the learning region that will be activated as a consequence of the interaction. In other words, the agent that has started the interaction will activate (learn) p per cent of the nodes, selected randomly (rounding always to the highest integer in the case of decimal numbers) from the learning region.[5] Since the number of nodes increases exponentially, we can infer that the higher the level of knowledge of the interacting agents is, the higher will be the learning opportunity. This mechanism reflects the idea that the 'absorptive capacity'[6] of each agent is a positive function of her/his level of education.

A final note has to be made on the 'incentive' mechanisms that generate knowledge flows. The model is structured as a 'gift economy' in which agents give away information for free. This model might better replicate behaviours which take place in particular environments such as research groups or university communities within which knowledge flows are generated not by direct payments but by a tacitly agreed reciprocity.

NETWORK CALCULATIONS

As discussed earlier, one of the targets of this work is to investigate the nexus between network architecture and knowledge diffusion dynamics. In order to address this question we will study the network properties of the model. More precisely, we will calculate the average path length and cliquishness of our network in different stages of the simulation:

$$\mathcal{L}(t) = \frac{1}{N}\sum_{x=1}^{N}\sum_{x\neq y}\frac{d(x,y)}{N-1} \tag{5}$$

and the average:

$$C(t) = \frac{1}{N}\sum_{x=1}^{N}\sum_{y,z=1}^{\Phi}\frac{X(y,z)}{|\Phi_x|(|\Phi_x|-1)/2} \tag{6}$$

where $X(y, z) = 1$ if y and z are connected at time t (no matter whether the connection is a first generation or next generation), and $X(y, z) = 0$ otherwise.

We shall compare our dynamic network with a random one at different stages throughout the simulation to show whether or not the small worlds architecture is emerging in our system. Since the number of connections in our network is changing over time (due to the mechanism by which agents make acquaintances of their acquaintances), in order to make an appropriate comparison we need to construct the random network with an equivalent number of connections. For calculating the average path length and cliquishness of a random network, we shall use the same approximation as Watts and Strogatz (1998), that is $\mathfrak{L}_{random}(t) \cong \ln N/\ln n$ and $C_{random}(t) \cong n/N$, where n is the average number of connections of each agent and N is the total number of agents. The criteria for identifying the network as small worlds are that $\mathfrak{L}(t) \cong \mathfrak{L}_{random}(t)$ and $C(t) \gg C_{random}(t)$.

If, when comparisons are made with the random network, we find that the Watts-Strogatz (Watts and Strogatz, 1998) criteria are observed, this will be evidence to suggest that a small worlds network structure is emergent from our model.

SIMULATION RESULTS AND INTERPRETATIONS

We ran several batches of simulations and we examined both learning behaviours and network properties. We performed simulation experiments with a population of 100 agents allocated over a wrapped grid of dimension 20 by 20 cells. Hence, the grid had an approximate overall density of one agent per four cells. Each agent had a visibility parameter that we tuned to study changes in learning behaviours as well as network structure. We started with $v = 2$, meaning that each agent can see the two cells situated in the four cardinal directions. Moreover, we endowed 10 per cent of the overall population with ICT platforms, meaning that approximately ten agents are members of the cyber-network.

The same random number seed was used for all the simulation runs, ensuring fewer artefacts present in the results. The model was programmed in the Strictly Declarative Modelling Language (SDML) developed at the CPM (Wallis and Moss, 1994) to support the modelling of social processes with multi-agent systems. The results were analysed using the graphical output capabilities of the SDML platform and the network analysis software toolkit UCINET 5.0 (Borgatti *et al.*, 1999).

Knowledge Diffusion Dynamics

We ran 400 cycles for each simulation, obtaining a long-term stationary state. When v was set equal to two we observed substantial increases in both mean and variance, suggesting a polarisation of knowledge distribution and an increase in the knowledge gap. Given the structure of knowledge expressed by the cognitive map, we calculated mean and variance based on the total number of activated nodes for each agent. Figure 9.4 shows these dynamics: first we plotted μ against time and we observed that the average number of activated nodes had grown substantially over the first 50 cycles, the pace of learning being approximately four nodes per cycle. Then, it speeded up remarkably, almost tripling the pace of learning (reaching approximately 11 nodes per cycle). This dynamic reflects the fact that agents first start interacting with their geographical neighbours, then they learn of the existence of acquaintances of their initial acquaintances and are therefore able to make better choices for interaction. Moreover, after several interactions they learn valuable information about their acquaintances' level of knowledge through the individual model of preference. In other words, they understand with whom it is worth interacting. After the first 120 cycles the average level of knowledge flattened out and then barely grew in the following 100 cycles until finally, at about 230 cycles, it reached its maximum value. This is due to the fact that the CM of some agents has become saturated. Finally, after about 230 cycles the mean curve levelled-off, meaning that the system has reached a stable equilibrium.

Subsequently, we plotted the variance in knowledge against time and we

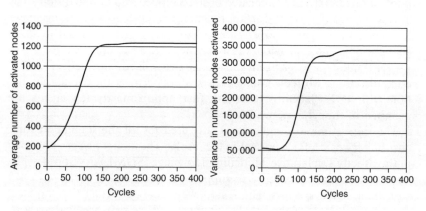

Source: Simulation results.

Figure 9.4   Changes in the mean and variance of knowledge ($v = 2$)

observed that σ^2 first decreases slightly over the first 50 cycles or so, where-upon it reached a turning point. After the first 150 cycles the variance slowed down considerably and finally reached a stationary state after 230 cycles. The variance pattern has added some useful information to our understanding: in the beginning, when everybody was interacting only with their closest neighbours, there were similar learning opportunities for each agent, the learning path being rather homogeneous. On the other hand, when agents had learned about of the existence of other acquaintances, and the network structure evolved, the society started dividing into clusters[7] or sub-groups of fast and slow catching-up agents, and the learning path became heterogeneous and unequal.

Looking at individual dynamics corroborates this interpretation. We can clearly see how the model generated multiple equilibria, suggesting the existence of unconnected sub-clusters of agents.

The groups converged to separate equilibria at very different intervals, one at 2044, one at 1532, one at 540, and several smaller groups at lower values. This is responsible for the high variance observed in Figure 9.4.

To explain the agent learning behaviour illustrated by Figures 9.4 and 9.5, we must consider the dynamics underlying the structure of knowledge in the model. The number of agents with fully saturated CMs increases

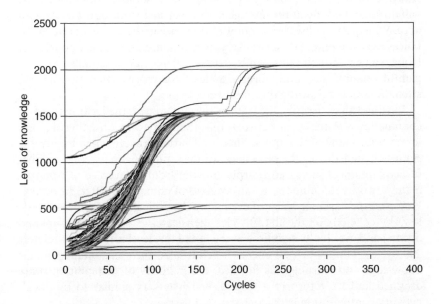

Source: Simulation results.

Figure 9.5 Changes in the average level of knowledge by individuals (v = 2)

over time, and as agents approach this state they have a reduced potential for learning, that is their learning region becomes smaller. However on the other hand, in the early stages of the simulation this region tends to widen in the CM of the majority of agents, giving the potential for greater gains. In addition, agents have increased opportunities to gain from interactions as CMs become more heterogeneous. For example, two agents with identical schooling will not be able to gain from an interaction in cycle zero, whereas later in the simulation they most likely will experience a small gain. This begs the questions: to what extent is the observed increase in knowledge due to the widening of the learning region (that is the structure of the CM), and to what extent is it due to agents making better choices for interaction (that is the preferential model of acquaintance selection)?

The efficiency of the learning mechanism was demonstrated through the exploration of a very similar model presented elsewhere (Morone and Taylor, 2004), where the authors discovered a more rapid diffusion process compared with simulations where there is no model of 'preferential acquaintance selection'. We leave this test of different learning mechanisms for further investigation.

More information on the structure of the network can be gathered by studying the dynamics through which agents make new connections. We will do so by looking at the average number of acquaintances and its variance. We expect to observe a monotonic increase in the number of acquaintances over the first few cycles: every interaction presents the opportunity to meet a new acquaintance, whilst agents will not start disconnecting nongainful relationships until several cycles have passed (that is when the strength level is below the threshold value).

Starting values describe the state of the system with the local-network in conjunction with the cyber-network: this situation is one consisting of a very low average number of acquaintances and variance as shown in Figure 9.6. As anticipated, during the early stages of the simulation the average number of acquaintances increased sharply, moving from an average of approximately two acquaintances, to an average of almost 20 after 30 cycles.[8] However, the variance behaved even more dynamically. It started off quite low, skyrocketed over the first 50 cycles, then decreased (with several ups and downs) and eventually stabilised at the initial low level after approximately 200 cycles. Thus, when all agents have attained their maximum possible knowledge and learning has finished, the majority of acquaintances are dropped and we return to a system, which is very similar to the local-network configuration with low mean and variance.

The variance behaviour during the learning period of the first 150–200 cycles is easily explained by considering the many disconnected agents and

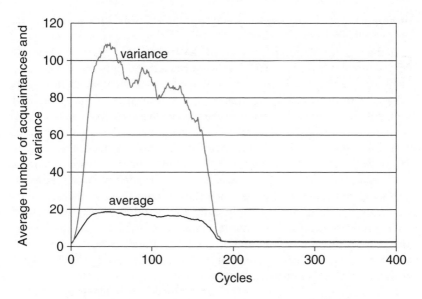

Source: Simulation results.

Figure 9.6 Average number of acquaintances and variance (v = 2)

sub-groups in the network. As the density of connections in the main population increases, these agents remain with relatively very few (or zero)
acquaintances, and this largely accounts for the high variance seen in
Figure 9.6. In this simulation experiment, only few agents have a very small
number of acquaintances, whilst the vast majority of agents are extremely
well connected. Clearly, this structure does not facilitate the equality of
knowledge flows, keeping the wrapped grid as a whole a rather un-cohesive
environment.[9]

Enhancing Knowledge Flows

One possible way to facilitate knowledge flows would be to make the global
simulation environment more cohesive by increasing the density of the
network. We could achieve this target by either reducing the grid size or,
alternatively, by increasing the visibility range of each agent. These two
options are technically very similar, as they increase the initial connectivity
(and make possible more subsequent connections), practically reducing the
geographical distance between agents. A useful example of the importance
of the cohesiveness of environments to enhance knowledge flows is provided by the literature on industrial districts. Several authors[10] pointed out

the importance of cohesiveness and geographical proximity in determining the overall efficiency of a district.

In the first simulation the density of the grid was one agent per four cells with a visibility equal to two. This produced a rather un-cohesive environment where groups of agents were isolated from each other. By raising the value of v from two to six we increase the cohesiveness of the global environment. In Figure 9.5 we report changes in the variance dynamics after changing the visibility value. We can clearly see how the variance behaves very differently according to the tuning of the visibility parameter: raising v from two to three, the model diverges at a slower pace and towards a much less unequal equilibrium. If we raise the v value to four and five, we observe a short-term behaviour during which the variance decreases, describing a converging pattern. Subsequently, after the first 100 cycles, the variance starts growing again and the model stabilises around a value of the variance not too dissimilar from the original one. Finally when v is set higher than five, the model shows a converging behaviour both in the short-term as well as in the long run steady-state.

By increasing v, we decrease the number of isolated agents and isolated sub-groups. Nevertheless, when the visibility is set equal to six, our simulation shows that convergence is not always complete (that is the model does not converge to zero variance and maximum mean), because in this case there is one agent who is totally isolated and hence unable to engage in interaction. None the less, 99 per cent of the population reach the highest possible level of knowledge in less than 250 cycles. Likewise, when visibility is increased, the distribution of acquaintances is more even.

In Figure 9.9 we can see that the average number of contacts per agent is higher than in the case $v = 2$. Throughout the simulation, agents maintain more connections: this number peaks at about 27 acquaintances and remains at a high level for nearly 200 cycles, producing a very dense network. Interestingly however, the variance is much lower than in the case $v = 2$, implying that agents, almost uniformly, maintain a high number of personal contacts. As in the previous case, the average number of acquaintances starts decreasing as soon as the model converges towards the long-run steady state around cycle 270.

In this second simulation, the mean number of acquaintances is much higher than the variance, reversing the result of the first simulation. The difference is largely attributable to the reduced number of disconnected agents, and the result illustrated in Figure 9.9 gives us a more accurate picture of the typical connectivity of agents following the preferential acquaintance selection model.

In conclusion, increasing the visibility range generates a more interconnected environment, which in turn produces improvements both in terms

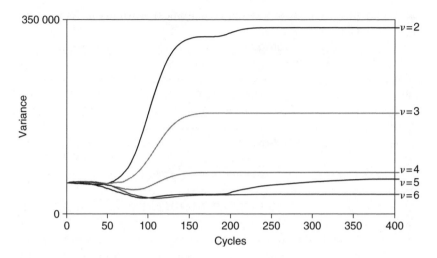

Source: Simulation results.

Figure 9.7   Knowledge variance transition, different values of v

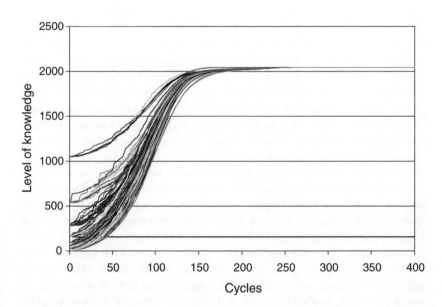

Source: Simulation results.

Figure 9.8   Changes in the average level of knowledge by individuals (v = 6)

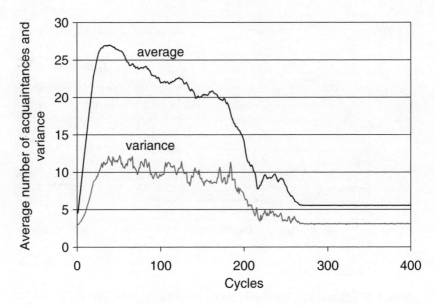

Source: Simulation results.

Figure 9.9   Average number of acquaintances and its variance (v = 6)

of overall efficiency (that is speed of knowledge diffusion) as well as in terms of equality of distribution. Given the structure of our model, an alternative way of enhancing knowledge diffusion would be increasing the percentage of agents endowed with ICT. So far, we have assigned an ICT platform to just 10 per cent of the population. Raising this value would represent an alternative way of bridging over the physical distance among agents and making the environment more cohesive.

When ICT penetration is boosted up to 30 per cent we can observe a rapid increase in the number of agents able to converge to the absolute maximum in the long-run steady state. None the less, almost 15 per cent of the overall population is unable to converge and appears to be fully disconnected and hence unable to interact at all. This implies that the overall variance would increase quite rapidly, converging to a high value.

By further increasing the ICT penetration to 50 per cent, however, we obtain a situation where almost all agents are able to converge to the highest possible level of knowledge exactly as we saw in the case where visibility was set equal to six.

As we can see in Figure 9.10, when we push ICT penetration up to 50 per cent (meaning that every second agent has access to the internet platform), the model converges to a long-run steady state, where more than 90 per cent

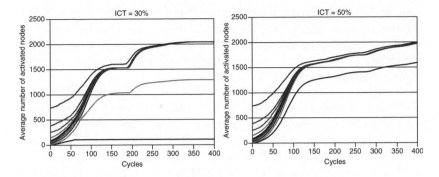

Source: Simulation results.

Figure 9.10 *Changes in the average level of knowledge by deciles.*
Different values of ICT penetration

of the agents reach the highest possible level of knowledge. None the less, 400 cycles did not prove sufficient to reach the steady state, meaning that the pace of convergence is much slower when compared to a model with high degree of visibility.

In other words, both actions to enhance knowledge flows (that is increasing the cohesiveness of the network by means of higher visibility, and increasing the ICT diffusion) will generate a long-term stationary state in which almost every agent converges. None the less, increasing the visibility seems to be a more efficient tool to reach this target. Knowledge flows more equally if we increase the size of each agent's neighbourhood (and hence local-network) rather than superimposing one large cyber-network over half of the population. In fact, this second option will account for greater chances of social exclusion even though it results in initially very much lower average path length and high cliquishness, as we will see in the following sub-section.

Calculating Network Properties

In this sub-section we present our results for the small world calculations (Table 9.1). We calculated average path length and cliquishness at different stages of simulations and for three different scenarios.[11] This has allowed us to compare the network properties with the knowledge diffusion results presented above. More precisely, we calculated small world properties at cycles 0, 10, 50, 100, 150, 200, 250, 300, 350 and 400; for the network with visibility equal to two and ICT penetration equal to 10 per cent, for the network with visibility equal to six and ICT penetration equal to 10 per

cent, and finally for the network with visibility equal to two and ICT penetration equal to 50 per cent. These results were then compared with those
characterising comparable random networks. In this way we can examine
the robustness of small world structures following the test first introduced
by Watts and Strogatz (1998).

In the first two cases, where ICT penetration was set equal to 10 per cent
and v varied (we did the calculations for v equals two and v equals six), the
same pattern was observed: cliquishness increased and average path length
decreased over the first 150 cycles as the system became more densely connected and knowledge flowed more intensively. After this period the system
started converging towards the long-run steady state equilibrium and, as it
stabilised, there were fewer gainful interactions and agents started disconnecting from their acquaintances. At this point, the average number of connections fell and cliquishness decreased, whilst the average path length
started increasing. Eventually the network reverted back towards the initial
configuration.

This, however, was not the case in the third simulation where ICT was set
equal to 50 per cent and v equalled two. The initial system was much more
densely connected due to the high level of ICT penetration. None the less,
agents could disconnect from their initial cyber acquaintances (unlike their
geographical neighbour acquaintances) and therefore we observed that
cliquishness dropped considerably after the first 150 cycles whilst the
average path length rose. In each case, the initial network is small world due
to the presence of the cyber-network which connects far-distant agents and
reduces the path length of the network.

What we can observe by looking at the network calculations is that in
every case the system preserves the most efficient network structure (that is
the small world) for the duration of the simulation; in particular, the learning period (that is the first 150–200 cycles) is characterised by very low
average path length and high cliquishness. In conclusion, small world properties are observed both when knowledge flows lead the system to convergence, and also when they lead to non-convergence. In other words, the
network structure does not affect directly the distributional aspects of
knowledge flows. Convergency patterns will be determined solely by the
existence of isolated agents and subgroups of agents.

AN EMPIRICAL APPLICATION OF THE MODEL

An interesting exercise to test the usefulness of the model presented in
this chapter would be applying it to an empirical case study. This would
allow investigating directly the risk of exclusion in a specific society and

Table 9.1   Small world calculation results

Cycle	Simulation		Random network	
	Average path length (among reachable pairs)	Cliquishness	Average path length	Cliquishness
First simulation results: $v = 2$ and ICT $= 10\%$				
0	5.9910	0.3497	4.2305	0.0297
10	2.5330	0.6203	2.0504	0.0945
50	2.2850	0.6910	1.6495	0.1631
100	2.0480	0.6999	1.6890	0.1528
150	2.1050	0.6903	1.7334	0.1425
200	3.1320	0.5995	3.0940	0.0443
250	4.3330	0.4609	4.5854	0.0273
300	4.0950	0.5015	4.6714	0.0268
350	3.5630	0.4677	4.8788	0.0257
400	3.9250	0.4135	4.8991	0.0256
Second simulation results: $v = 6$ and ICT $= 10\%$				
0	3.1280	0.4514	2.5375	0.0614
10	2.3390	0.4541	1.8583	0.1192
50	1.9090	0.6677	1.4224	0.2547
100	1.9830	0.6695	1.4663	0.2312
150	2.0180	0.7038	1.4806	0.2243
200	2.3560	0.4811	1.7853	0.1319
250	3.1630	0.3533	2.5678	0.0601
300	3.1780	0.3530	2.5678	0.0601
350	3.2200	0.3758	2.5702	0.0600
400	3.1910	0.3742	2.5726	0.0599
Third simulation results: $v = 2$ and ICT $= 50\%$				
0	1.7370	0.7734	1.2754	0.3699
10	1.5580	0.9712	1.2299	0.4228
50	2.0970	0.7397	1.5596	0.1916
100	2.2250	0.7233	1.6132	0.1737
150	2.2930	0.7901	1.6288	0.1690
200	3.5110	0.3798	2.8793	0.0495
250	5.9450	0.4088	4.1419	0.0304
300	6.0930	0.3732	4.2046	0.0299
350	5.7700	0.3863	4.1918	0.0300
400	6.6450	0.3929	4.2046	0.0299

Source: Simulation results.

developing a model which might bring insight to the knowledge diffusion process in a well-identified context. This kind of exercise was carried out by the authors who applied the model to the Chilean case (Morone and Taylor, 2004). As we will see, several interesting results were obtained.

The data used to calibrate the model was a sub-sample of the 1998 edition of the *Encuesta de Ocupación y Desocupación* (one of the most comprehensive household surveys collected in Santiago de Chile), providing us with the following useful variables: district of residence, years of schooling, kind of schooling, and use of computers at work. These variables were used to distribute agents over the geographical grid, to build the CM of each agent and to construct the cyber-network.

The model's environment was defined as a grid that resembled the geographical configuration of the metropolitan area of Greater Santiago de Chile. The grid was divided into 34 portions, each corresponding to a defined district of Santiago, having thus different dimensions and population densities. Defining the grid as a two-dimensional geographical region has added into the model a core-periphery aspect, with some districts being located in a central position and others in a peripheral one. Each agent was initially assigned a district and then allocated, randomly, to a cell within that district. Depending on the geographical location, agents were endowed with acquaintance lists, and – depending on the empirical data – few agents were selected as members of the cyber-network. Moreover, each agent was initially endowed with a different cognitive map, which depended upon her/his level and kind of education (measured as years of schooling and kind of school attended). Each column corresponded to a higher level of education.

The results concerning the knowledge diffusion process were very interesting: in presence of high levels of (knowledge) inequality there was a high risk of exclusion for those agents initially endowed with low level of education – an ignorance trap where agents were never able to catch up. Moreover, looking into the spatial dimension of the exclusion process, we found that the ignorance trap mechanism is more likely to take place if an initial situation of low level of knowledge is coupled with geographical exclusion. In other words, those people who start with a high level of individual learning (that is schooling) will always be able to escape from the ignorance trap mechanism, while more backward people might remain trapped if their low level of knowledge is cumulated with geographical exclusion.

These findings are extremely important from a policy prescription perspective. Based upon the theoretical results obtained in this chapter, a twofold policy action could be suggested in order to avoid the occurrence of an ignorance trap: the policy maker should aim at reducing the geographical gap between centre and periphery. This policy could be either implemented through the development of relevant infrastructure, bridging the centre-periphery distance, which would correspond to an increase of the visibility range of our model population, or through the development and improvement of ICT connections. In other words, the exclusion risk could be minimised through the development of a more comprehensive cyber-network, so that also peripheral agents will have the same opportunity to interact with central and semi-peripheral agents.

CONCLUSIONS

In this chapter we addressed the issue of knowledge diffusion, developing a simulation model to investigate the complex learning process which occurs among agents interacting in informal networks. In our model, agents exchange knowledge by means of face-to-face interactions, and every time a knowledge transfer occurs, the new knowledge acquired is confronted and linked with previous knowledge. In other words, knowledge is acquired not through a simple additive process, but by a more articulated combinatory process.

We studied how, within this framework, knowledge flows. Particularly, we investigated the occurrence of different long-run steady states for different levels of network cohesiveness and ICT penetration. We found a critical level, by tuning the visibility parameter, above which convergence in knowledge levels occurs. A converging long-run equilibrium was also achieved by increasing the ICT penetration. None the less, we showed how this latter option was less efficient, as convergence was slower. We conclude from this finding that a more effective measure aimed towards generating more evenly-distributed knowledge flows should focus upon enhancing local-network connectivity rather than extending the cyber-network coverage.

Subsequently, we studied the network properties of different systems, showing how the model consistently preserved a small world structure, presenting desirable properties in terms of overall knowledge flows.

As a suggestion for further research, we would like to point out the importance of better investigating the real nexus between network cohesiveness and ICT penetration. In other words, we suggest studying the relation between geographical proximity and cyber proximity in order to understand if these two system properties are substitutable or, as we would foresee, complementary in promoting knowledge flows.

ACKNOWLEDGEMENTS

The authors are grateful to Nick von Tunzelmann, Scott Moss, Robin Cowan and Ed Steinmueller for helpful comments in different stages of the work. Finally, the authors wish to thank all participants in the seminar at CESPRI – University of Milan 'Bocconi' (Milan, 07-03-2003) for comments and suggestions. The usual disclaimers apply.

NOTES

1. For a more detailed review see Morone and Taylor, 2004.
2. In this way we assume that agents are constrained by 'bounded rationality' in the sense that they respond to utility signals without this meaning that they maximise utility (Katz, 2001).
3. See, for instance, Wenger (1998).
4. We define the cognitive map only as a function of X and N because at this stage we are not interested in the depth of knowledge.
5. In the simulation model p is set equal to 0.1.
6. We refer explicitly to the work of Cohen and Levinthal (1989) on returns from R&D. The concept of individual absorptive capacity was already developed in Morone (2001).
7. We will return to this point in the following section while studying the network structure.
8. It is worth noting that the average number of acquaintances reported here does not include the cyber acquaintances as it is constant over time.
9. It is worth clarifying this point: the presence of prestigious agents facilitates knowledge flows but the network structure does not.
10. See among others: Marshall (1952); Becattini (1990); Dei Ottati, (1994).
11. C was calculated by taking the average over all agents of the proportion of an agent's acquaintances that are themselves acquainted. This was a straightforward calculation made by means of querying the database of SDML at the appropriate stage of the simulation. L was calculated by importing the relational data into UCINET 5.0 and using the Networks-Properties function to produce a matrix of path lengths between each node. The average path length was determined by finding the density of the matrix. More detailed information on these calculations is available upon request.

REFERENCES

Acemoglu, D. and J. Angrist (1999), 'How large are the social returns to educations? Evidence from compulsory schooling low', NBER, Working Paper, 7444.

Akerlof, G. (1997), 'Social distance and social decisions', *Econometrica*, **65**, 1005–27.

Ancori, B., A. Bureth and P. Cohendet (2000), 'The economics of knowledge: the debate about codification and tacit knowledge', *Industrial and Corporate Change*, **9** (2), 255–87.

Anderlini, L. and A. Ianni (1996), 'Path dependence and learning from neighbours', *Games and Economic Behaviour*, **13**, 141–77.

Appleton, S. and A. Balihuta (1996), 'Education and agricultural productivity: evidence from Uganda', *Journal of International Development*, **8**(3), 415–44.

Arrow, K. (1962), 'The economic implications of learning-by-doing', *Review of Economic Studies*, **29**, 155–73.

Ashenfelter, O. (1991), 'How convincing is the evidence linking education and income?', Industrial Relations Sections, Working Paper, 292.

Ashenfelter, O. and A. Krueger (1992), 'Estimates of the economic returns to schooling from a new sample of twins', NBER, Working Paper, 4143.

Bala, V. and S. Goyal (1995), 'A theory of learning with heterogeneous agents', *International Economic Review*, **36**(2), 303–23.

Bala, V. and S. Goyal (1998), 'Learning from neighbours', *Review of Economic Studies*, **65**, 595–621.

Becattini G. (1990), 'The Marshallian industrial district as a socio-economic notion', in F. Pyke, G. Becattini and W. Sengenberger (eds) *Industrial Districts and Inter-firm Cooperation in Italy*, Geneva, International Institute for Labour Studies.

Becker, G. S. (1964), *Human Capital, a Theory and Empirical Analysis, with Special Reference to Education*, New York: NBER.

Bénabou, R. (1993), 'Working of a city: location education and production', *Quarterly Journal of Economics*, **58**, 619–52.

Berningaus, S. and U. Schwalbe (1996), 'Evolution, interaction, and Nash equilibria', *Journal of Economic Behaviours and Organization*, **29**, 57–85.

Beyer, H. (2000), 'Education and income inequality: a new look', *Estudios Publicos*, 77.

Borgatti, S. P., M. G. Everett, and L. C. Freeman (1999), UCINET 5.0 Version 1.00, Natick, MA: Analytic Technologies.

Bravo, D., D. Contreras, Madrano (1999), 'The return to computer in Chile: does it change after controlling by skill bias?', *mimeo*, Department of Economics, University of Chile.

Breschi, S. and F. Lissoni (2003), 'Mobility and social networks: localised knowledge spillovers revisited', *mimeo*, paper presented at the DRUID Academy Winter 2003 Conference.

Brock, W. and S. Durlauf (1995), 'Discrete choice with social interaction I: theory', NBER Working Paper, 5291.

Card, D. (2001), 'Estimating the return to schooling: progress on some persistent econometric problems', *Econometrica*, **69**(5), 1127–60.

Case, A. and L. Katz (1991), 'The company you keep: the effects of family and neighbourhood on disadvantaged families', NBER Working Paper, 3705.

Chwe, M. S-Y. (2000), 'Communication and coordination in social networks', *Review of Economic Studies*, **67**, 1–16.

Clark, G. (1984), *Innovation Diffusion: Contemporary Geographical Approaches*, Norwich: Geo Books.

Cohen, W. M. and D. A. Levinthal (1989), 'Innovation and learning: the two faces of R&D', *The Economic Journal*, **99** (September), 569–96.

Coleman, J. (1966), *Equality of Education Opportunities*, Washington DC: US Government Printing Office.

Cornes R., and T. Sandler (1996), *The Theory of Externalities, Public Goods and Club Goods*, Cambridge, MA: Cambridge University Press.

Cowan, R., P. A. David and D. Foray (2000), 'The explicit economics of knowledge codification and tacitness', *Industrial and Corporate Change*, **9**(2), 211–53.

Cowan, R. and N. Jonard (1999), 'Network structure and the diffusion of knowledge', MERIT Working Papers, 99–028.

Cowan, R. and N. Jonard (2000), 'The Dynamics of Collective Invention', MERIT Working Papers, 00–018.

Dei Ottati G. (1994), 'Trust, interlinking transactions and credit in the industrial district', *Cambridge Journal of Economics*, **18**, 529–46.

Dougherty, C. R. S., and E. Jimenez (1991), 'The specification of earning functions: tests and implications', *Economics of Education Review*, **10**(2), 85–98.

Durlauf, S. (1996), 'Neighborhood feedbacks, endogenous stratification, and income inequality', in W. Barnett, G. Gandolfo and C. Hillinger (eds), *Dynamic Disequilibrium Modelling*, Cambridge: Cambridge University Press.

Ellison, G. (1993), 'Learning, local interaction, and coordination', *Econometrica*, **61**, 1047–71.

Ellison, G. (2000), 'Basins and attraction, long run stochastic ability and the speed of step-by-step evolution', *Review of Economic Studies*, **67**, 17–45.

Ellison, G. and D. Fudenberg (1993), 'Rules of thumb of social learning', *The Journal of Political Economy*, **101**(4), 612–43.

Ellison, G. and D. Fudenberg (1995), 'Word-of-mouth communication and social learning', *Quarterly Journal of Economics*, **110**(1), 93–125.

Epstain, J. and R. Axtell (1996), *Growing Artificial Societies*, Cambridge, MA and London: The MIT Press.

Goethals, G., G. Winston and D. Zimmerman (1999), 'Students educating students: the emerging role of peer effects in higher education', in M. E. Devlin and J. W. Meyerson (eds), *Future Forums: 1999 Papers*, New Haven, CN: Forum Publishing.

Glaeser, E. L., B. Sacerdote, and P. Scheinkman (1996), 'Crime and social interactions', *Quarterly Journal of Economics*, **111**, 507–48.

Goyal, S. (1996), 'Interaction structure and social change', *Journal of Institutional and Theoretical Economics*, **152**, 472–94.

Granovetter, M. (1973), 'The strength of weak ties', *American Journal of Sociology*, **78**, 1360–80.

Haveman, R. and B. Wolf (1994), *Succeeding Generations: On the Effect of Investments in Children*, New York: Russell Sage Foundation.

Jovanovic, B. and R. Rob (1989), 'The growth and diffusion of knowledge', *Review of Economic Studies*, **56** (198–9), 569–82.

Katz, J. (2001), 'Structural reforms and technological behaviour. The sources and nature of technological change in Latin America in the 1990s', *Research Policy*, **30**, 1–19.

Kiefer, N. (1989), 'A value function arising in economics of information', *Journal of Economic Dynamics and Control*, **7**, 331–7.

Lucas, R. (1988), 'On the mechanics of economic development', *Journal of Monetary Economics*, **22**, 3–42.

Mansfield, E. (1968), *Economics of Technological Changes*, New York: Norton.

Marshall, A. (1952), *Principles of Economics*, London: Macmillan.

Milgram, S. (1967), 'The small world problem', *Psychology Today*, **2**, 60–7.

Mincer, J. (1974), *Schooling, Experience and Earnings*, New York: Columbia University Press.

Morone, P. (2001), 'The two faces of knowledge diffusion: the Chilean case', Universidad de Chile, Departamento de Economia, Working Paper, 178.

Morone, P. and R. Taylor, (2001), 'Knowledge diffusion dynamics and network properties of face-to-face interactions', proceeding of the 6th Workshop on Economics and Heterogeneous Interacting Agents (WEHIA), Maastricht 7–9 June, The Netherlands.

Morone, P. and R. Taylor, (2004), 'Small world dynamics and the process of knowledge diffusion. The case of the metropolitan area of Greater Santiago De Chile', *Journal of Artificial Societies and Social Simulation*, **7**, 1.

Morris, S. (2000), 'Contagion', *Review of Economic Studies*, **67**, 57–68.

Murnane, R., J. B. Willett and F. Levy (1995), 'The growing importance of cognitive skills in wage determination', *Review of Economics and Statistics*, **77**, 251–66.

Nelson, R. and E. Phelps (1966), 'Investment in humans, technological diffusion and economic growth', *American Economic Review*, **56**(1/2), 69–75.

Nonaka, I. and N. Takeuchi (1995), *The Knowledge Creating Company*, Oxford: Oxford University Press.

OECD (1996), *Employment and Growth in the Knowledge-Based Economy*, Paris.

Polanyi, M. (1962), *Personal Knowledge*, London: Routledge.

Psacharopoulos, G. (1994), 'Returns to investment in education: a global update', *World Development*, **22**(9), 1325–43.

Rauch, J. (1993), 'Productivity gains from geographic concentration of human capital: evidence from the cities', *Journal of Urban Economics*, **34**, 380–400.

Rogers, E. M. (1995), *Diffusion of Innovation*, 4th edition, New York: Free Press.

Rosenberg, N. (1982), *Inside the Black Box: Technology and Economics*, Cambridge: Cambridge University Press.

Ryan, B. and N. Gross (1943), 'The diffusion of hybrid seed corn in two Iowa communities', *Rural Sociology*, **8**(1), 15–24.

Saviotti, P. P. (1998), 'On the dynamic of appropriability, of tacit and codified knowledge', *Research Policy*, **26**, 843–56.

Slicher van Bath, B. H. (1963), *The Agrarian History of Europe, A.D. 500–1850*, London: Arnold.

Steinmueller, W. E. (2000), 'Will new information and communication technologies improve the "Codification" of knowledge?', *Industrial and Corporate Change*, **9**, 361–76.

Summers, A. and B. Wolfe (1977), 'Do schools make a difference?', *American Economic Review*, **67**(4), 649–52.

UNDP (1999), *Human Development Report 1999*, New York and Oxford: Oxford University Press.

Wallis, S., and S. Moss (1994), *Efficient Forward Chaining for Declarative Rules in a Multi-Agent Modelling Language*, available online at: http://www.cpm. mmu.ac.uk/cpmreps

Watts, A. (2001), 'A dynamic model of network formation', *Games and Economic Behaviours*, **34**, 331–41.

Watts, D. J. (1999), *Small Worlds*, Princeton: Princeton University Press.

Watts, D. and S. Strogatz (1998), 'Collective dynamics of small-world networks', *Letters to Nature*, **393** (June), 440–2.

Wenger, E. (1998), 'Communities of practice: learning as a social system', *System Thinker*, **9**(5).

Wilson, R. J. and J. J. Watkins (1990), *Graphs: An Introductory Approach*, New York: Wiley.

World Bank (1999), *World Development Report 1998/1999*, New York: Oxford University Press.

PART IV

Measuring and Modelling for Knowledge-based Economies

10. A non-parametric method to identify nonlinearities in global productivity catch-up performance

Bart Los

INTRODUCTION

Economic performances of countries cannot be solely explained by tendencies or policy measures within the countries themselves. Individual countries are parts of an intricate system of ever-changing interdependencies. Some of these interdependencies have a purely economic character, whereas others are of another nature but have strong implications for economic performance. A very important aspect of economic performance is productivity growth. Increases in productivity provide opportunities to attain higher levels of well-being, both in developed and underdeveloped countries. Consequently, economists have directed much effort at descriptions and explanations of international differences in productivity levels and their growth rates. Especially within the popular field of convergence analysis, interdependencies between countries play an important role, although this role is often implicit (at best).

The notion of productivity convergence refers to the idea that productivity levels of countries would become more similar over time. Although this 'definition' could (and maybe should) be qualified in many respects, it can serve well to summarize the types of interdependencies that could yield productivity convergence as emphasized by the two main strands of theory in this field.

Traditional mainstream economists focus on the international mobility of capital. Due to the law of diminishing returns to capital accumulation, new investment will be directed towards countries with still higher returns. By assumption, these have low capital intensities and productivity levels. Because technological progress is generally assumed to be exogenous and uniform across capital intensities, such international investment flows should equalize productivity growth rates and levels in the long run. Scholars who adhere to the technology gap approach adopt a different viewpoint.

They stress the non-immediate international diffusion of technology pertaining to productivity-enhancing innovations. Backward countries would need time to imitate or assimilate such technology, both in embodied and in disembodied form, but would eventually be able to do so. Consequently, more backward countries would 'catch up' faster than less backward countries. This mechanism would ultimately equalize productivity growth rates, leaving a constant proportional productivity gap between the leader country and the follower countries.[1]

In this chapter, we will focus on the technology gap approach, although the core methodology we propose would be easily applicable to mainstream analyses as well. As said, the basic idea of technology gap models is that the dynamics of productivity differences is governed by two opposing forces. The differences tend to be enlarged by innovation in the leader country, while they tend to be reduced by catch-up through technology spillovers to lagging countries. The joint effect of these tendencies can be captured in a very simple regression equation, originally suggested by Abramovitz (1979):[2]

$$\dot{g}_i = \alpha + \beta g_i^0 + \varepsilon_i \tag{1}$$

In this equation, g_i represents the productivity gap, defined as the logarithm of the ratio of the productivity levels of country i and the leader country. The superscript 0 refers to the value in the initial year. In terms of the simplest technology gap model that one could imagine, the intercept α refers to the rate of innovation by the leader, and the slope coefficient β to the ability of countries to benefit from the pool of technology spillovers, which is larger for countries with a large gap (a strongly negative value of g^0). The simple theory thus predicts a positive value for α and a negative value for β, which would imply that all lagging countries would converge towards an equilibrium productivity gap in the long run.

A more advanced model would allow backward countries to innovate independently from the leading country. In this case, estimates for α should be interpreted as the average difference between rates of innovation attained by the backward countries and the leader country. Of course, the autonomous rate of innovation by backward countries can be endogenized to some extent by including right-hand side variables like 'number of patent applications' and 'educational attainment' by country i (see, for example, Fagerberg, 1988; Baumol et al., 1989). The rate of catch-up β, though, is generally assumed to be identical across countries, whereas economic historians like Gerschenkron (1962), Ohkawa and Rosovsky (1973) and Abramovitz (1979, 1986) emphasized the fundamental difference between potential spillovers (indicated by g^0 in Equation (1)) and actual spillovers. According to this literature, the degree to which lagging countries are able to turn potential spillovers into actual spillovers is dependent on their social and technological capabilities, which can be proxied by schooling, R&D, patent and infrastructural indicators, among others.[3] Differences in capabilities could yield complex patterns of convergence and divergence among countries, if only because equilibrium gaps become country-specific.

This chapter adds to the mostly recent literature that seeks to develop methods to identify nonlinearities in catching-up performance and link these to the presence or absence of sufficient capabilities. In the next section we will briefly evaluate some important, earlier, related methodologies. The third section will be devoted to the introduction of a simple nonparametric test that alleviates some of the problems pertaining to the methods in use. In the fourth section, we will describe the data used to illustrate the methodologies. In the fifth and sixth sections the results will be discussed. The final section concludes.

ANALYSIS OF GROWTH NONLINEARITIES: STATE OF THE ART

The usual, linear specification of the catch-up Equation (1) suggests that countries will converge to a situation in which the technology gap between the follower countries takes on a negative, constant equilibrium value, unless the exogenous rates of innovation are equal ($\alpha = 0$).[4] This equilibrium value equals α/β, as can be derived in a straightforward way by setting the left hand side of Equation (1) to zero and solving the right hand side for the gap. The widely found empirical fact that there is no tendency towards such a common gap is not in line with this result. Country-specific values for α could cause this, but the evidence cited by economic historians suggests that country-specific values for the catch-up parameter β are at least equally or probably even more important. A simple linear relation like Equation (1) cannot capture this idea, even if additional regressors would be added.

At least two approaches have been pursued to deal with such nonlinearities.[5] First, Verspagen (1991) derived a nonlinear regression equation. Second, Durlauf and Johnson (1995), Fagerberg and Verspagen (1996) and Cappelen *et al.* (1999) proposed piecewise linear estimation techniques, as did Hansen (2000). Below, we will discuss these contributions briefly.

The Nonlinear Regression Approach

The point of departure of Verspagen (1991) is the observation that Equation (1) is a special case of a more general specification of the dynamics of the technology gap:

$$\dot{g} = \alpha + \beta g e^{-g/\delta} \quad (\delta > 0) \tag{2}$$

Verspagen (1991) argues that the parameter δ can be considered as an indicator of the 'intrinsic learning capability' of a country. Equations (1) and (2) are identical if and only if $\delta = \infty$. In this specific case, actual spillovers equal a fixed fraction of the potential spillovers indicated by the gap itself. As mentioned, this situation will lead to an equilibrium gap of which the size depends on the relative strength of the innovation parameter and the catch-up parameter. For finite values of δ, however, Verspagen (1991) shows that convergence to such an equilibrium gap is not warranted. If δ is lower than the threshold level $\delta^* = \alpha e/\beta$, the productivity gap will tend to infinity, irrespective of the size of the initial gap. In other words, falling behind is the certain outcome of the model. For finite values of the intrinsic learning capability that exceed δ^*, two equilibria exist. If the initial gap is too big (relative to δ), falling behind will result. If the initial gap is relatively small, however, the gap will tend towards a stable value. This value is always larger than α/β.

In his empirical analysis, Verspagen (1991) allowed δ to vary across countries, assuming a common α and β. By means of nonlinear least squares techniques, he estimated a model derived from Equation (2) with δ modelled as a simple function of either educational attainment or electricity generating capacity. The results for a comprehensive sample of 114 countries in the period 1960–85 by and large indicates that the nonlinear specification outperforms linear equations that involve the same variables, in particular if the intrinsic learning capability was measured by education variables. In an analysis of a somewhat more complex model along similar lines, Verspagen (1992) came to the conclusion that more than one-third of the countries in his sample had intrinsic learning capabilities that did not exceed the implicitly computed threshold value δ^*. Only three countries had higher intrinsic learning capabilities, but faced an initial gap so large that it prevented them from catching up with the world leader, the United States. The remaining countries belonged to the category of countries characterized by convergence in productivity growth rates.

The Piecewise Linear Regression Approach

Multiple productivity growth regimes could also prevail in mainstream models based on production factor accumulation. Azariades and Drazen

(1990), for example, suggested that returns to scale may be increasing locally, due to surpassing a 'threshold value' for an accumulable input. Durlauf and Johnson (1995) analysed this issue empirically. The scope of their 'regression tree' analysis is not confined to mainstream theory-inspired investigations, though. For ease of exposition, we will discuss the methodology with reference to the simple technology gap Equation (1).

The main idea is that the parameters α and β may not be homogeneous across an entire sample of countries. Instead, threshold values of some variables might identify different regimes of innovativeness by laggards and/or their ability to catch up. These variables could for example relate to social and technological capabilities, such as schooling or initial productivity. The Durlauf and Johnson (1995) approach basically amounts to simultaneously identifying the apparently most important threshold variable and estimating the value of this variable. The relevant criterion is the maximum reduction of the residual sum of squares obtained by ordinary least squares estimation, added over the two subsamples implied by the 'split'. The estimates (α_1, β_1) and (α_2, β_2), for the first and second subsample respectively, together constitute a piecewise linear function. This procedure is repeated for each of the two subsamples and, if any, the smaller subsamples that result from subsequent splits, until the residual sum of squares cannot be reduced any further or the number of observations within a subsample would become smaller than twice the number of parameters to be estimated. It should be noted that the first split does not preclude other variables to be the threshold variable in subsequent steps.

In usual regression analysis, adding explanatory variables will reduce the residual sum of squares. Without putting a 'penalty' on adding regressors, specifications with many regressors would always be preferred over simpler specifications. One way to avoid such 'overparametrization' is to base the choice of variables on a minimization of the sum of the residual sum of squares and a penalty roughly proportional to the number of regressors (Akaike's information criterion). With respect to reducing the residual sum of squares, adding splits has effects similar to adding regressors. Durlauf and Johnson (1995) propose a variant of Akaike's criterion, in which the penalty is roughly proporional to the number of splits. Application of this criterion ('pruning the regression tree') generally leads to a limited number of splits, the actual number depending on the weight of the penalty function relative to the residual sum of squares. This eventual weight is determined using a rather complicated cross-validation procedure.

In their study inspired by the mainstream augmented production function, Durlauf and Johnson (1995) identify four productivity growth regimes for the period 1960–85. The first split divides the sample of 96 countries into a low-initial productivity subsample (14 countries) and a higher-initial productivity subsample (82 countries). The second subsample was further subdivided, into a low-literacy subsample (34 countries) and a higher-literacy subsample (48 countries), which could be split into an intermediate-initial productivity subsample (27 countries) and a high-initial productivity subsample (21 countries). The estimated coefficients vary wildly across subsamples.

The piecewise linear regression approach also got some attention from authors who have been investigating cross-country productivity growth differences from a catching-up perspective. Fagerberg and Verspagen (1996) included unemployment rates to split their sample of European regions into three subsamples.[6] They found that the effects of EU support through R&D subsidies and investment loans for productivity growth were quite different across the high-, intermediate- and low-unemployment subsamples, which led the authors to consider European regions as 'at different speeds'. In a follow-up study, Cappelen *et al.* (1999) restricted the analysis to a single split for each threshold variable, but considered many more variables. Besides R&D activity levels and unemployment rates, structural characteristics as the shares of agricultural employment (viewed as a retarding factor for growth) and the shares of industrial employment (viewed as an engine of growth) were considered as splitting variables and found to be useful. Other variables, such as population density, population growth and physical infrastructure led to less convincing results.

Assessing the Significance of Nonlinearities in Growth Regressions

Many growth theories suggests that nonlinearities play an important role in the productivity growth process. The empirical work reviewed above yielded interesting results that are often in line with intuition. Nevertheless, at least one pressing question remains. Do nonlinear estimation methodologies perform significantly better (in a statistical sense) than ordinary linear techniques?

Verspagen (1991) subjected his nonlinear regression results to two specification tests, a 'nested' and a 'non-nested' test. Discussion of these rather complicated tests goes beyond the scope of this paper, because the method we will propose in the next section belongs to the class of piecewise linear regression techniques. It should be mentioned, though, that Verspagen (1991) presents strong evidence for the claim that his nonlinear equation outperforms its linear counterpart.

Until the recent contribution by Hansen (2000), almost nothing could be said about the significance of splits found in the piecewise linear regressions. As discussed already, Durlauf and Johnson (1995) relied on a rather ad-hoc 'pruning' procedure to arrive at an apparently reasonable number of splits. In the absence of a known distributional theory for regression trees, it seems impossible to draw strong conclusions on significance levels. Fagerberg and Verspagen (1996) do not report what criterion they used to find exactly three unemployment rate-determined productivity growth regimes. Cappelen *et al.* (1999) are much more explicit on this issue. They base their decision on the significance of a single split on the *F*-statistic used in well-known Chow-tests for structural change. As is explained by Hansen's (2001) very accessible article on dating structural breaks in time series, this procedure leads to over-rejection of the null hypothesis of a single productivity growth regime. The Chow-test assumes that the location of the possible split (for example, an unemployment rate of 0.12) is given beforehand, and not derived from the data. In the procedure by Cappelen *et al.* (1999), however, the location of the split is first estimated by the rate of unemployment for which the reduction of the sum of squared residuals is largest. In general, this will be a split between an observation for the unemployment rate that yields a very negative residual in the linear regression based on the entire sample and an observation that yields a very positive residual, or the other way round.

Hansen (2000) suggested a technique to determine the significance of splits on the basis of asymptotic theory.[7] First, the threshold value of the split variable is estimated in the way first put forward by Durlauf and Johnson (1995). Next, a Lagrange Multiplier test (based on a kind of boot-strapping procedure) is used to get an indication of the significance of the split. This is a parametric test, since it is assumed that the errors are normally distributed around zero. Hansen (2000) finds point estimates of the location of splits that are quite close to the estimates obtained by Durlauf and Johnson (1995). Interestingly, he is also able to present confidence intervals for the location, based on a parametric Likelihood Ratio principle. With regard to the first split (initial income is the threshold variable), the asymptotic 95 per cent-confidence interval appears to be very wide. Actually, for as many as 40 of the 96 countries in the sample, no definite answer can be given to the question to which of the two regimes they belong. Hansen's (2000) approach can formally not be extended to testing for multiple splits, but repeating the same procedure for both subsamples can at least give some good indications of the presence and location of more splits.

This review of existing methods that deal with potential nonlinearities leads us to two interim conclusions, which should offer a justification for the content of the next sections.

First, Verspagen's (1991) nonlinear regression framework is attractive in many respects:

1. it is derived from a simple but elegant theory of productivity growth;
2. it yields sensible results; and
3. it survives exposition to specification tests against linear specifications.

A potentially serious drawback, however, is that the model supposes linearity at a lower level. It assumes that capabilities to assimilate spillovers are proportional to variables like schooling and infrastructure. It could well be that this relation has a different shape in reality, which would lead to a different nonlinear relation between productivity growth and the initial gap. Such an alternative nonlinear specification might do better than Verspagen's nonlinear equation in specification tests. This does not seem to be a viable way to proceed, however, because theory does not offer any clue about the 'right' specification of the relation between capabilities and the inputs that shape capabilities. Empirical clues can neither be obtained, since capabilities are not observable.

Second, the piecewise-linear regression approach is based on an almost opposite modelling perspective. The procedure is entirely data-driven. No functional specification is required a priori, apart from the choice of variables that are included in the 'grand equation'. Theory starts to play a role only at the stage in which the results have to be judged on their plausibility. Significance results rely on asymptotic theory and normality assumptions, which may well be untenable if samples are small. An advantage is that confidence intervals for the location of thresholds can be constructed.

In the next section, we will propose a non-parametric, exact way to test for the presence of two catching-up regimes. We will also propose a non-parametric, though asymptotic, way to construct a confidence interval for the location of the threshold.

BASIC METHODOLOGY AND EXTENSIONS

This section consists of two subsections. In the first subsection, we will explain how the location of a threshold is estimated and its significance will be assessed. The second subsection deals with the construction of confidence intervals for this location.

Point Estimation of a Threshold Value

In statistical terms the problem of detecting two catch-up regimes and assessing the significance of the splitting variable reads as follows. Consider the model

$$\dot{g}_i = \alpha_H + \beta_H g_i^0 + \varepsilon_i, \quad \forall x_i > x_0$$
$$\dot{g}_i = \alpha_L + \beta_L g_i^0 + \varepsilon_i, \quad \forall x_i \leq x_0 \quad i = 1, \ldots, n \quad x_0 \in X \qquad (3)$$

x denotes the splitting variable, and x_0 the threshold value of this variable. It is assumed that the errors ε_i are independent and identically distributed. In order to rule out threshold values very close to the minimum and maximum values of x in the sample (which would yield regimes which would be relevant for just one or two countries) the range X will be chosen in such a way that a reasonable number of countries will be included in both regimes.[8]

$$H_0:(\alpha_H, \beta_H) = (\alpha_L, \beta_L) = (\alpha, \beta) \quad \forall x_0 \in X$$
$$H_1: \exists\, x_0 \in X \text{ for which } (\alpha_H, \beta_H) \neq (\alpha_L, \beta_L)$$

It should be noted that the alternative hypothesis does not make a distinction between situations in which the two regimes differ with respect to one parameter and situations in which both parameters differ across regimes.[9] The procedure we propose to test H_0 against H_1 can best be described as a sequence of steps.

Step 0: Estimate

$$\dot{g}_i = \alpha + \beta g_i^0 + \varepsilon_i, \quad i = 1, \ldots, n$$

Store the sum of squared residuals (*SSR0*). This involves estimating the ordinary linear catch-up Equation (1), for all observations.

Step 1: Order the n countries according to a splitting variable x. For analysis of catching-up performance x should be some variable that affects the social capabilities of countries. The regressor g^0 may act as such, but x is not necessarily included in the piecewise linear function itself. Country 1 has the lowest absorptive capacity, country n the highest. Now, estimate the linear convergence equation for pairs of ordered subsamples. In the first subsample, the first n_1 countries are included, the second subsample contains the $n - n_1 = n_2$ remaining countries. This is done for all values of n_1, as long as both subsamples contain at least a pre-specified number of countries.[10] For each estimation, store the sums of squared residuals *SSR1abs* (corresponding to the first subsample) and *SSR2abs* (second subsample). To complete Step 1, determine the value of n_1 for which *SSR1abs* + *SSR2abs* is found to be lowest and denote $\hat{x}_{n1}$ as the 'potential split' or 'potential threshold value'. Note that Step 1 is exactly identical to the first part of the procedures adopted to arrive at the earlier estimators of piecewise linear functions, as discussed in the previous section.

Step 2: Repeat Step 1 many times (for instance 10 000 times), with x^a as an artificial splitting variable. Each time, the values of x_i^a are obtained by means of a random number generator. Consequently, random orderings of countries are used to obtain artificial 'potential threshold values'. Store *SSR1rand* + *SSR2rand* for each of these. Finally, calculate the fraction of random orderings for which *SSR1rand* + *SSR2rand* is lower than *SSR1abs* + *SSR2abs*. This fraction equals the level of significance of $\hat{x}_{n1}$. If this significance level is lower than a pre-specified level, two catching-up regimes are identified. The 'point' estimate for the critical level of the absorptive capacity variable is in between its value for the countries n_1 and $n_1 + 1$ in the ordering.

In brief, the test procedure outlined above boils down to investigating whether a theoretically sensible splitting variable yields a larger reduction of the sum of squared residual than the large majority of random, theoretically nonsensical, splitting variables.

Confidence Intervals for the Threshold Value

The test procedure indicates whether the splitting variable x defines two productivity growth regimes or not. If so, it also yields a point estimate of the value of x that constitutes the boundary between the two regimes. In statistical terms, this point estimate is dependent on the distribution of the errors. Hence, drawing another hypothetical sample by assigning other realizations of the error generating process and applying the test procedure could yield a different point estimate for the threshold value. Repeating this redrawing many times (for instance 10 000 times) would give a distribution of estimated threshold values. One could cut-off the lowest $0.5 * \theta$ per cent and the highest $0.5 * \theta$ per cent of the estimated threshold values to obtain a $(1 - \theta)$ per cent confidence interval for x_0.

The main problem associated with this approach is that the true distribution of the errors ε is not known. Often, see for example, Hansen (2000), a normal distribution with a fixed variance is assumed. In the case of growth regressions, this assumption seems hard to defend, if only because a glance at the performances of formerly low-productivity countries indicates that these vary across a much wider range than the performances of initially high-productivity country. Heteroscedasticity seems omnipresent and the usefulness of the normal distributions is rather doubtful, as is the justification of the use of test statistics based on this assumption.

Instead of relying on questionable assumptions regarding the distribution of unobserved errors, we propose to use the observed distribution of residuals as an estimate of the actual distribution of errors. We apply a bootstrapping methodology (Efron, 1979, is the classic reference). That is, we start from expected values for $(g_i^0, x_i, i = 1 \ldots n)$ obtained from Model (3) and its least squares estimates (including the threshold value x_0). To each of these expected values we add a randomly drawn residual $\hat{u}_i$ from the distribution obtained for the least squares estimators of Model (3). These drawings are done with replacement, as the distribution of residuals is considered as a discretized version of the actual continuous distributions. This solution to the problem of unobservability of errors allows for the construction of confidence intervals by means of the procedure outlined above.[11]

EMPIRICAL ILLUSTRATION

Data

In this section, we will apply the test for multiple catch-up regimes and the procedure to construct confidence intervals as proposed in the previous section on country-level data. The majority of these are taken from the GGDC Total Economy Database (University of Groningen and The Conference Board, 2003). To include as many observations as possible, the labour productivity variable considered is GDP per worker, instead of, for example, GDP per hour worked. The average annual growth rates are computed over the period 1960–2000. The initial levels are evaluated for 1960. Productivity growth and the initial gap are defined as relative to the growth and initial level of the USA.

Following Verspagen (1991) and Durlauf and Johnson (1995), we consider educational attainment as a variable that might delineate multiple regimes. Many alternative measures of educational attainment are available, and a choice between them is mainly a matter of taste. We choose the average number of schooling years for the entire population (males and females) over 25 years old in 1960 as the variable of interest. These data were taken from Barro and Lee (2001). It should be mentioned that we deliberately choose to included educational attainment in 1960 as a threshold variable, instead of educational attainment in a specific year in between 1960 and 2000, or an average value of this variable for this time period. We agree with Durlauf and Johnson (1995) that one of the latter approaches would imply some endogeneity of the threshold variable, because a good productivity growth performance in early years could allow a country to spend more funds on education. Admittedly, a drawback of our choice is that levels of variables as far back as 1960 are supposed to explain patterns that were partly shaped less than ten years ago.[12]

These choices with regard to variables and time interval left us with 44 observations. Roughly speaking, the sample seems to cover the world's economies rather well. Nevertheless, the rich OECD countries seem to be over-represented, while both (formerly) centrally-led economies and African economies are under-represented.[13] The countries in the sample and the values of the variables of interest are included in Appendix A.

Test for Thresholds

Estimation of Equation (1) for the entire sample yields a result that does
not point towards convergence:

$$\dot{g} = 0.00797 + 0.00125g^0$$

According to standard heteroscedasticity-consistent t-tests, the slope is far
from significantly different from zero. The intercept is significantly positive
(p-value: 0.034). This would point towards a general tendency for countries
to converge to the US productivity levels. This would be caused by better
abilities to innovate than the USA, which is of course highly counter-
intuitive. Within the sample of lagging countries, however, no convergence
in labour productivity levels seems to occur. This could lead to a conclusion
that catching-up is no important factor in the process of productivity
growth. It should be noted that the (admittedly simple) model has an
extremely poor fit. Actually, only 0.5 per cent of the total variation of
growth rates can be explained. $SSR0$ used to compute this value of R^2 equals
0.01018. Figure 10.1 presents the datapoints and the estimated technology-
gap equation. The conclusions drawn above are quite clearly reflected in this
diagram, in which the dashed line indicates the estimated equation.

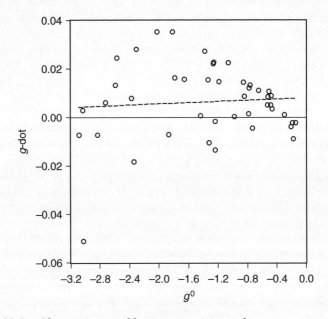

Figure 10.1   Observations and basic regression results

Next, we re-estimated the model, but now allowed for a threshold effect. Following Durlauf and Johnson's (1995) lead, we experimented with two potential threshold variable candidates. First, we looked at the initial labour productivity gap g^0. Second, we repeated the analysis for the educational attainment variable described in the previous section. In both cases, we decided that at least five countries should be included in a subsample. This minimum size falls within the trimming bounds of 5 to 15 per cent of the number of observations, as suggested by Hansen (2001).

For the initial gap as the splitting variable, the sum of squared residuals appears to be minimimal for $n_1 = 9$ and $n_2 = 35$. The sum of squared residuals ($SSR1abs + SSR2abs$) is reduced to 0.00718. Application of the same procedure for educational attainment yields subsample sizes of $n_1 = 15$ and $n_2 = 24$. In this case, the sum of squared residuals turns out to be somewhat lower, 0.00652. Irrespective of the choice of threshold variable, the estimates for both parameters appear insignificant (p-values above 0.2) for the first subsample. For these, low-initial productivity and low-schooling subsamples, tendencies towards convergence seem absent. For the second subsamples a much clearer picture emerges. The estimated intercepts are not significant. This points to a situation in which the 'intrinsic' abilities to innovate are in general not different from the USA. For the catch-up parameter β, significant negative estimates are found. For the initial gap threshold variable, this estimate equals -0.01141, with a small associated p-value of 0.002. Schooling as a threshold variable yields a point estimate of -0.01264 and a p-value of 0.0004.

As mentioned, the sum of squared residuals is smaller for the educational attainment threshold variable than for the initial labour productivity gap threshold variable. It remains to be seen, though, whether the reduction is sufficiently large to conclude that a threshold is present indeed. We performed Step 2 of the testing procedure outlined in Section 3 10000 times. In only 318 cases, the sum of squared residuals appeared to be lower than found for the educational attainment threshold variable and $n_1 = 15$. Thus, in view of the p-value of 0.032, educational attainment is found to define two catching-up regimes.[14] Further, it should be noted that we could not reject the null hypothesis of a single regime against the alternative of two regimes identified on the basis of initial productivity gaps. The p-value for this test was 0.107.[15]

A natural question to ask is whether the labour productivity dynamics is best characterized by two regimes. It might well be that three or more regimes are present. This is hard to test in a statistically sound way, as was also stated by Hansen (2000) for his parametric analysis. A first, and arguably not too bad indication can be obtained by repeating the testing procedure for the two subsamples. Thus, we first look at the 'low-schooling' subsample of 15 countries and tested for a single regime for this sample against the alternative of two regimes based on either initial gap or educational attainment. This subsample does not show any symptoms of multiple regimes. The *p*-values (again based on 10 000 random orderings) are 0.715 and 0.609 for the initial productivity gap variable and the schooling variable, respectively.

Next, we run the same procedure for the 'high-schooling' subsample of 29 countries. This yields a very significant threshold value, with a *p*-value of only 0.0022.[16] The 'medium-schooling' sample consists of only six countries, mostly located in East Asia: Korea, Singapore, Spain, Sri Lanka, Taiwan and Thailand. This subsample is characterized by a rather high point estimate for α (although just insignificant at 5 per cent, according to a *t*-test) relative to the high-schooling subsample. For both subsamples, the catching-up parameter β estimate is insignificant. This leaves us with a rather uncomfortable result: medium-schooling countries might well be the only countries with a positive innovation differential to the USA, whereas theory would suggest that this should only be the case for countries with a high educational attainment. Further, and maybe even more striking, catching-up to the world productivity leader does not seem to play a role within any of the three subsamples. An alternative, reasonable explanation can be offered, however. The model could suffer from omitted variables. The 'medium-schooling' subsample might therefore be a group of outliers under a single productivity regime, instead of being governed by a separate regime. An indication of the potential power of this explanation is given by the results found if we require each subsample to contain at least seven (instead of five) observations. In that case, a still very significant split ($p = 0.014$) is identified for $n_1 = 13$ and $n_2 = 16$. The estimated equations are

$$\text{medium-schooling subsample:} \quad \dot{g} = -0.00319 - 0.01245g^0$$
$$\text{high-schooling subsample:} \quad \dot{g} = -0.00734 - 0.02543g^0$$

The coefficients in these equations all have *p*-values well below 5 per cent, except for the intercept in the medium-schooling subsample. More importantly, these results are much more in line with theory. That is, in general, follower countries do not have higher innovative abilities than the world productivity leader. Further, countries with higher educational attainments were catching-up at a faster rate. For the methodology, however, these results indicate a weakness: if the number of observations is small, clustered outliers can well affect the results if trimming is relatively weak. Therefore, more research is required to prescribe rules-of-thumb for the minimum subsample size.

Confidence Intervals for Thresholds

As discussed in more general terms on pp. 238–40, the analysis on catching-up regimes presented in the previous section yields a point estimate for threshold value between different regimes. This estimate of the threshold value depends on a single realization of a stochastic process, however. In this section, we will apply the procedure outlined on pp. 240–41 to produce a confidence interval for the threshold value of the schooling variable. We will restrict our analysis to the first split, which breaks our sample into just two subsamples.

In fact, our point estimate is not a 'real' point estimate. The actual point estimate tells us that the threshold value would be located in the range of average years of education of the population of 25 years old and over between 3.02 and 3.14. These educational attainment values relate to Peru and Singapore, the most 'schooled' country of the low-schooling subsample and the least schooled country of the high-schooling subsample, respectively. More precise point estimates are impossible to obtain, without strong assumptions on error distributions. Although this issue might have been more important if our estimated threshold had been located in between two countries that differed strongly with respect to their educational attainments in 1960, this identification problem is not the topic of this subsection.

Our main concern is illustrated by Figure 10.2. On the horizontal axis, the values of the educational attainment variable are depicted. The values on the vertical axis indicate the sum of squared residuals that are obtained by

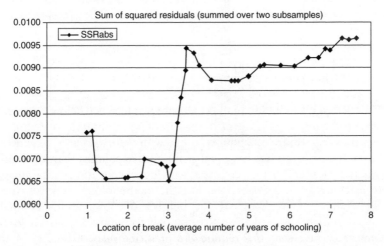

Figure 10.2   Sensitivity of sum of squared residuals to location of break

splitting the sample for a specific value on the horizontal axis. These values are obtained in the process of testing for the significance of a threshold variable. The leftmost point thus refers to the sum of squared residuals obtained for the minimal size of the first subsample, that is $n_1 = 5$. Analogously, the rightmost point is the observation for the opposite extreme, $n_2 = 5$.

The minimum value is found for $n_1 = 15$. For smaller values of the threshold variable, however, the sum of squared residuals is almost as low. For higher values, the reduction in comparison to the single regime case is much smaller. Thus, we expect that other realizations of the stochastic error-generating process will often yield point estimates of the average number of years of schooling that indicates the border between the two regimes well below 3.0, and relatively seldom above that value.

The results for 10 000 replications of the procedure are summarized by Figure 10.3. The diagram presents the frequency distribution of the estimated n_1s, that is, the size of the low-schooling subsample. This frequency distribution is in line with our expectations. Most observations are for $n_1 = 15$, a value found for approximately 20 per cent of the observations. Further, much of the distribution's mass is found for smaller values of n_1, while relatively few replications yield high values. Actually, only about 17 per cent of the replications yield a low-schooling subsample that contains 16 or more countries.

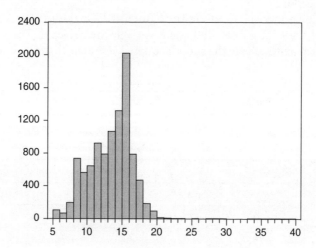

Notes:
Horizontal axis: number of countries in low-schooling subsample.
Vertical axis: frequency (10 000 observations in total).

*Figure 10.3   Frequency distribution of estimated low-schooling
               subsample size*

As argued on pp. 240–41, the empirical distribution function allows us to construct confidence intervals for the threshold value. A two-sided 90 per cent confidence interval is found by eliminating the 500 lowest values of n_1 and its 500 highest values. For n_1, this yields the interval [8, 17]. The corresponding values of the average number of years of schooling are [1.45, 3.23]. This can be regarded as a rather wide interval. Of course, similarly constructed 95 per cent confidence intervals are even wider, [7, 18] for n_1 and [1.20, 3.32] for the educational attainment variable, respectively.

This analysis provides a first indication of the range within which the threshold value is located. In the literature on bootstrapping, it is stressed that the reliance on point estimators such as our least squares estimator of the threshold value and the coefficients of the two productivity dynamics equations in Model (1) is only warranted if these are unbiased. If not, bias correction procedures should be applied.[17] At present, we do not have reasons to believe that our estimators are unbiased, but we should prove this conjecture by means of simulation analysis.

CONCLUSIONS

In this chapter, we offered a non-parametric method to test whether a very simple catching-up model of labour productivity growth should account for the possibility that multiple catching-up regimes co-exist. Further, we proposed a way to construct confidence intervals for the threshold value between two such regimes, by means of bootstrapping techniques. The methods were implemented for a small dataset on labour productivity dynamics for aggregate economies in the period 1960–2000. We did not find evidence for two or more regimes if the labour productivity gap to the world leader (the USA) was used as an indicator of social capabilities. For an educational attainment variable, however, the test pointed to at least two regimes. The confidence intervals for the threshold value of this schooling variable appeared to be rather wide, in particular towards the lower end of the schooling spectrum.

An attempt to find evidence for a second threshold showed that the method is not flawless if the number of observations is very limited. In that case, the results appeared to be very sensitive to the minimum number of observations contained in a subsample. The method does not endogenously decide on this argument, thus introducing some arbitrariness. More investigations into this issue might reveal that related literature on parametric suggests solutions to this problem.

Another caveat refers to the construction of confidence intervals. Implicitly, we assume that our point estimators are unbiased. Although we do not see a reason why this would not be the case, we should study the validity of this assumption thoroughly. If the assumption would turn out to be untenable, we should leave our very simple and intuitive methodology and opt for a more complex alternative. The basic idea, however, could remain unchanged. This also holds for a test that could cope with heteroscedasticity.

In this chapter, we emphasized methodological issues, instead of the economic interpretation of results. For instance, we did not discuss the plausibility of the result that multiple regimes are found for schooling as a potential splitting or threshold variable, while the initial productivity gap did not give reason to multiple regimes. This is an interesting finding in itself, though, because more neoclassically-oriented studies into the existence of multiple productivity growth regimes found contrary results. A study which would apply our methodology to related datasets could tell more about the robustness of this result, as could application of our methodology to a different (probably more advanced) model.

A final question to be discussed is of a more fundamental nature. Is it natural to suppose that worldwide labour productivity growth could be regarded as being governed by a finite number of linear regimes, as we implicitly assume? Or should we adopt the viewpoint that there is a smooth continuum of 'regimes', that relate the productivity performance of countries to each other in a nonlinear way? Some very preliminary analyses on the same database, using varying coefficient models (for example, Hastie and Tibshirani, 1993) seem to suggest that this might prove a promising avenue of research. Nevertheless, we feel that refinement and application of the techniques proposed in this paper deserves attention in our future work.

ACKNOWLEDGEMENTS

Earlier versions of this paper were presented at EMAEE 2003 (Augsburg, 10–12 April) and a Technology and Economic Growth workshop (Maastricht, 11 June 2003). I would like to thank Bart van Ark, Paul Bekker, Marcel Timmer and Bart Verspagen for very useful suggestions. My research has been made possible by a grant from the Dutch Organization for Scientific Research NWO.

NOTES

1. This description is purposefully simplified. Since its inception by Solow (1956) the mainstream view has been modified in many respects, for instance by including human capital as a separate production factor that captures some aspects of innovation (for example, Mankiw *et al.*, 1992). Moreover, many adopters of the technology gap perspective (Gerschenkron (1962) is generally seen as the classic study) feel that sufficient capital

good accumulation is a precondition for innovation and catch-up (for example, Fagerberg, 1988). Bernard and Jones (1996), Basu and Weil (1998) and Los and Timmer (2005) offer approaches that combine elements from both perspectives on convergence in different ways.

2. Abramovitz (1979) actually computed rank correlation coefficients between the left hand side and right hand side variables (although not standardized by the performance of the leader), and found an inverse relationship.

3. To our knowledge, Nelson and Phelps (1966) were the first to relate the availability of human capital to the speed of technology diffusion in the framework of a formal model. The importance of technological capabilities at the firm level was assessed empirically by Cohen and Levinthal (1989), who coined this concept 'absorptive capacity'. Note that governmental policies can affect the availability of capabilities, as opposed to variables like geographical location found in many studies that try to explain productivity growth differentials.

4. If $\alpha < 0$, follower countries would eventually overtake the productivity level of the initial leader. Although productivity leadership has historically changed a couple of times, it has done so only among a very limited number of countries. Hence, it may be appropriate to confine our theoretical analysis to non-negative values of the intercept.

5. Durlauf (2001) views careful treatment of nonlinearities (as suggested by modern mainstream growth theories) as one of the most promising avenues for research in applied growth econometrics.

6. Fagerberg and Verspagen (1996) used a simplified version of the Durlauf and Johnson (1995) methodology, in which only one splitting variable was considered at a time. Initial labour productivity and EU-funded R&D activities did not produce as large reductions in the sum of squared residuals as unemployment rates did.

7. Papageorgiou (2002) used the Hansen (2000) technique to identify growth regimes caused by differences in trade openness.

8. See Hansen (2001), who also suggests this 'trimming' to save desirable distributional properties of his test statistic.

9. The test outlined below supposes that the errors are homoscedastic, that is, they have an identical variance. In growth regressions including developing countries, this assumption is hardly defendable. The F-test and the tests by Durlauf and Johnson (1995) and Hansen (2001) share the same weakness.

10. This corresponds to X in Model (3).

11. This procedure could be refined, for instance by adoption of methodologies to account for differences between the estimate of the threshold value and its actual value. In this chapter, we do not consider these. Results should therefore be taken with some caution.

12. Verspagen (1991) opted for the alternative choice, by defining one of his social capability indicators as a weighted average of electricity generating capacities over years for which productivity growth rates were analysed.

13. Although this assertion is rather speculative, the under-representation of low-productivity countries might well lead to underestimation of the number of productivity growth regimes (in view of the trimming procedure, which implies that each subsample should at least contain a predetermined number of observations).

14. Figure 10.1 suggests that Zaïre (the observation in the extreme southwest of the diagram) might drive the result of multiple regimes. A robustness check in which this observation was excluded did not yield qualitatively different results. The threshold value remained identical and the p-value of the test decreased to below 0.01.

15. Interestingly, application of the procedure adopted by Cappelen *et al.* (1999) would have yielded strong evidence in favour of multiple initial gap-based regimes. Their Chow-test (2, 40 degrees of freedom) would yield a value of 8.355, which corresponds to a p-value of only 0.0009. Careful inspection of Figure 10.1 shows that $n_1 = 9$ implies that the last observation included in the 'low-initial productivity' subsample has the second most negative residual in the one-regime regression, while the first observation included in the 'high-initial productivity' subsample appears to yield the third most positive residual. The Chow-test is only valid if the threshold value is chosen independently from the data.

16. Again, the initial productivity gap threshold variable did not produce a significant split at reasonable levels of significance.
17. If one or more estimators would be biased, this would invalidate the choice of the distribution of observed residuals as an approximation for the distribution of unobserved errors.

REFERENCES

Abramovitz, M. (1979), 'Rapid growth potential and its realization: The experience of capitalist economies in the postwar period', in E. Malinvaud (ed.), *Economic Growth and Resources, Volume 1*, London: Macmillan, pp. 1–30.

Abramovitz, M. (1986), 'Catching up, forging ahead, and falling behind', *Journal of Economic History*, **46**, 385–460.

Azariadis, C. and A. Drazen (1990), 'Threshold externalities in economic development' *Quarterly Journal of Economics*, **105,** 501–26.

Barro, R. J. and J-W. Lee (2001), 'International data on educational attainment: Updates and implications', *Oxford Economic Papers*, **53**, 541–63.

Basu, S. and D. N. Weil, 'Appropriate technology and growth', *Quarterly Journal of Economics*, **113**, 1025–54.

Bernard, A. B. and C. I. Jones (1996), 'Technology and convergence', *Economic Journal*, **106**, 1037–44.

Baumol, W. J., S. A. Batey Blackman and E. N. Wolff (1989), *Productivity and American Leadership: The Long View*, Cambridge MA: MIT Press.

Cappelen, A., J. Fagerberg and B. Verspagen (1999), 'Lack of regional convergence', in J. Fagerberg, P. Guerrieri and B. Verspagen (eds), *The Economic Challenge for Europe: Adapting to Innovation Based Growth*, Cheltenham UK: Edward Elgar, pp. 130–48.

Cohen, W. M. and D. A. Levinthal (1989), 'Innovation and learning: The two faces of R&D', *Economic Journal*, **99**, 569–96.

Durlauf, S. N. (2001), 'Manifesto for a growth econometrics', *Journal of Econometrics*, **100**, 65–9.

Durlauf, S. N. and P. A. Johnson (1995), 'Multiple regimes and cross-country growth behaviour', *Journal of Applied Econometrics*, **10**, 365–84.

Efron, B. (1979), 'Bootstrap methods: Another look at the jackknife', *Annals of Statistics*, **7**, 1–26.

Fagerberg, J. (1988), 'Why growth rates differ', in G. Dosi, C. Freeman, R. R. Nelson, G. Silverberg and L. Soete (eds), *Technical Change and Economic Theory*, London: Pinter, pp. 432–57.

Fagerberg, J. and B. Verspagen (1996), 'Heading for divergence? Regional growth in Europe reconsidered', *Journal of Common Market Studies*, **34**, 431–48.

Gerschenkron, A. (1962), *Economic Backwardness in Historical Perspective*, Cambridge MA: Belknap Press.

Hansen, B. E. (2000), 'Sample splitting and threshold estimation', *Econometrica*, **68**, 575–603.

Hansen, B. E. (2001), 'The new econometrics of structural change: Dating breaks in US labor productivity', *Journal of Economic Perspectives*, **15**, 117–28.

Hastie, T. and R. Tibshirani (1993), 'Varying-coefficient models', *Journal of the Royal Statistical Society B*, **55**, 757–96.

Los, B. and M. P. Timmer (2005), 'The "appropriate technology" explanation of productivity growth differentials: An empirical approach', *Journal of Development Economics*, **77**, 517–31.

Mankiw, N. G., D. Romer and D. N. Weil (1992), 'A contribution to the empirics of economic growth', *Quarterly Journal of Economics*, **107**, 407–37.

Nelson, R. R. and E. S. Phelps (1966), 'Investment in humans, technological diffusion, and economic growth', *American Economic Review, Papers and Proceedings*, **56**, 69–75.

Ohkawa, K. and H. Rosovsky (1973), *Japanese Economic Growth*, Stanford: Stanford University Press.

Papageorgiou, C. (2002), 'Trade as a threshold variable for multiple regimes', *Economics Letters*, **77**, 85–91.

Solow, R. M. (1956), 'A contribution to the theory of economic growth', *Quarterly Journal of Economics*, **70**, 65–95.

University of Groningen and The Conference Board (2003), *GGDC Total Economy Database*, http://www.eco.rug.nl/ggdc (accessed on 10 February 2003).

Verspagen, B. (1991), 'A new empirical approach to catching up or falling behind', *Structural Change and Economic Dynamics*, **2**, 359–80.

Verspagen, B. (1992), 'Uneven growth between interdependent economies', Ph.D. Thesis, University of Limburg.

APPENDIX A: SAMPLE CHARACTERISTICS

Countries are ordered according to their initial labour productivity gaps. Column headers refer to the following variables:

INITGAP: natural logarithm of GDP/worker of country in 1960 to GDP/worker of the USA in 1960 (source: University of Groningen and The Conference Board, 2003).

GROWTH: average annual growth rate of GDP/worker of country in 1960–2000 minus average annual growth rate of GDP/worker of the USA in 1960–2000 (source: University of Groningen and The Conference Board, 2003).

SCHOOLING: average number of schooling years of entire population aged 25 and over (source: Barro and Lee, 2001).

	INITGAP	GROWTH	SCHOOLING
1 Kenya	−3.090541	−0.007369	1.20
2 Burma	−3.034502	0.002940	0.97
3 Zaïre	−3.032776	−0.051021	0.56
4 Bangladesh	−2.834400	−0.007212	0.79
5 India	−2.725251	0.006144	1.45
6 Pakistan	−2.591427	0.013305	0.63
7 Thailand	−2.569596	0.024413	3.45
8 Indonesia	−2.368618	0.007990	1.11
9 Ghana	−2.337197	−0.018392	0.69
10 Sri Lanka	−2.306328	0.028008	3.43
11 Korea	−2.022904	0.035356	3.23
12 Philippines	−1.863815	−0.007191	3.77
13 Taiwan	−1.812441	0.035236	3.32
14 Malaysia	−1.783009	0.016348	2.34
15 Turkey	−1.653433	0.015677	2.00
16 Brazil	−1.438171	0.000661	2.83
17 Singapore	−1.381946	0.027299	3.14
18 Portugal	−1.331659	0.015496	1.94
19 South Africa	−1.322980	−0.010448	4.08
20 Spain	−1.266535	0.022186	3.64
21 Japan	−1.259673	0.022714	6.87
22 Peru	−1.240228	−0.013421	3.02
23 Colombia	−1.239998	−0.001749	2.97

		INITGAP	GROWTH	SCHOOLING
24	Greece	−1.188852	0.014757	4.64
25	Ireland	−1.062227	0.022590	6.45
26	Mexico	−0.976179	0.000298	2.41
27	Finland	−0.851216	0.014406	5.37
28	Israel	−0.840021	0.008762	6.99
29	Chile	−0.783847	0.001528	4.99
30	Austria	−0.779124	0.012089	6.71
31	Italy	−0.765787	0.013393	4.56
32	Argentina	−0.735929	−0.004476	4.99
33	Hongkong	−0.652546	0.011030	4.74
34	Sweden	−0.525499	0.005093	7.65
35	Norway	−0.518960	0.008504	6.11
36	Belgium	−0.508081	0.010663	7.46
37	Denmark	−0.485456	0.005024	8.95
38	France	−0.478826	0.008937	5.78
39	UK	−0.462938	0.003472	7.67
40	Australia	−0.295109	0.001064	9.43
41	Switzerland	−0.210945	−0.003858	7.30
42	Netherlands	−0.189182	−0.002390	5.27
43	New Zealand	−0.178020	−0.008866	9.56
44	Canada	−0.141383	−0.002200	8.37

11. Self-reinforcing dynamics and the evolution of business firms

Giulio Bottazzi and Angelo Secchi

Recent empirical analyses on different datasets have revealed a common exponential behaviour in the shape of the probability density of the corporate growth rates. In this chapter we propose a very simple simulation model that, under rather general assumptions, provides a robust explanation of the observed regularities. The model is based on a stochastic process describing the random partition of a number of 'business opportunities' among a population of identical firms. This model exactly reproduces the empirical findings in the limit of a large number of firm. We show, however, that even in a moderately small industry the agreement with asymptotic results is almost complete.

INTRODUCTION

One of the traditional problems in the Industrial Organization literature concerns the statistical properties of the size of firms and its dynamics. Recently a new strand of analysis, pioneered by Stanley et al. (1996), focused on different aspects of the firm growth process. The most robust empirical finding in this literature (see also Bottazzi and Secchi (2003) and Bottazzi et al. (2003)) concerns the tent-shape of the growth rates distribution. In the first part of this work we review evidence concerning this finding from US and Italian manufacturing industries. In the second part we present a model able to provide an economic interpretation of the mentioned empirical findings.

The literature offers few stochastic models aimed at the explanation of this kind of regularities in industrial dynamics. Moreover, from the seminal work of Gibrat (1931) to the more recent contributions of Geroski (2000) and Amaral et al. (2001), a large part of these models presents a noticeable theoretical shortcoming: they do not assume any interdependence between the histories of different firms (for a critical review of the relevant literature see Sutton (1997)). A different kind of model, originally proposed by

Simon (see Ijiri and Simon (1977)) and later reconsidered by Sutton (1998), makes the assumption that there is a finite set of pre-existing 'growth' opportunities (or equivalently, a constant arrival of new opportunities) and that firms' growth process is conditioned by the number of opportunities they are able to catch. Roughly speaking, one could say that these models, generically known as 'islands models', try to provide a first account of the competitive behaviour among firms based on the idea that firms, to maintain and expand their business, need to seize the most out of a scarce resource.

In the present chapter we build a stylized model of firm dynamics where this idea of 'competition' is introduced. The model is similar to the previously cited tradition, at least in its aspiration to meet both the requirements of simplicity and generality. A stochastic model is used and each firm is considered a different realization of the same process. Similarly to what happens in the 'islands models', this symmetry is however broken at the aggregate level, in the sense that the total growth of the firms' population is bounded by a finite set of sector-specific opportunities.

The novelty of our approach resides in the way in which we design the random distribution of opportunities among firms. The assumption, common in the Simon-inspired models, that a random 'assignment' of opportunities across firms can provide a zero-level approximation of a competitive dynamics, in other terms a 'competition with random outcome', provides only a partial characterization of the dynamics. Indeed the implied random process of 'assignment' must be specified. In providing this specification, we depart from the original 'splitting' procedure, found in this literature, and we introduce a different statistic to describe the outcome of the 'random competition'. From a theoretical point of view the distinctive feature of this statistic resides in its ability to represent self-reinforcing mechanisms in which the probability, for a given firm, to catch a new opportunity depends on the number of opportunities already caught. In a more phenomenological perspective one could, however, say that the fundamental justification of choosing a different description for the 'opportunities assignment' relies on the possibility of obtaining much better description of the empirical findings. Rephrasing William Feller: 'We have here an instructive example of the impossibility of selecting or justifying probability models by A PRIORI argument' (Feller, 1968; 41).

In the next section we briefly review the relevant empirical findings. In the third section we propose a new stochastic simulation model of the growth process which we analyse in the fourth section. We conclude in the final section.

EMPIRICAL MOTIVATION

Some years ago in a series of papers based on the COMPUSTAT database Stanley *et al.* (1996) and Amaral *et al.* (1997) analysed the probability distribution of the (log) growth rates of many US manufacturing firms. These studies were performed at the aggregate level using observations in the time frame 1974–93 and on companies with primary activity[1] belonging to the SIC code range 2000–3999. The authors found that the growth rates followed a tent-shape distribution, and in particular, they proposed to describe the empirical observations using a Laplace (symmetric exponential) functional form

$$f_L(x; \mu, a) = \frac{1}{2a} e^{-\frac{|x-\mu|}{a}}.$$ (1)

In the present section we add further evidence extending the analysis of the COMPUSTAT database to a higher level of disaggregation.

We consider COMPUSTAT data for more than one thousand US publicly traded firms in 15 different two digit sectors (SIC code ranges between 2000–3999) of the manufacturing industry. We perform the analysis on the time window 1982–2001.

We also analyse a new databank, called MICRO.1, developed by the Italian Statistical Office (ISTAT).[2] MICRO.1 contains longitudinal data on a panel of several thousands of Italian manufacturing firms, with 20 or more employees, over a decade and belonging to more than 50 different three digit industrial sectors.

In both analyses, we use sales as a definition of the size of the firm. We do not present here a detailed statistical description of the business companies and their dynamics; for an in depth analysis of the COMPUSTAT database see Bottazzi and Secchi (2003) while a more extensive description of the MICRO.1 database can be found in Bottazzi *et al.* (2003). Our aim here is to show that there exists a robust property concerning the growth rates distributions that seems largely invariant both across countries and sectors.

Let $S_{i,j}(t)$ represent the sales of the *i*-th firm in the *j*-th sector at time *t*, we consider the normalized (log) sales

$$S_{i,j}(t) = \log(S_{i,j}(t)) - <\log(S_{i,j}(t)) >_j$$ (2)

where $<. >_j$ stands for the average over all the firms of sector *j*. The log growth rates are defined as:

$$g_{i,j}(t) = s_{i,j}(t+1) - s_{i,j}(t)$$ (3)

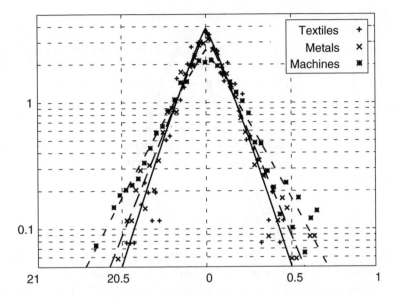

Figure 11.1   Growth rates densities for Italian textiles (ATECO 172), treatment of metals (ATECO 285) and machinery (ATECO 295)

In Figures 11.1–11.4 we report the growth rates density for six different sectors of Italian and US manufacturing considered, respectively, at three and two digits level. These sectors were chosen because they are both numerous and technologically diverse. Their activities indeed range from shoe-making to the treatment of metals for industrial purposes. The different years of data are pooled together since the differences across time in the distribution shape are negligible for any sector. As can be seen, the Laplace distribution well describes the observations even in the MICRO.1 database and at a high level of disaggregation.

A SIMULATION MODEL OF FIRM GROWTH

In the broad literature about the growth dynamics of business firms, there exists a well established tradition that describes the modification of the size of a business firm, over a given period of time, as the cumulative effect of a number of different 'size' shocks originated by the diverse accidents that affected the firm in that period (see, among many contributors, Kalecki (1945); Ijiri and Simon (1977); Steindl (1965) and more recently Amaral *et al.* (2001); Geroski (2000); Sutton (1998)). These models of growth are

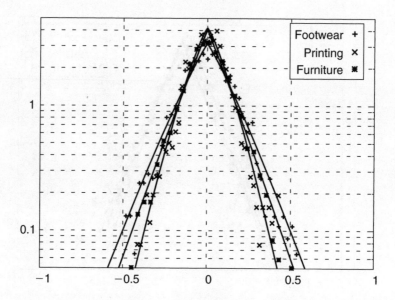

*Figure 11.2   Growth rates densities for Italian footwear (ATECO 193),
               printing (ATECO 222) and furniture (ATECO 361)*

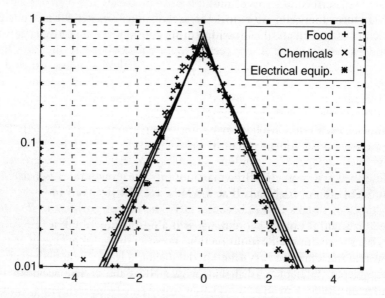

*Figure 11.3   Growth rates densities for US food (SIC 20), basic
               chemicals (SIC 28) and electrical equipment (SIC 36)*

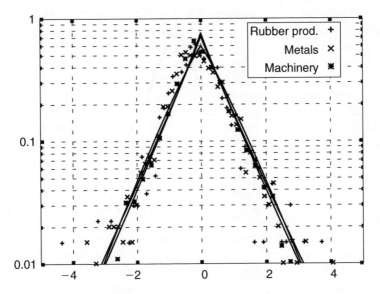

Figure 11.4   Growth rates densities for US rubber products (SIC 30), metals (SIC 33) and industrial machinery (SIC 35)

usually described in terms of multiplicative processes and then it is natural to use logarithmic quantities to describe the 'status' of a given firm. Consider a firm i and let $s_i(t)$ be the logarithm of its size at time t. One can write

$$g_i(t;\, T) = s_i(t + T) - s_i(t) = \sum_{j=1}^{G_i(t;T)} S_j(t) \qquad (4)$$

where the firm growth in the period $[t, t + T]$ is described as a sum of $G_i(t;\, T)$ 'shocks' each one having a finite effect ε on firm size[3]. In the oldest and probably most controversial model of Gibrat (1931) the shocks are assumed independent random variables, so that the firms' growth is described as a geometric Brownian motion. The growth rates associated to different non-overlapping time periods are independent and when the number of shocks $G_i(t;T)$ becomes large the rate of growth $g_i(t;\, T)$ tends, for the Central Limit Theorem, towards a normal distribution.

We showed in the previous section, however, that this is not the case in the real world: in two very different databases, at least when yearly data are considered, a Laplace distribution fits the data much better than a Gaussian. Since Gibrat's model cannot yield an equilibrium distribution of the growth rates that resembles the observed one, we are led to conclude that some of the assumptions adopted are not appropriate.

Probably the most noticeable drawback of Gibrat's idea resides in the implicit assumption that company growth processes are completely independent. This is equivalent to assuming that any form of competition is absent even among firms operating in the same sector and selling on the same market. This assumption sounds rather implausible. To this respect, a different theoretical tradition, dating back to the early work of Simon and recently renewed by Sutton (1998), has been developed with the aim of introducing in Gibrat-type stochastic models a stylized description of competition and entry dynamics.

These models assume the existence of a finite number of business opportunities available to firms. All the firms compete to take up these opportunities and their growth process is measured by the number of opportunities that they are able to seize. These models, however, assume equiprobability of incumbent firms to capture new business opportunities. In this case the unconditional distribution of the random variable G_i for a given firm is binomial; hence in the limit of many small opportunities one obtains again, via the Law of Large Numbers, a Gaussian form for the growth rates distribution.

The remainder of this section is devoted to presenting a model showing that if one modifies this basic assumption of 'equal assignment probabilities' of each opportunity the shape of the growth rates distribution changes and is no longer Gaussian. We describe the growth of a firm as a two step process. In the first step there is a random assignment among firms of a given number of business opportunities leading to a possible realization of the random variables G_i. These opportunities represent all the variegated 'accidents' that can plausibly affect the history of a business firm, encompassing, for instance, the exploitation of technological novelties, the reaction to demand shocks and the effects of managerial reorganizations. The assigned business opportunities, in the second step, act as the source of micro-shocks affecting the size of the firm according to Equation (4).

We run a computer experiment considering a fixed number of firms N and a fixed number M of business opportunities. At each round of the simulation, the M opportunities are randomly assigned to the N firms. Instead of assuming, as common in the aforementioned models, that the assignment of each opportunity is an independent event with constant probability $1/N$, we introduce the idea of 'competition among objects whose *market success* . . . [is] cumulative or self-reinforcing' (Arthur, 1994, 1996). Economies of scale, economies of scope, network externalities and knowledge accumulation are just few examples of possible underlying economic mechanisms that are able to generate these effects of positive feedbacks within markets, businesses and industries. We model this idea with a process where the probability for a given firm to obtain a new opportunity is proportional to the number of opportunities already caught. We do that assigning the opportunities to firms one at a time in M successive steps. When the mth ($m < M$) opportunity is to be assigned, we assign it to firm i with probability

$$p_i = \frac{1 + l_i(m)}{N + M - 1} \tag{5}$$

where $l_i(M)$ is the number of opportunity already assigned to it. Since $\Sigma_i l_i(m) = m - 1$, it is easy to check that the constraint $\Sigma_i \, p_i$ is satisfied.

After M steps this assignment procedure provides a particular partition of the M opportunities among the N firms. Let $m_i(t)$ equal the number of opportunities assigned to firm i during round t. Now the $m_i(t)$ opportunities become the source of an equal number of 'micro-shocks' affecting the size of the firm. We assume that these micro-shocks are randomly and independently drawn from a distribution $F(\varepsilon; v_0)$ of fixed variance v_0 and, since we are interested only in the distribution of the relative growth rates, zero mean. The total growth of firm i is obtained adding $m_i(t) + 1$ independent micro-shocks. If $s_i(t)$ stands for the (log) size of firm i at the beginning of each round, the growth equation reads

$$s_i(t + 1) = s_i(t) + g_i(t) = \sum_{j=1}^{m_i(t)+1} \varepsilon_j(t) \tag{6}$$

Notice that the random growth rates g_i are identically, but not independently, distributed across firms, due to the global constraint $\Sigma_i m_i = M$. In order to study the behaviour of this model we ran the previous procedure for many rounds and collected the relevant statistics of the growth rates distribution.

SIMULATIONS

The mechanism presented in the previous section is rather parsimonious in terms of the required parameters. Indeed it is able to provide a uniquely defined distribution for the firm growth rates when only three components are specified: the number of firms operating in the market N, the total number of 'business opportunities' M representing the 'sources' of the firms growth events and the effect that these events have on the size of the firm, captured by the micro-shocks probability distribution $F(x; v_0)$.

In this section we analyse extensively the properties of the mechanism presented. Our aim is to understand under which conditions this mechanism is able to reproduce the empirical regularities described on pp. 256–7.

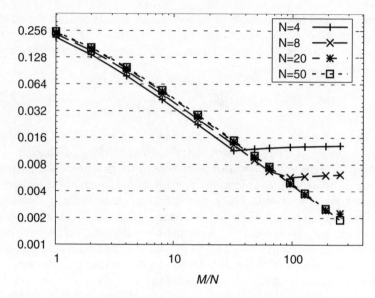

Figure 11.5   *The absolute deviation* D *as a function of the average number*
of micro-shocks per firm M/N *for different values of* N.
Micro-shocks are normally distributed

To this purpose we consider the probability distribution of our model $F_{\text{model}}(x; N, M)$ computed from the repeated simulation described in the previous section. We compare it with the Laplace $F_L(x)$ using different values for the total number of firms N composing the sector, for the total number of opportunities M, and for the shape of the micro-shocks distribution F. Since the variance of the growth rates can be perfectly reproduced with a tuning of the micro-shocks variance, we consider unit variance distributions and set $v_0 = N/M$.

We use the maximum absolute deviation as a measure of this agreement

$$D(N, \lambda) = \max_{-\infty < x < +\infty} |F_{\text{model}}(x; N, \lambda) - F_L(x)| \qquad (7)$$

where $\lambda = M/N$ is the average number of opportunities per firm. The values of D for different values of N and λ are plotted in Figures 11.5 and 11.6 for, respectively, Gaussian and Gamma distributed micro-shocks. For a fixed value of N, as λ increases, the value of D decreases and eventually reaches a constant asymptotic value. This constant regime, for the lower values of N, can be clearly seen in Figure 11.5. When N is large, the curves for different values of N collapse and D becomes a function of λ. This can be directly checked observing that the curves for the largest values of N are

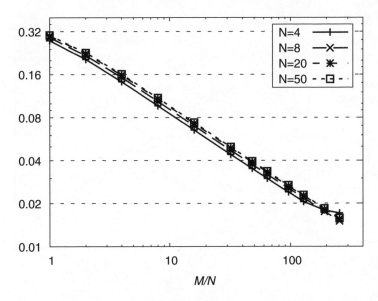

Figure 11.6   *The absolute deviation* D *as a function of the average number*
of micro-shocks per firm M/N *for different values of* N.
The micro-shocks distribution is a Gamma with shape
parameter 1

basically superimposed in both Figures 11.5 and 11.6. The variation of D as a function of λ, until the constant regime sets in, is perfectly fitted by a power-like behaviour

$$\log(D(N \gg 1, \lambda)) \sim a\log(\lambda) + b. \tag{8}$$

The fitted parameters on a population of $N = 500$ firms are $a = -0.970 \pm 5.210^{-3}$, $b = -0.84 \pm 2.210^{-2}$ for the Gaussian case and $a = -0.560 \pm 2.610^{-3}$, $b = -1.04 \pm 1.110^{-2}$ for the Gamma. The remarkable increase in the value of D for the latter is due to the large skewness of the distribution.

Using the absolute deviation D one is able to characterize the statistical significance of the agreement between the model and the Laplace distribution. More precisely, one can compare the value of D defined in Equation (7) with the Kolmogorov-Smirnov statistics, that is the maximum absolution deviation $D^*(N)$ between the empirical distributions of two finite samples of size N composed by independent random variables extracted from a Laplacian. With this comparison we are able to assess in what region of the parameters space the two distributions, F_L and F_{model}, provide analogous results from a statistical point of view.

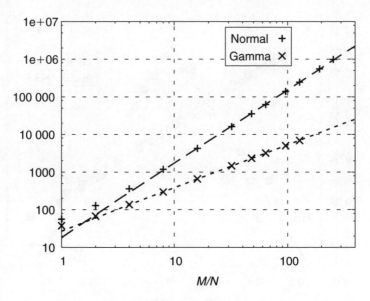

Figure 11.7   N* *as a function of* λ = M/N *for Normal and Gamma*
                distributed micro-shocks. The straight lines are obtained using
                Equation (8) to approximate the value of D

In particular, we can compute the number of observations[4] $N^*(D, r)$
needed to reject, with a given significance r, the null hypothesis of
Laplacian distribution if a maximum absolute deviation D is observed. If
one chooses for r the standard value of 0.05 the behaviour of $N^*(D(N \gg$
$1, \lambda), 0.05)$ as a function of λ is reported in Figure 11.7 for the same micro-
shocks distributions, Normal and Gamma, used in Figures 11.5 and 11.6.
Even for relatively small values of $\lambda \sim 20$, the discrepancies between our
model and the Laplace distribution can only be statistically revealed using
rather large samples, with more than 500 observations.

We now turn to study the fitness of our model with the empirical findings
presented on pp. 256–7. Notice that the exact tuning of all the parameters of
the model is not feasible. While the number N of firms in the different sectors
is known, and the final variance v can be obtained from the relevant samples,
nothing can be said about the number of opportunities M and the shape of
the related shocks F, whose nature was left largely unspecified in the
definition of the model. Nevertheless, since the number of firms per sector is
high (on average $N = 130$), one can use the N large limit in Equation (8) for
an estimate of the discrepancy to obtain a lower bound on the value of λ for
different micro-shock densities F. From Figure 11.6 it appears that even with

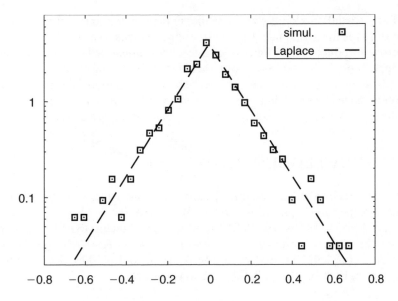

Figure 11.8　*The model growth rates probability density with $N = 100$,*
$\lambda = M/N = 16$ and micro-shocks normally distributed. The
statistics is collected over seven independent realizations to
provide direct comparability to the empirical plots on pp. 257–9.
The theoretical Laplace density with unit variance ($a = 1/\sqrt{2}$)
is also shown

skewed F, a number of opportunities per firm ≥ 20 is enough to obtain a rather good agreement: indeed the typical number of observations for a sector, in our empirical analysis around 1000, lies near or above the considered N^*.

Finally, we check the fitness in a specific case. We run simulations of the model with $N = 100$ and $\lambda = 16$. Results reported in Figure 11.8 show that the agreement is good even if the value of λ is low.

We can conclude that the model presented on pp. 257–61 does generate, for a wide range of parameters values, growth rates distributions that are almost identical to the Laplace, hence providing a complete explanation of the 'stylized fact' described on pp. 256–7.

CONCLUSION

We present a new model of the growth dynamics accounting for competition among firms that try to seize the most out of a limited market size.

The essential novelty of this model lies in the use of a self-reinforcing procedure for the assignment of business opportunities to firms. This mechanism introduces a sort of 'positive feedback' effect between the various opportunities that tends to group them into possibly big chunks.

Our model well replicates the tent-shape distribution of growth rates observed in empirical data. The generality of our approach is coherent with the robustness and the essential invariance of the empirical findings.

ACKNOWLEDGEMENTS

Comments by Mikhail Anoufriev, Carolina Castaldi and Roberto Gabriele have helped in shaping this chapter. We would like to also thank Elena Cefis, Roberto Monducci (ISTAT) and Andrea Mancini (ISTAT). Support of the Italian Ministry of University and Research (grant n. A.AMCE.E4002GD) and of the S. Anna School of Advanced Studies (grant n. E6003GB) is gratefully acknowledged.

NOTES

1. The different lines of business inside the same multi-activity firm were completely aggregated.
2. The database has been made available to our team under the mandatory condition of censorship of any individual information.
3. In empirical studies, the time lag T can range from 3 months for quarterly data, to 30–50 years for the longest databases.
4. This number can be written

$$N^*(D, r) = \frac{1}{2}(Q_{ks}^{-1}(r)/d - 0.12 + (Q_{ks}^{-1}(r)/d - 0.12)^2 - 0.44)^2$$

where Q_{ks} is the distribution of the Kolmogorov-Smirnov statistics (see for example Press *et al.* (1993)).

REFERENCES

Amaral, L. A. N., S. V. Buldyrev, S. Havlin, H. Leschhorn, F. Maass, M. A. Salinger, H. E. Stanley and M. H. R. Stanley (1997), 'Scaling behavior in economics: I. Empirical results for company growth', *Journal de Physique I France*, **7**, 621–33.
Amaral, L. A. N., P. Gopikrishnan, V. Plerou and H. E. Stanley (2001), 'A model for the growth dynamics of economic organizations', *Physica A*, **299**, 127–36.
Arthur, B. W. (1994), *Increasing Returns and Path Dependence in the Economy*, Ann Arbor: University of Michigan Press.
Arthur, B. W. (1996), 'Increasing returns and the new world of business', *Harvard Business Review*, **74**(4), 100–9.

Bottazzi, G. and A. Secchi (2003), 'Common properties and sectoral specificities in the dynamics of U.S. manufacturing companies', *Review of Industrial Organization*, **23**, 217–32.

Bottazzi, G., E. Cefis, G. Dosi and A. Secchi (2003), 'Invariances and diversities in the evolution of manufacturing Industries', L. E. M. Working Paper, S. Anna School of Advanced Studies, Pisa.

Feller, W. (1968), *An Introduction to Probability Theory and Its Applications*, Vol.I, Third Edition, New York:Wiley & Sons.

Feller, W. (1971), *An Introduction to Probability Theory and Its Applications*, Vol.II, Second Edition, New York:Wiley & Sons.

Geroski, P. A. (2000), 'Growth of firms in theory and practice' in N. Foss and V. Malinke (eds), *New Directions in Economics Strategy Research*, Oxford: Oxford University Press.

Gibrat, R. (1931), *Les inégalités économiques*, Paris: Librairie du Recueil Sirey.

Hall, B. H. (1987), 'The relationship between firm size and firm growth in the US manufacturing sector', *Journal of Industrial Economics*, **35** (4), 358–606.

Hart, P. E. and S. J. Prais (1956), 'The analysis of business concentration', *Journal of the Royal Statistical Society*, **119**, 150–91.

Hymer, S. and P. Pashigian (1962), 'Firm size and rate of growth', *Journal of Political Economy*, **70**, 556–69.

Ijiri, Y. and H. A. Simon (1977), *Skew Distributions and the Sizes of Business Firms*, Amsterdam: North Holland Publishing Company.

Kalecki, M. (1945), 'On the Gibrat distribution', *Econometrica*, **13**, 161–70.

Press, W. H., S. A. Teukolsky, W. T. Vetterling and B. P. Flannery (1993), *Numerical Recipes in C*, 2nd edition, Cambridge: Cambridge University Press.

Simon, H. A. and C. P. Bonini (1958), 'The size distribution of business firms', *American Economic Review*, **48**, 607–17.

Stanley, M. H. R., L. A. Nunes Amaral, S. V. Buldyrev, S. Havlin, H. Leschhorn, P. Maass, M. A. Salinger and H. E. Stanley (1996), 'Scaling behaviour in the growth of companies', *Nature*, **379** (6568), 804–6.

Steindl, J. (1965), *Random Processes and the Growth of Firms*, London: Griffin.

Subbotin, M. T. (1923), 'On the law of frequency of errors', *Matematicheskii Sbornik*, **31**, 296–301.

Sutton, J. (1997), 'Gibrat's legacy', *Journal of Economic Literature*, **35**, 40–59.

Sutton, J. (1998), *Technology and Market Structure, Theory and History*, Cambridge, MA: MIT Press.

Index